CHILDREN: THE VANISHED CHILDHOOD

About the Authors

Swati Ghosh (b. 1977) is a passionate development professional working for more than 15 years in social development field. She obtained Ph.D. degree in social work in the year 2012 from Visva-Bharati University. The academic exposure helped her to get associated with various leading National and International Developmental Organizations and she gained experience in social development field of India, Bangladesh and Nepal. Her real life experience helped her to specialize in Child Protection, and she was selected as a National Level Trainer. Her papers were also selected for presentation at different levels like "World Health Congress", "American Evaluation Association, in Chicago". She also received Dympna Meaney Women's Leadership Development Award from Dublin, Ireland in 2015 that aims to connect women leaders from Latin America, Africa and Asia with skills building opportunities to strengthen their contribution to global human rights.

Debotosh Sinha (b. 1962) currently is a Professor in the Department of Social Work, Visva-Bharati.

Apart from classroom teaching, fieldwork supervision, guiding Ph.D. students and other administrative assignments he has to his credit a number of articles and papers published in different reputed journals along with contribution of chapters in various books. He also authored three books on social work.

He was also a visiting faculty from time-to-time to University of Tampere (Finland), University of Stockholm, University of London and Glasgow, University of Dhaka, Shahjalal University of Science and Technology and Rajshahi University of Bangladesh. He also visited a number of countries (Italy, Norway, China, Indonesia, Hong Kong, Malaysia, Thiland, South Korea and so on) to attend seminars, conferences on for some other academic purposes.

Dr. Sinha had also conducted a number of research projects sponsored by his own university as well as Ministry of Social Justice and Empowerment, National Human Rights Commissions and other Ministries of Government of India. He is also been closely associated with a number of social action groups and voluntary bodies.

CHILDREN : THE VANISHED CHILDHOOD
(AN EMPIRICAL STUDY)

By

Swati Ghosh
Debotosh Sinha

CONCEPT PUBLISHING COMPANY PVT. LTD.
NEW DELHI - 110 059

ISBN-13: 978-93-5125-259-7

First Published 2017

Published and Printed by

Concept Since 1974

Concept Publishing Company Pvt. Ltd.
A/15-16, Commercial Block, Mohan Garden
New Delhi-110059 (India)
T: 25351460, 25351794, *F*: 091-11-25357109
E: publishing@conceptpub.com, W: www.conceptpub.com

Cataloging in Publication Data--Courtesy: D.K. Agencies (P) Ltd. <docinfo@dkagencies.com>

Ghosh, Swati, 1977- **author.**
Children : the vanished childhood : an empirical study / by Swati Ghosh, Debotosh Sinha.
pages cm
Study conducted in Kolkata, West Bengal, India.
Includes bibliographical references and index.
ISBN 9789351252597

1. Street children--India--Kolkata--Social conditions. 2. Street children--India--Kolkata--Economic conditions. 3. Street children--Abuse of--India--Kolkata. 4. Street children--Government policy--India--Kolkata. I. Sinha, Debotosh, author. II. Title.

HV887.I42K65 2017 DDC 362.760954147 23

Dedicated to the memory of those social workers and activists who have unhesitatingly sacrificed their lives for the progress and well-being of the marginalized sections of the society.

And

To those social workers who are still working tirelessly among the deprived classes, like the street children, striving against all odds to bring justice, care, love and support to them, and relating them to the mainstream of life.

PREFACE

We tend to believe that children are the future of the country and this belief also seems to help us to forget that the same children are the citizens of this nation and they also have their rights and responsibilities like any other adult citizen. With time, it has been realized that children do have knowledge, sensitivity, and dedication to bear the responsibilities and raise their voice for their own rights. This understanding led the Government of India to ratify the Convention on the Rights of the Child (CRC) and make statutory provisions with an aim of providing them the opportunities and facilities to grow in a healthy manner, which includes an environment of freedom and dignity. The Government changed its legislation to protect children from abuse and exploitation, which led to the changes made by the Government in the socio-legal system of the country. "The Juvenile Justice (Care and Protection of Children) Act was enacted in the year 2000, which was amended in 2006 to plug some of its loopholes". To translate the said act into action and to develop programmes for the development of children, the Government of India formed a separate Ministry for Women and Child Development and designed schemes on "Integrated Child Protection Scheme (ICPS)".

The ICPS is a centrally sponsored scheme aimed at building a protective environment for children in difficult circumstances, as well as other vulnerable children, through Government-Civil Society Partnership. It brings together multiple existing child protection schemes of the Ministry under one comprehensive umbrella, and integrates additional interventions for protecting children and preventing harm. ICPS, therefore, would institutionalize essential services and strengthen structures, enhance capacities at all levels, create database and knowledge-base for child protection services, strengthen child protection at family and community level, ensure appropriate inter-sectoral response at all levels. The scheme has set-up a child protection data management system to formulate and implement effective intervention strategies and monitor their outcomes. Regular evaluation of the programmes and structures are being conducted.

To further promote the rights of the children, the Ministry drafted a bill called "Offences Against Children Act, 2006". Hence, the Juvenile Justice (Care and Protection of Children) Act, 2000 has given a new dimension to the whole Juvenile Justice System of the country. The Act recognizes the rights of children to participate in and made state machineries responsible for child protection. It presents more significance on treatment, care, protection and developmental needs of children by adopting a child friendly approach in the adjudication and disposition of the matters for the best interest of the children. The present move by State and Central Government is obviously a big step towards the long-term goal and it is possible only due to the strong advocacy initiatives taken by many child rights activists.

India is the home for largest number of children in the world but unfortunately, the majority of its children continue to remain in distress and turmoil. Among various social problems of the modern era, child protection occupies an important place. Along with many other social problems, the problem of child abuse has emerged as a result of rapid urbanization and industrialization. This has pushed many families to fall in the vicious cycle of poverty resulting into unplanned growth of the cities. Such families are forced to settle on the streets without any shelter and basic amenities of life. Hence, the children of such families remain deprived and are exposed to the risk of abuse, exploitation and lack of participation in the society with their basic rights. Unfortunately, the lack of entitlements and formal identity, extreme poverty, absence of state protection and exploitation forced them to adopt deviant coping strategies for their sustainability. They do not get a fair chance of protection from the state protection machineries due to their illegitimate status in the city. This study was an attempt to understand the socio-economic status of street families and its impact on the child protection. In the whole gamut of Juvenile Justice Administration, police plays a significant role in child protection. The study seeks to assess the interface between the children of families living on the streets and the police system, which are an integral part of juvenile justice system. Though child participation is still tentative, uneven and relatively unevaluated, the researchers strongly feel that children are one of the important stakeholders in the whole process. If given an opportunity, the children can think and express what they consider appropriate for them. If adults listen to and make space for children, they can actively participate in the policy development, implementing and evaluating of all matters affecting their rights. Therefore, the present endeavour of us aims to raise a voice for children living with families on the streets, who are still invisible in the policy documents and, it hopes to contribute to bring about a sustainable change in the protection and overall development process through a harmonized effort.

Swati Ghosh
Debotosh Sinha

ACKNOWLEDGEMENTS

First of all, we would like to share our gratitude with all the children and their families living on the streets, who participated in this study. We deeply appreciate their patience and efforts to comprehend their problems, shared many mournful experiences, enthusiastically participated in sharing their views, and voiced their opinion with their real life experience.

We are thankful to Mr. Partha Roy, ex-Deputy Director, CINI ASHA who helped us to enrich our professional skills through providing opportunity to work in different aspects of child rights. This was the organization that had exposed us in the area of child protection, provided the opportunity to work closely with police and the other juvenile justice system and enlightened our research quest through the exposure in various training programme.

We would like to convey our thanks to GOAL India and colleagues for their necessary support and cooperation. We would like to appreciate the effort of Biswajit Koyal, Munmun Sinha and Mantu Ghosh who had helped us during the process of data collection.

Our sincere thanks and utmost gratitude to all the library staff of Visva-Bharati as well as other libraries we consulted; nevertheless, who tolerated our erratic borrowing habits and extended their helping hands as and when required.

Swati Ghosh
Debotosh Sinha

CONTENTS

LIST OF TABLES

LIST OF FIGURES

1

INTRODUCTION

They abandoned me, now what will become of me? What will be?
How good it is to be prepared for the pitfalls of life.

I am the future. Nothing will happen, nothing will change.
I am a child of the street.
From the centers, from the corners.
The days pass and I am here, where everything is seen.

Where the struggle for survival is constant. And for a piece of bread, they robbed my life. They robbed me and left without an affection. They left me marginalized for you. What fault have, I, a child, a kid with nothing in life. Do you understand?

Delivered to the life of streets. I, a being without love. I cry for affection, for the maternal breast, I cry.

Even though they can criticize me-why don't they do something to help us?

I need affection. I need closeness and guidance.
It is not my fault that I am a street child, that I am an abandoned child.
Do you know what I want? I only want the right to be a person, to be able to dream like every one of having liberty.
Have you ever imagined the life of an abandoned child? Without any help?
Abused my life?

Meeting face to face with brute liberty? I do not want to be given up like a freak to life. Let me be a person, at least to be happy, to be a child, to believe in fairy tales, to believe that Santa Claus, to feel human warmth.

Let me live my childhood
Is it much to ask?

— **Gaura Rosa da Silva**, Brazil

The most vulnerable group of children in physical, psychological and organizational terms is surely the **'Street Children'** who live, work, sleep and sometimes dies uncared and unprotected. Most of these children are destitute or abandoned, who spend their time mostly on the streets and also sleep on the streets and in public places.

Majority of the children on the streets are working children who are thoroughly exploited and oppressed. These children are not even counted or considered part of any statistics. Therefore, they are not of any concern to any legislation or subjects of any policies or there are any programmes or benefits for them.

Life of street children violates all the survival, protection and development rights of their child. Environmental degradation, migration and displacement of families have led to exodus to cities and expansion of slums and pavement dwellings. Child care and development are seriously hampered in these families. Women in the single-parent families and female headed households are worst affected as they have the main responsibility for the children, but they are neither trained nor experienced. The children most often spend their time on the street. Large number of street children suffers destitution, neglect, abuse and exploitation. They are subjected to harassment and eviction by the municipal authorities because of their unauthorized occupation of city roads and vacant places.

Neither the **Juvenile Justice Act of 1986** nor the **National Policy for Children 1974** recognizes the needs of street children or mentions them in the Policy. **The National Plan of Action** includes them in the category of children in especially difficult circumstances. Only recently, schemers have been launched with a view to support and strengthen voluntary organizations engaged in the welfare and development of the street children, to enable them to reach out to a large number of such children.

The first aim of the scheme is to provide integrated community-based non-institutional basic services for the care, protection and development of the street children, facing destitution. The second aim is programme intervention for reduction of exploitation and abuse and withdrawal of children in hazardous work. The scheme has been focusing on the preventive and rehabilitative aspects.

"Every child is a sacred gift to mankind". Every child is born blissful and radiates immense love for everyone who becomes part of his life. India has 400 million children, which is more than any other country in the world. But, unfortunately, our society is unable to reciprocate uniform level of care and protection to each young citizen.

As one of the signatory of UN Convention on the Rights of the Child, Government of India had vowed to ensure rights to all children without discrimination. Yet, we are far from realizing it. It is not uncommon to find children living in poverty being deprived of their basic rights to survival, protection, care and opportunity to develop, and participate in the affairs of mainstream society. Furthermore, the situation of children living on streets is worsened by immense poverty, dismal environmental conditions and lack of protection mechanism.

The need to work for children was well recognized by both national and international agencies before many decades. But all the efforts put together were unable to make a mark in the problem. With the introduction of global market policy, industrialization and added pressure of expanding population has seriously affected the village economy. Thousands of families lost their household income and were pushed out of villages to the pavements in cities with hopes to survive. People from both rural and urban areas are forced to diversify their livelihood options. Broadly speaking, the growth of street families and the upshoot of a vicious poverty cycle, employment and lack of coordination between rural and urban policy-makers have made the scenario much dismal. With globalization and significant growth in economic sector, India has become one among the ten fastest developing countries of the world. The population scientists are expecting further growth in urbanization by 2030. This will accelerate the process of migration and more families will be emigrating in the cities in search of alternative livelihood options. Consequently, this will result in the faster increase of the number of families living on streets as well. Though India is experiencing a high growth in urbanization, no comprehensive effort has yet been taken by the policy-makers to absorb the steady inflation of poor families in urban areas. Thus, all the cities of India will have increased number of families settled in unauthorized lands and encroachments on the roadsides. This process of rapid urbanization will have a negative impact on children, especially without an integrated policy approach and proper protection mechanism for the children of these families.

The problems of street-living families are not a new phenomenon in India, but still the children of these families are invisible in official records. In reality, very little attention has been given so far for the children of street-living families to ensure that the mark of set by the universal standard was met. Children of these families live in appalling and inhuman conditions and are the victims of the social, economic and political complicacies. Living on the fringe of society and the disadvantaged by the pressures of poverty and insecurities, children are exposed to various forms of physical, economical and sexual exploitations. Their basic minimum rights ate grossly violated and they are debarred from the mainstream development of the society. Children are forced to take up adult responsibilities from their tender age to substitute their family pressure. Unfortunately, such children are the most vulnerable group struggling to survive without basic services and protection. In many cases, children are oppressed and exploited not only by others but also by their own family members.

For many years now, organizations have been talking about child protection from all kinds of abuses perpetrated against them by enforcing laws. After the ratification of UN Convention on the Rights of the Child, Government of India amended various legislations among which **Juvenile Justice (Care and Protection) Act, 2000 [amended]**, is one of the important legislations that gave a new dimension to child protection and juvenile justice system of the country. But in reality, violence against children of street families is an observable phenomenon. Because of immense poverty, ignorance and illegitimacy of stay, children's rights are even violated by protective machineries of the State. They do not get fair treatment of services from the justice authorities, who are legally responsible to protect every citizen's rights. Thus, children resort to their own survival mechanism and acquire different survival traits to satisfy their needs and protect their interest. These factors lead to personal, family and social disorganization which ultimately causes insanity, delinquency and other anti-social behaviours among street living children.

JJ Act, 2000 is considered as an umbrella of all the child related laws which offer more significance on treatment, care, and protection and development needs of children by adopting a child friendly approach in the adjudication and disposition of the matters for the best interest of the children. For the first time, in our country, an act has given focus on voice of the children towards identification and solution of their own problems and encourages children to produce themselves before the juvenile justice system in case of violation of their basic rights.

Child rights movements are not new in origin. We can track the history of child rights back from 1800s, which was initiated in United States. However, the first effective attempt to promote children's rights was the Declaration of the Rights of the Child in 1923, which was adopted by the League of Nations in 1924. In 1989, the legally binding Convention on the Rights of the Child was adopted by the United Nations. It laid down a universal set of standards and guiding principles to be adhered by all the countries to protect and safeguard rights of the children. It is mostly widely and rapidly ratified rights treaty in history. In Article **Number 54** the Convention incorporates the whole spectrum of human rights — civil, political, economic, social and cultural — and set out the specific ways these should be ensured for children and young people. This Convention also respects and recognizes the protective responsibilities of parents, other primary groups of society and the cultural values of the children's community. On the other hand, it ensures the legal and other protective measures, before and after the birth of the child, against the family members and primary groups for ensuring protection of children against maltreatment. After this convention, all children were considered as a political, economic, socio-cultural as well as spiritual entity with their own rights. Consequently, the Convention also recognized children's right to participation in arenas where children can satisfy several aspects of their personhood and grow up in as a responsible citizen of the country.

Unlike any other countries of the world, the Government of India ratified the Convention in 1992 and amended various legislations to recognize children's rights adopted in the convention. However, it seems that change is taking place in the socio-legal system of the country. A separate Ministry for Women and Child Development formed a scheme on Integrated Child Protection Scheme was in place as on August 17th, 2006. Further, the Bill Offences Against Children Act, 2000 was drawn up by the **Women and Child Development Department**, under the Central Government's, **Ministry of Human Resource Development**.

Despite the enactment of all these legislations, a strong gap is extremely visible between the law enforcement bodies and primary beneficiaries. These policies and legislations on the whole suffered from weak implementation, owning to scant attention to the issues of child rights, resulting in scare resources, minimal infrastructure and inadequate services to address the problem. In the year 2005, total expenditure on children's health, education, development and protection together amounted to just 3.86 per cent in India's budget and rose to 4.91 per cent in 2006-07. However, the shares of resources for child protection were an abysmally low of 0.034 per cent in both 2005-06 and in 2006-07 financial years. It reflects Government's attitude and negligence in child related issues, especially protection of the children.

Though, the JJ Act encourages children and other primary beneficiaries to access the system, but does not emphasize to ensure the services are physically accessible to the children. Among the law enforcement agencies, police has a decisive role in child protection by the implementation of the JJ system. They are the first persons to be called for intervention and have a very important role in investigation of cases. In the era of this social modernization, the reaction of Indian police was found to be halting to respond to the violation of rights of children because of the unchanged core laws and administrative orientation. Indian police administration continued to be oriented with the anachronistic model of British administration and culture that confronts a dilemma and lack of commitment to any specific ideology of child rights and newly formed JJ Act.

Even after the amendment of JJ Act, in the year 2000, no guidelines have yet been designed to equip police personnel to deal with child related cases. Police personnel are still more concerned about punitive aspect of crime rather than protective part. But on the other hand, JJ Act, 2000, talks about setting up of a **Special Juvenile Police Unit (SJPU)** in every district and city to coordinate and upgrade police to interface with children. Except for some states, a few personnel from each police station has been identified as **Child Welfare Officer** and have been given additional responsibility to deal with the child related cases.

In the JJ Act, the priority has been given to the voice of the children towards identification and solution of their own problems. However, because of lack of orientation and administrative limitation, police do not encourage children to directly lodge any complaint without an adult. They are not still oriented to give due respect to children's opinion. They think children take whimsical decision and any legal actions should not be taken based on the opinion of these innocent children. It has been routinely observed that police cannot earn the trust of children and thus cannot establish communication with them. Hence, priorities are not given to ensure children's participation in identification and solution of their problem in legal measures. Further, illegitimacy of stay restraints street living families to access the required support from the law enforcement machineries. Thus, children of these families are widely discriminated and are also abused by the law enforcement authorities.

All the strategies adopted so far for the protection of children have domineering focus on institutional and less focus on creating supportive and protective environment within the community to protect children from abuse. Furthermore, no comprehensive studies has yet been undertaken to assess the interface between the police and the children. We are all aware that success of any intervention depends upon the involvement of the primary beneficiaries. All the strategies, taken so far for the welfare of children are practically preconceived ideas of a particular class of people. Lack of coordination among lateral service provider as well as among non-governmental agencies is an integral problem of planning and implementation of any programme in India which make these problems to continue eternally. Thus, none of the strategies took so far for the welfare of the children yields any fruitful result in the solution of the actual problem.

Against this backdrop, this study is an endeavour to understand the interface of Juvenile Justice Administration and the primary beneficiaries', i.e. children and their parents. Among them, children living on the streets of Kolkata with their families have been selected as the core respondents. Among the gamut of while juvenile justice system, the study only can captures the interface of street living children with the police, which is one of the important agencies in Juvenile Justice Administration.

The study assumes that abuse of children living on street, as in any other developing countries, is a phenomenon, which is widespread and their access to the legal system for justice protection and care is poor. Efforts were made through this study to recognize different forms of abuse that children of street living families face; socio-economic conditions that build insecurities within the children and their families. Attempt has been made also to understand the implementation of Juvenile Justice System for the protection of children of street living families. To understand these factors, the researchers have made an attempt to capture the views of children and their families towards their own rights; different abusive experiences that the children face; various protective mechanisms that their children and their families resort to.

At the end, an attempt has also been made to draw together the opinion of families and their children towards an effective and friendly police system which can help them to access the legal system to safeguard their rights. Though it appears ambitious undertakings, but the study is aimed to voice the opinion of children for the long-term policy level changes.

In tune with the above scenario, the followings are the key **objectives** of this study.

- To elicit the socio-economic profile of respondents.
- To identify types of abuses being perpetrated against children both by family members and outsiders.
- To know the existing self-protection mechanism of children living on streets against violation of basic rights.

- To know the perception of children towards the existing law and other machinery and their opinion towards creating a child friendly police system.
- To ascertain the opinion of parents of deprived urban children regarding the enforcement of law to safeguard right's of the children.
- To know the perception of parents towards abuse by family members and outsiders.

With globalization and significant growth in economic sector, India has become one of the top 10 growing economy in the world. The population studies anticipate sharp growth in urbanization and urban poverty by the year 2030. Realizing the problem of shrinkage of income opportunities, the Government of India had undertaken various industrial policies with the expectation to trigger employment opportunities within the village area through attracting foreign and domestic investments. The lack of harmonized attempt among the political parties to promote a balance between agriculture and industrialization, created political turmoil and halted the implementation of livelihood promotional initiatives in West Bengal.

In the face of rising demands of urbanization, more families will be attracted towards cities and will be forced to live in a disagreeable environment without support system for their children. And, protection of children of street living families would continue to be an important issue in near future unless a comprehensive understanding was developed and measures were taken. Also, the State like West Bengal would continue to suffer from the inflow of migrant population because of shrinkage of income opportunities in rural economy and Kolkata being an important location for commercial and communication in the North-East Indian states, Kolkata would continue to experience faster expansion of street living families.

Though India is experiencing a high growth of urbanization, no comprehensive effort has yet been taken by the policy-makers to absorb the steady inflow of poor families in urban areas. Thus, all the cities of India will have increased number of families settled in unauthorized lands and encroachments of the roadside. Consequently, this process of chaotic urbanization will have a negative impact on children. Without an integrated policy approach and proper protection mechanism for the children of these families, the issue is bound to deteriorate.

Kolkata has been selected as the universe of the study to get an overview of child abuse and protection issues in the context of children living with their families on the streets.

- This study offers an integrated perspective on the impact of socio-legal structure of street living families on child abuse. It tries to understand perception of children and their families regarding child rights, different forms of abusive experiences and various types of protection mechanism adopted by the families and their children.
- It has been recognized in UNCRC that the primary responsibility of parents is to ensure the adequate standard of living to their children and responsibility of state to oversee and ensure this responsibility is fulfilled. This study will give an overview of the environment which the street living families can offer to their children. Also, it will encompass the socio-economic and legal constrains of these families that prevent them to fulfil their responsibilities.
- An attempt has been made through this study to assess the interface between the children of street living families' and police system, which are an integral part of juvenile justice system. The study reveals abusive experiences of the children subjected by the law and order machineries that are mainly responsible to protect children from abuses.
- Because of lack of faith on the protection machineries of the state, children and their families sought to develop their own protection mechanism to survive in the complex society. This study attempts to identify a few of these community based protection mechanisms adopted by these families to protect their interest.
- An attempt has been made in the study to understand different forms of violence that are faced by the children in different settings. In most of the cases, it may remain as children are scared to disclose such incidences. Many a time, parents of the children also persuade to hide those to avoid social stigma. The study also surfaced different abusive experience of children perpetrated in different settings.
- This study is an endeavour to understand the role of police system among the whole gamut of juvenile justice authorities' in the protection of children of families living on the streets. The study also tries to draw together the expectation of children towards police system and voice their opinion on **"child friendly approach"** which has been recognized under JJ Act, 2000.
- Though, participation of children is still tentative, uneven and relatively unevaluated but the researchers strongly feel that given

the opportunity, the children can think and express what they think is fit for them. It is a initiative to involve children in identification of their own rights and issues affecting their interest. It is also an attempt to provide a space for children in decision-making related to implementation of the law for their own protection. Thus, the outlook captured in the study reflects the need and understanding of children towards their own rights; perception of their own abuse and also record their recommendations towards creating a child friendly police system.

- The study analyses various aspects of Juvenile Justice Act and the Police Act of the country and tries to draw a synergy between these two acts for the effective implementation of Juvenile Justice System.

In summary, the study aims to voice for the children living with their families on the streets. They may be invisible in the policy papers, but there is a hope and insight to bring about a long-term change in the protection and overall development process through a synchronized effort. And this study is one more step in that direction.

2

THEORETICAL UNDERPINNINGS

Even though our study is mainly concentrating on street living children and their families, but the tyranny and exploitation the children face are basically due to different forms of abuse and which are responsible for their famished condition which is writ large on their countenance. These abuses also had forced them to be on the street and lead a miserable life. So, we are keen to highlight some of the theories of child abuse propounded by various social scientists from time-to-time from their perception which would help the readers to get an idea of what are the causes of abuse and why it so happens to them.

Over the years there has been a substantial amount of research done trying to understand the origins and causes of child abuse. Precise links have been established between a child's victimization and behavioural problems later on in life such as problems in school, delinquency, violence, and adult criminality. At present there are six theories that have been developed to understand the root causes of abuse which are briefly depicted below:

Social Learning Theory

According to this theory, behaviour is learned through two methods:

- We either learn by being rewarded for our actions (instrumental learning); or
- We observe and imitate the behaviour of those around us (modelling).

Some social scientists assume that abused children learn to be abusive using these two methods and continue their abusive behaviour into adulthood. This pattern of learned aggression is commonly referred to as the "cycle of violence" or the intergenerational transmission of violence. The broad-based application of the cycle of violence theory is questioned, pointing to findings that only 20-30 per cent of child abuse and neglect victims become involved in abusive and criminal behaviour. Interventions based on social learning theory commonly have the purpose of stopping current and preventing future child abuse and neglect by teaching both the parent and child appropriate relationship skills within the family.

Attachment Theory

Attachment theorists believe humans develop behaviour as a result of how their caregivers nurture them. According to attachment theory, the type of bond develops between child and caregiver affects the child's later relationships. There are **four** bonding types:

Secure — The securely attached child freely explores his/her surroundings and is easily comforted.

Preoccupied — Children with preoccupied attachment will move easily between their caregiver and a stranger when looking for comfort, but will simultaneously resist the comfort given.

Dismissive — Children who experience dismissive attachment show distrust of the caregiver and have an inability to be comforted.

Fearful — This attachment pattern is characterized by erratic and confused behaviour as the child is unable to recognize which behaviour gain favourable attention from the caregiver.

Secure attachment patterns are thought to develop from a consistent and nurturing caregiver, whereas the insecure attachments are the result of inconsistent, emotionally neglectful and/or abusive caregiving. Several researchers have cited that as many as 80 per cent of abused infants and children exhibit insecure attachment patterns.

Ecological Theory

Ecological theory holds that abuse and neglect result from multiple factors. These are divided into four systems: individual, family, community, and culture. For individuals and families involved in child abuse and neglect, the degree of influence by each of these four systems may differ dramatically. A child who has been sexually abused may be committed to school, involved with peers but dissociated from the family. In another family, a sexually abused child may be disconnected from the community and isolated from peers. If child maltreatment is the result of multiple factors from various systems, then in order to be effective, programmes need to address each factor and system.

Family System Theory

This theory is similar to ecological theory in that both focus on the entire family unit when assessing the needs and service approach for responding to child abuse and neglect. Family system theory however focuses primarily on the family and is a process of identifying problems as the consequences of dysfunctional relationships among family members. For example, in cases of incest where the father is the perpetrator, the possibility that the mother's reluctant intervention may appear to be tacit approval would be explored as a contributing factor in the repeated abuse. Critics are concerned with the theory's failure to recognize the influence of power and society on human behaviour. Some critics worry that the discussion of the victim's and bystander's roles in the abuse may be overemphasized and relieve the perpetrator of responsibility.

Self-Efficacy Theory

This theory focuses on how personal characteristics of the child, and especially the parent, influences family functioning. Self-efficacy theory addresses how a parent's expectations of effectiveness impact their motivation and behaviour. An individual's expectations dictate if they will start and continue actions to achieve a goal. This theory may help bridge a gap between knowledge and behaviour. A gap between knowledge and behaviour is apparent when parents know they should not hit their children, but are unable to seek out methods to achieve this goal. Self-efficacy theory states that this knowledge/behaviour gap is due to the parents' belief that they cannot behave in a manner that would stop them from abusing their children. Self-efficacy theory is limited because it does not incorporate a developmental perspective.

Resilience Theory

Historically, child abuse and neglect research and interventions were grounded in the belief that inevitably the victim is damaged by the trauma. However, factors such as severity of abuse, frequency of abuse, age of the victim, and relationship to the perpetrator can predict later adjustment. Additionally, factors such as social support, parental warmth, and the victim's healthy relationship with a supportive adult can influence the child's healthy development and avoidance of delinquent behaviour. Resiliency does not explain why abuse and neglect occur, rather, it explains why children may not inevitably be damaged by child abuse and neglect. It may also explains how the "cycle of violence" can be interrupted.

Finkelhor's Precondition Theory

Finkelhor states that a close examination of the literature on child sexual abuse reveals that four underlying factors have typically been used to explain the occurrence of abuse; usually in the form of single factor or **level II** theories. These factors are as follows:

(a) Sex with children is emotionally satisfying to the offender (Emotional congruence);
(b) Men who offend are sexually aroused by a child (sexual arousal);
(c) Men have sex with children because they are unable to meet their sexual needs in more socially appropriate ways (blockage); and
(d) These men become disinhibited and behave in ways they would not normally behave (disinhibition).

He suggests that the first three factors explain why some individuals develop a sexual interest in children and the fourth why this interest is manifested in sexually abused behaviour. These factors may be complementary or work antagonistically or even synergically.

The key idea in Finkelhor's theory is that these four sets of factors can be grouped into four preconditions that must be satisfied before the sexual abuse of a child occurs. These preconditions comprise motivation to sexually abuse a child; overcoming of internal inhibitions; overcoming of external inhibition; and dealing with a child's possible resistance to the abuse. Factors one, two, and three, emotional congruence, sexual arousal to children, and blockage, are all linked to precondition 1. That is, the motivation to behave sexually with a child. The final factor, disinhibition, relates to precondition 2, overcoming internal inhibition. The remaining preconditions are more to do with the how of the offence process and seem not to relate to the causal factors. These preconditions are hypothesized to occur in a temporal sequence and each is necessary for the next to occur. Additionally, Finkelhor proposes that the model provides a typology of child molesters.

Hall and Hirschman's Quadripartite Theory

Their model of sexual aggression against children is based on four components: physiological sexual arousal, cognitions justifying sexual aggression, affective dyscontrol, and personality problems. These serve both as motivational precursors that increase the probability of sexually aggressive behaviour occurring, and also define offender and offence sub-types based upon relative prominence of each factor. They suggest that physiological, affective, and cognitive factors are all primarily state and situation dependent (**state factors**) while personality problems represent enduring vulnerability factors (**trait factors**). This implies that personality deficits are the source of offenders' vulnerability to sexually abuse children.

A key idea in their model is that while each of the above factors may contribute to a sexual offence, usually one factor is prominent for each child molester and constitutes their primary motive. This means that it will exert a greater influence on the other factors and "push" individuals over the offence threshold. That is, from a position of being able to control deviant sexual impulses to one in which they commit a sexually abusive act. Hall and Hirschman regard this interaction as synergistic in nature stating that the activation of one factor (primary motivational precursor) functions to increase the intensity of the others. This may in turn propel an individual above the critical threshold for performing a sexually deviant act.

Each one of the above factors is hypothesized to characterize a particular type of child molester, with distinct treatment needs. The first sub-type has deviant sexual arousal and strong sexual preference for children. In a sense this category represents the classic preferential offender who tends to commit offences against large number of children. Treatment would revolve around the reduction of deviant sexual arousal using range of conditioning strategies, for example, directed masturbation. Offenders who are characterized by cognitive motivation typically misinterpret children's behaviour as revealing sexual intent and also possess good self-regulatory and planning skills (**incest offenders**). Therapy may involve the challenging of their sense entitlement and the modification of other dysfunctional cognitions. The third group of offenders is defined by their susceptibility to negative affective status, and frequently behaves in an impulsive and unplanned manner (**situational offenders**). Treatment would center on such individuals learning how to control and regulate their negative emotions. The final sub-groups of offenders are those who have developmentally elated personality problems and experience difficulties establishing intimate adult relationships and functioning effectively in the world (**fixated offenders**). Treatment for this group would be prolonged and intensive requiring the modification of entrenched and maladaptive interpersonal strategies and beliefs about themselves and other people.

Marshall and Barbaree's Integrated Theory

Marshall and Barbaree's Integrated Theory proposes that the sexual abuse of children occurs as a consequence of a number of interacting distal and proximal factors. This important model was developed as a general theory of sexual offending and has been used to explain the development, onset, and maintenance of child sexual abuse.

From the perspective of the Integrated Theory it is the transition to adolescence that is particularly challenging for a vulnerable individual. Negative childhood experiences leave offenders without the necessary social competence to develop and maintain heterosexual relationships. It is at this stage that individuals are most receptive to acquiring sexual preferences and associated behaviours. In a sense, the onset of puberty represents a critical period for the acquisition of enduring sexual scripts, interests and attitudes. The massive increase of sex hormones during this period increases the salience and potency of sexual cues. A lack of effective self-regulation and social competence, means that some individuals are more likely to be adversely affected by these hormonal and biological challenges and, therefore, likely to learn to meet their sexual or emotional needs in a deviant manner. A failure to successfully distinguish between sexual and aggressive needs may result in their fusion and a subsequent tendency to impose one's own immediate needs upon others. The task of discriminating between sex and aggression is a difficult one for adolescent males because they originate from the same neural substrates and are thought to be subjectively similar. That is, the underlying neural structures are hypothesized to cause qualitatively similar experiences. In addition, a vulnerable individual may rely upon deviant sexual activity (fantasizing, etc.) to cope with lowered mood and a sense of powerlessness. If adolescent males feel inadequate or ineffective they will be more vulnerable to accepting socio-cultural messages conveying a dysfunctional picture of masculinity and all that this entails. That is, they may believe males to be superior to women and come to regard heterosexual relationships purely in sexual terms. The subsequent presence of situation factors such as stress, intoxication or sexual stimuli, will either overwhelm a person's inadequate coping mechanisms and result in a sexual offence, or encourage him to actively seek deviant sexual activity as a way of meeting his needs for intimacy and/or personal effectiveness. The reinforcing effects of deviant sexual activity and the development of cognitive distortions maintain offending. This reinforcement may be positive (e.g. sexual arousal, sense of power) or negative (e.g. reduction of low mood) in nature.

Marshall and Barbaree state that it is possible for any individual to offend, depending on their circumstances. The greater the degree of vulnerability possessed by an individual, the less intense stressors need to be for a sexual offence to occur. While a lesser degree of vulnerability means that situational factors will need to be considerably stronger in order to overwhelm inhibitions against committing a sexual crime.

A valuable contribution of the Integrated Theory is to articulate the nature of male's predisposition to sexually abuse children in terms of vulnerability. An individual's vulnerability to commit a sexual offence is viewed as dimensional, anchored at one end by extreme weakness and at the other by resilience. Resilience is hypothesized to consist of characteristics (abilities, skills, attitudes, preferences, values and beliefs) that enable individuals to resist the temptation, and the opportunity, to sexually offend. Considerable importance is attributed to early causal factors in the integrated theory but the influence of transient situational variables is also acknowledged. Sexually aggressive behaviour is viewed as multiply determined and Marshall and Barbaree provide a rich description of the critical adverse developmental antecedents and resulting vulnerabilities thought to continue to culminate in sexual offending.

The Pathway Model of Child Sexual Abuse

It is clear that each of the three major theories of child sexual abuse has serious limitations. An unresolved issue concerns the direction any future theoretical development should take. In our view, it is worth building on the virtues of each of the three major theories in order to construct a more comprehensive explanation of child sexual abuse. Briefly, Finkelhor's Theory neatly links offenders' psychological vulnerabilities with the offence process, Hall and Hirschman comprehensively address the issue of typology, while Marshall and Barbaree convincingly describe the way developmental adversity can result in vulnerability to sexually abuse a child. It would be a waste of intellectual resources to simply dismiss these theories as inadequate and start from scratch. Ideally, a comprehensive theory of child sexual abuse should incorporate the strengths of each of the above three theories.

Outline of the Pathway Model

The casual mechanisms implicated in child sexual abuse are hypothesized to be multiple and associated with distinct systems of factors. That is, most theorists accept that a satisfactory explanation of child sexual abuse will be multifactorial. These factors include: ***developmental adversity, cultural values and belief systems, family context, biological variables, psychological deficits, and situational variables.*** Many of the causal mechanisms will exert both a distal and proximal influence, for example, cultural factors will influence the early socialization of an offender and also function to reinforce or precipitate his current offending behaviour. It is suggested that the clinical phenomena evident mange child molesters are generated by four distinct, and interacting, types of psychological mechanism; ***intimacy and social skill deficits, distorted sexual scripts, emotional dysregulation, and cognitive distortion.*** Learning events, biological, and cultural factors exert an influence through their effects on the structure and functioning of these sets of mechanisms.

A mechanism is a set of psychological process that causes specific outcomes or effects. That is, a mechanism is what makes things work or function and a dysfunctional mechanism is one that fails to work as intended or designed. Examples of dysfunctional mechanisms include impaired cognitive or behavioural skills and mental states such as maladaptive beliefs and desires. Psychological mechanisms generating child sexual abuse constitute *vulnerability* factors.

The Psychoanalytical Approach

The earliest proposed explanation for the occurrence of sexual abuse was Freud's psychoanalytic theory which derived from his clinical work with female clients who disclosed childhood sexual abuse, often at the hands of their fathers. Freud was the first to postulate that the trauma of childhood sexual abuse resulted in later psychic damage. This was the basis of his **'seduction'** theory which he presented along with detailed case studies at a major forum in 1896. The idea that fathers were sexually abusing their daughters caused such an outrage in conservative nineteenth century Vienna that Freud was ridiculed and shunned by peers. In fact, **Seduction Theory** was so poorly received that Freud never again publicly referred to it. In 1933, in his Introductory Lecture on Psychoanalysis, he stated:

> "I was driven to recognize in the end that these reports (of sexual abuse) were untrue and so came to understand that the hysterical symptoms are derived from fantasies and not from real occurrences".

Adult sex offenders are viewed as pathologically disturbed and sexually perverted as a result of poor psycho-sexual development. The distortions in the offenders' psycho-sexual development are seen as the result of failure in his mother's parenting.

To explain incest, Freud's Oedipus Complex casts the daughter as the active desiring agent who wishes her father to become her love object. The child is seen as **'seductress'** while the father is seen as the passive, innocent object of his daughters; seduction: an overtly displayed invitation which he cannot help but act upon. This normalizes sexual acts between parents and children by seeing them as **NATURAL** rather than **ABUSIVE** and places the responsibility clearly on the child's victim.

Associated with the concept of the seductive child is the view of the mother as being responsible for the occurrence of incest. There are numerous ideas around this but central idea is that the child has natural affection needs which are not met by the mother. The mother is seen as cold and rejecting of the child who turns to the father as a source of security and affection through sexual channels. Another view is that the mother sexually deserts her husband who must then turn to the daughter for sex. The mother's behaviour is explained essentially in terms of poor resolution of her own Oedipus Complex through which generates a situation in which her daughter acts out her own incestuous desire.

In summary, the psychoanalytical model attempts to deny the reality of childhood sexual abuse and incest and in **PROVEN** cases places the blame firmly on the child or the mother.

The Victim Precipitation Approach

This approach considers offenders and victims as mutually interacting patterns where the victim, through signs, eye contact, gestures and words, or by being present at certain venues or being out alone sometimes encourages rape. Things like accepting a ride home, responding in a friendly manner in conversation, accepting a dinner invitation, visiting a male friend at home or inviting a male friend into her own home may be misread or intentionally rationalized by the perpetrators as a sign of consent to sexual intercourse. In other words, a woman is raped because she failed to accurately communicate her desire not to have sex.

The Family Dysfunction Approach

In contrast to the psychoanalytic model which focuses on the individual psyche as the cause of sexual assault, this approach focuses on the family unit as dysfunctional. The notion of the dysfunctional family was first proposed in the 1940's as an outgrowth of family psychiatry and the influence of Classic Freudian theory on this approach cannot be ignored. It is a notion that has been popular in explaining the etiology of a number of disorders with the basic premise that disorders arise from pathological family dynamics.

Family dysfunction theory has become one of the most widely held explanations for the manifestation of incest and together with its treatment methods has been adopted by many government and statutory authorities in Australia, U.S., and the U.K. In this view, incest is seen as an overall symptom of family maladjustment and it proposes that all members of the family are responsible for causing it to occur even though apparently uninvolved, in particular, the mother. Underpinning this approach is a system of family norms which are used as a yardstick for measuring different degrees of family pathology. A family in which incest is occurring is seen to be dysfunctional as it does not conform to socially approved goals or values and normal family hierarchies based on age and sex have been destroyed. In a dysfunctional family incest is utilized to reduce tension and maintain balance within the family while ensuring that the family's pathology is kept a secret.

In this view the mother is seen to have failed fundamentally. *Firstly*, she is seen as a dysfunctional wife who does not fulfil her assigned role as sexual provider for the husband, or her nurturing role as mother and protector of her child. She does this by absenting herself either emotionally or physically from her children by working outside of the home, pursuing outside interests and activities, or through illness, hospitalization, escaping into depression, or by being emotionally and/or sexually frigid.

Secondly, this view assumes that the mother's failure to provide adequate nurturing means the love-starved and seductive child turns to and accepts the sexual advances of the sex-starved father as a substitute for the mother's love.

Thirdly, both the mother and father are seen as dysfunctional adults who seek a role reversal and disintegration between generational boundaries with the child cast in the role of satisfying the sexual needs of the father while assuming a protective role towards the mother. The mother supposedly engineers the incestuous relationship by placing enormous responsibilities on the child such as housework, child-care and wifely duties towards her father.

What we see in this formulation is, once again, the collusive mother and it is this collusion which is seen to be the cornerstone of family pathology. In fact, it is argued by many family dysfunction theorists that the mother knows consciously or unconsciously that incest is taking place, but chooses to deny it even when confronted by her daughter, by failing to take any preventive action or by blaming the daughter for the incest. Thus, in this view, the real abuser is an incestuous family is the mother.

Psychological Approach

Psychological approaches to what causes sexual assault have focused on the abuser rather than on the victim or the family. Psychologists have focused their attention at two levels:

- identifying a personality profile of sex offenders; and
- on isolating the motivations of abusers.

The search for a personify profile of sex offenders has focused on establishing the existence of fixed and stable personality traits that are predictive of sex offenders. A range of studies of diverse population samples have been conducted using differential research techniques and perhaps unsurprisingly, research results have been contradictory and inconclusive. Some of the personality characteristics that have been consistently identified include social introversion, feeling of masculine inadequacy and the need to exercise a high level of dominance and control in family relationships. This later characteristics is particularly true of incest offenders.

Abusers have been found to be highly adept at rationalization and displacing responsibility and blame onto others rather than the self. The inability of researchers to consistently define particular characteristics as indicative of sex offenders has nevertheless contributed to our knowledge of sexual abuse. The huge amount of demographic and clinical data that has been collected has helped to dispel many of the myths and stereotypes about who commits sexual abuse. It has become clear that abusers come from all social backgrounds and are not confined to socially or economically deprived families. In addition, they do not suffer from any mental illness nor do they necessarily have other criminal tendencies. In fact, the sex offender is often and otherwise law-abiding '***guy next door***' type.

In terms of motivations for abuse, a common finding has been that alcohol or alcoholism contributes to a reduction in internal inhibitions to commit sex offences and/or incest. Poor impulse control is also seen as a common problem. In terms of child sexual abuse offenders, a distinction has been drawn between the **fixated** and the **regressive** abuser. The fixated abuser has been conditioned from childhood and adolescence to be primarily sexually attracted to younger children. While the regressive abuser, in response to stress, which exacerbates existing feelings of inadequacy and impairs normal impulse control, thereby allowing abuse to occur.

The Feminist Approach

The many limitations of previous approaches meant that considerable reinterpretation of the causes for sexual assault was needed. With the emergence of the women's movement in the 1960's and 70's, people began to tell of their experiences of sexual assault and so a more accurate identification of the problem became possible. This victim centred awareness prompted research and investigation in an attempt to address the key issues of sexual assault. In particular,

- Why is it men who rape?
- Why is it women and children who are primarily the victims of sexually abusive behaviour?

The feminist approach is a sociological analysis which over the past three decades has focused on two important and previously largely ignored aspects of sexual assault.

- The unequal power relationships between men and women and adults and children; and
- The abusers' responsibility for initiating and/or maintaining sexual assault.

In examining differential power relationships within society and the family this approach argues that the most adequate explanation of the motivation for, and incidence of, sexual assault is found in the complex interplay between existing social structures, conventional attitudes and socialization, in particular, the differential gender socialization of males and females in patriarchal society. A fundamental contribution offered by the feminist approach is that it does not focus exclusively on incestuous abuse within the family. In interpreting sexual abuse as a sexual power relationship rooted in differential gender socialization and male power in patriarchal society, it is able to broaden its focus to include the dynamics of extra-familial as well as intra-familial sexual and incestuous abuse, all of which rely on males exerting their sexual power over women.

The research has overwhelming demonstrated that sexual abuse is not a problem of individual pathology occurring between '***pathological men and seductive women and children***'. Instead it shows that sexual assault is an extension of the current legal, social, economic and political systems in which we live which manifest and reinforce male dominance over women and children. The manifestation of male power relationships is well documented. In the areas of education, employment, health, income security, law and decision-making, women and children come out second best. Unequal power relationships between men, women and children are embedded in social organizations like the family where they become internalized by individuals. Masculine dominance over females is further linked to the patriarchal nature of heterosexual relationships. In a culture where men are socialized to view women as a means of satisfying their emotional, sexual and daily needs, a similar objection of children is only a step away. The messages that females receive through such power structures and female socialization serve to emphasize women's powerlessness, passivity and their role as victim. When internalized these messages generate submissive, compliant and self-effacing behaviour which offer little or no protection against sexual abuse.

Examinations of male power within the family show that abusers tend to see their wives and children as property which they can exploit in any way they wish, including sexually. Incest is thus seen as a just one expression of 'normal' male/female relations in a patriarchal society. Analysis of reported findings of perceived masculine inadequacy and social isolation of incestuous fathers have led to speculation that this prompts abusers to enforce patriarchal rule within the family where it is '**socially acceptable**' for them to be in-charge. Within the family the abuser is able to reconstruct traditional patriarchal domination in which, by means of threat, physical violence or coercion, he is not only obeyed but serviced by his wife and children.

Differential gender socialization, in particular male sexual socialization, is manifested and reinforced through the media, school curricula, sex store-typed expectations and role definitions, and gender specific child rearing practices. Male sexual socialization is a major factor in abusive behaviour, particularly child abuse. Sexuality contains culturally moulded components which include values, feelings and attitudes, as well as biological drives, which account for stereo-typical gender roles in the expression of sexuality. There are four distinct features of masculine sexual socialization that predispose men toward sexually abusing women and children.

1. Men are socialized to express their dependency or intimacy needs through sex, and have not always been encouraged to act as nurturers.
2. Men tend to have sex as a form of reconfirmation when their ego has encountered any kind of rebuff.
3. Many men experience sexual arousal outside of the context of a relationship but are more specifically aroused and stimulated by the genitals of their preferred sexual object. Whether these belong to an adult or a child may become largely irrelevant.
4. Men are socialized to desire sexual partners who are younger and smaller than themselves.

Impaired nurturing and diminished capacity for affection, along with putative masculine identity, restricts the forming of genuine relationships while encouraging sexual contact only with complaint submissive women who have inferior status. In addition, as male gender identity is more dependent on sexual success. The sexually inadequate male may prefer a child as a sexual partner to bolster an inadequate adult ego. Such socialization makes male sexual exploitative behaviour towards women and children increasingly comprehensible.

Included in this approach is the analysis of the role of pornography in perpetuating and legitimizing sexual abuse and in particular child sexual abuse. The virulence of child pornography and the increase of child sex rings demonstrate that not only do men exert their sexual power over children, more fundamentally they find them erotically desirable. Such analysis provides powerful evidence against the notion that child sexual abuse is a problem of parenting. It is instead a function of masculine socialization. It is this social context which both creates and is reinforced by sexual assault and abuse and in which sexual abuse plays an important role in maintaining the *status quo*. In this view, rape is seen as a **SOCIAL** rather than **NATURAL** fact. It is produced by a certain kind of society and not by immutable human nature and it is argued that the attempt to treat rape and sexual abuse as a natural and inevitable pat of human behaviour, through defining psychological structures or developing elaborate theories, is a way to avoid having to do anything about it. But if we view it as social fact, it can be eliminated through social change.

The Four Pre-Conditions Model

To bridge the gap between psychological and sociological interpretations of sexual abuse, Finkelhor (1984) proposed a multi-factor model which has explanatory power on both levels. In reviewing all the causal factors that researchers and clinical have isolated as contributing to sexual abuse. Finkelhor developed a hierarchical model which included individual factors related to the victim, abuser and the family as well as social and cultural factors. It provides an adaptable and flexible framework which can accommodate new research to enhance our understanding of why sexual abuse occurs. The model accounts for both intra and extra familial sexual abuse. This perspective clearly places responsibility with the abuser. Finkelhor's model has more explanatory power than other approaches in that it incorporates both psychological factors such as:

- The motivation of the abuser;
- The existence of internal inhibitors; and
- Ego strength of the child.

As well as sociological factors such as:

- male socialization,
- pornography,
- social tolerance of erotizing children,
- unequal power relationships between men and women, and
- the patriarchal prerogatives of fathers and men.

This model also views potential victims as not necessarily passive, but possessing the power to resist.

Finally, Finkelhor's model provides vital enhancement to treatment in that it allows for evaluation and intervention on all four levels. Capitalizing on the strengths while implementing problem-solving techniques to ameliorate the weakness may facilitate cessation of abuse and prevent its re-occurrence.

All the factors known to contribute to child sexual abuse are grouped into **four** pre-conditions. These are:

1. ***Motivation*** — The potential abuser needs to have some motivation to sexually abuse. There are three fundamental components subsumed under the motivation to sexually abuse children.

- ***Emotional congruence*** in which sexual contact with a child satisfies profound emotional needs.
- ***Sexual arousal*** in which the child represents the source of sexual gratification for the abuser.
- ***Blockage*** when alternative sources of sexual gratification are either not available or are less satisfactory.

These components are not actual pre-conditions and not all three need to be present for sexual abuse to occur. The three components do explain not only the instances of abusers who are not sexually motivated, but enjoy degrading victims and welding power, but also the paedophilic and the sexually motivated abuser.

2. ***Internal Inhibitions*** — The potential abuser must overcome internal inhibitions that may act against his motivation to sexually abuse. No matter how strong the sexual interest in children might be, if the abuser is inhibited by taboos then he will not abuse. Arguably, most people have some inhibitions against the sexual abuse of children. Disinhibition is not a source of motivation, it merely releases motivation. The second pre-condition aims to isolate factors that account for how inhibitions are overcome. While preconditions 1 & 2 account for the abusers behaviour, pre-conditions 3 & 4 consider the environment outside the abuser and child which controls whether and whom he abuses.
3. ***External Inhibitors*** — The potential abuser must overcome external obstacles and inhibitions prior to sexual abuse. External inhibitors that may restrain the abuser's action include family constellation, neighbours, peers and societal sanctions as well as the level of supervision a child receives. Although a child cannot be supervised 24 hours per day, lack of supervision has been found to be a contributing factor to sexual abuse as has physical proximity and opportunity. External inhibitors are easily overcome if the potential abuser is left alone with an unsupervised child.
4. ***Resistance*** — Finally, the potential; abuser has to overcome the child's possible resistance to being sexually abused. This capacity to resist may operate in a very subtle covert way and does not necessarily involve over protestations. Abusers may sense which children are good potential targets, who can be intimated or co-coerced to keep a secret or otherwise

manipulated. Abusers report that they can almost instinctively pick out a vulnerable child on whom to focus their sexual attentions while ignoring those who might resist. Frequently, these children may even be unaware that they are being sexually approached and have little or no capacity to resist. Some of the risk factors that inhibit the capacity to resist include emotional insecurity and deprivation, etc.

Knowing which factors make children vulnerable to abuse is essential in formulating prevention programmes. Isolating behaviours that constitute a risk, while emphasizing those that enhance resistance or avoidance can empower children to protect themselves. This is not to say that children who are not vulnerable are not abused. Many children may be forced or co-coerced despite displaying resistance and avoidance behaviours. Some instances of abuse are the result of force, threat or violence and no matter how much resistance that displays it will not prevent the abuse. Pre-condition 4 has **three** possible outcomes:

(a) The child may resist but still be abused through force or violence.
(b) A child may resist but be overcome through coercion.
(c) The child may resist by overtly saying no and running away, or covertly by displaying a confident and assertive manner which conveys strong messages to the abuser not to try for fear of detection or exposure.

The four-pre-conditions for sexual abuse come into play in a logical sequence. The abuser must firstly have the motivation and be able to overcome any internal inhibitions. When these have been overcome the potential abuser will need to overcome external inhibitions and finally the resistance of the child.

3

GLIMPSES OF LITERATURE

Many researchers have taken interest to study the needs of the children living on the streets from a "rights perspective" to ensure access to basic rights. Besides, few intensive studies have also been conducted to get an overview of the socio-economic profile of such children in relation with the types of violence, risk factors associated with different environmental settings, attitudes of children towards policies and other officials and opinion of various stakeholders towards the protective measures for children. With the experience of the researchers, it has been increasingly realized the need to seek the opinion of the children before designing studies of programmes for them. But still, it is hard to find studies that are conducted to seek children's opinion for formulating a policy or adapting developmental initiatives based on their feedback. Hence, this research was undertaken to actively explore opinion of children based on their experience to develop a child friendly system within our society, which will guarantee a favourable environment for the development of children, especially for those who are forced to live with or without their families on the streets.

Here, an attempt has been made to knit together outcomes of different national and international conventions, policies and research studies. During the review of literature, books, paper clippings and editorials were reviewed to get a holistic picture of the issue. The entire discussion has been sub-divided into following sections:

Section 3.1

This section gives an overview of the child rights movement and reviews of different international treaties. It also outlines the universal set of standards that are adhered by all the participating countries.

Section 3.2

This section glosses over approaches and policies amended by different countries to promote rights of children. It also gives a view of Government of India and its policy level amendments to ensure rights of children in India.

Section 3.3

Here a reflection is given on the global picture of violence against children taking place in different settings.

Section 3.4

Inspite of many studies conducted for increasing the knowledge base about street children, the terminologies and its definitions still vary amongst various users. This ambiguity which exists among definitions is not only seen at local level but can also be found in the official documents and publications by various international agencies. Thus, in this section, definitions used by different agencies and studies available were reviewed and an attempt was made to draw a holistic profile of a particular group of street children. Further, there is an attempt to capture the socio-economic profile of children living on the streets with their families, violence against them, push actors for delinquency and mechanisms adopted by justice authorities to treat them.

SECTION 3.1

Child Rights Movements

Child rights movements started in USA in 1800s while working with the orphan children in different establishments. The National Child Labour Committee (NCLL), an organization dedicated to the abolition of all child labour was formed in the 1980s. It managed to pass a law, which was struck down by the Supreme Court two years later for violating a child's right to contract his work. Later, in the year 1907, the US Congress adopted the mission of "promoting the rights, awareness, dignity, well-being and education of children and youth as they relate to work and working". In 1924, Congress made first attempt world-wide to pass a National Labour Law with focus to protect children from harm at work. Unfortunately, the bill was dropped due to various reasons. But in 1938, President Franklin D. Roosevelt signed the Fair Labour Standards Act, which placed limits on many forms of child labour. This was a major step towards eradication of child labour. But the movement was stalled again when the Second World War broke out and adult men were at war. Women and children entered the workforce again to keep the country running. On the other side, children in Europe worked as intelligence collectors, and for other underground resistance workers in opposition to the Hitler's regime.

In the early twentieth century movement began to promote the idea of children's rights as distinct from those of adults and as requiring explicit recognition. In 1917, following the Russian Revolution, the Moscow branch of the organization, Proletcult, produced a Declaration of Children's Rights. However, the first effective attempt to promote children's rights was the declaration of the Rights of the Child in 1923, which was adopted by the League of Nations in 1924. This was accepted by the United Nations (UN) on its formation and updated in 1959, and replaced with a more extensive UN Convention on the Rights of the Child in 1989. In the past two decades there was a greater international attention turned towards protection of children's rights. In the 1980s, mounting concern for the rights of children resulted in several child focused international treaties (Children's right movement, wikipedia retrieved, 2008).

The primary child rights instruments in the history of child rights movements are as under (Amanda, 2004).

Chronology of Human Rights Treaties in the Twentieth Century

1921 Declaration for the Suppression of the Traffic in Women and Children.

1924 Declaration of the Rights of the Child.

1926 Slavery Convention.

1930 Slavery Convention.

1948 Universal Declaration of Human Rights.

1949 Convention for the Suppression of the Traffic in Persons and of the Exploitation of Prostitution of Others.

1956 Supplementary Convention of the Abolition of Slavery, The Slave Trade, and Institutions and Practices similar to Slavery.

1960 Convention on Discrimination in Education.

1962 Recommendation on Consent to Marriage, Minimum Age for Marriage and Registration.

1966 International Convenant on Civil and Political Rights.

1966 International Convenant on Economic, Social and Cultural Rights.

1967 Declaration on the Elimination of Discrimination against Women.

1975 Convention on Reduction of Statelessness.

1979 Convention on the Elimination of All Forms of Discrimination against Women.

1985 The Minimum Rule for the Administration of Juvenile Justice.

1989 Indigenous and Tribal Peoples' Convention.

1989 Convention on the Rights of the Child.

1990 The UN Standard Minimum Rules for the Protection of Juvenile Deprived of their Liberty.

1990 The UN Guidelines for the Prevention of Juvenile Delinquency.

1997 The UN Guidelines for Action on Children in the Criminal Justice System.

1999 International Labour Organization (ILO) Convention 182.

1999 Convention Concerning the Prohibition and Immediate Action for the Elimination of the Worst Forms of Child Labour.

2000 Optional Protocol to the Convention on the Rights of the Child on the sale of children, child prostitution and child pornography.

Other generally applicable instruments are as under:

- The UN Standard Minimum Rules for Non-Custodial Measures' (The Tokyo Rules).
- The UN Basic Principles on the use of Restorative Justice Programmes in Criminal Matters.
- The Convention Against Torture.
- The Basic Standard Minimum of Rules for the Treatment of Prisoners.

A recent child specific instrument which has an increasing relevance to Juvenile Justice is the ILO Convention 182, in the year 1999, concerning for the elimination of worst forms of child labour. So far, the convention identified children, who are used by other young people or by adults, to commit offences as a worst form of child labour. At the regional level, many countries have ratified their own charters to promote the rights and welfare measures for the children.

Convention on the Rights of the Child (CRC), 1989

The Convention on the Rights of the Child adopted in 1989 in UN is the most widely and rapidly ratified human rights treaty in the history. It provides a universal set of standards to be adhered by all countries to protect children and child offenders from being abused. UNICEF describes the CRC as a milestone to establish "non-negotiable minimum standards and obligations" for the treatment of children. Thus, the philosophy and the basic minimum standard outlined in this section can help us to relate the research outcomes with the set minimum standard. In 1989, the convention redefined a child as every human being below the age of 18 years. The standards of the convention on the Rights of the Child were derived after a decade long negotiation by governmental, non-governmental organizations, human rights advocates, lawyers, health specialists, social workers, educators, child development experts and religious leaders from all over the world. It came out as a consensual agreement while respecting the tradition and cultural values for the protection and harmonious development of the child. All countries had ratified this convention and have become State Parties to the Convention as of November 2003 except United States of America and Somalia. UNICEF had described the CRC as establishing "non-negotiable standards and obligations" for the treatment of children.

Thereafter, child's needs have become legally binding rights. This convention recognizes that all members of human family has inherent dignity and deserves equal and inalienable rights without distinction of any kind. It encompasses the whole spectrum of children's specific human rights including civil, political, economic, social and cultural *viz.* 41 individual articles. The UNCRC also lays down four general principles, which together form a guiding tool for a holistic interpretation of the UNCRC. These principles are as under (Petren, Alfhild *et al.*, 2000):

- Non-discrimination (Article 2).
- The best interest of the child (Article 3).
- The right to survival and development (Article 6).
- The right to express an opinion and to be heard (Article 12).

The basic principle of this convention is to give full consideration to the best interest of the child. In forty one substantive articles, it establishes that children should be benefitted from special protection measures and assistance. It lays emphasis to access education and health care services for children to enable them to develop their potentialities, abilities and talents to the fullest potential and grow up in an environment of happiness, love and understanding. It also states that children should have the right to be informed about the participative in achieving their rights in accessible and active manner. It recognizes that all the state parties shall undertake every measure to implement and promote child rights to protect children from any form of discrimination. CRC also deals with broad range of issues including juvenile justice and also establishes provisions to monitor the compliance of each signatory country (UNCRC, 1989).

The convention laid emphasis on the following **four** basic rights of children:

- Right to Survival.
- Right to Development.
- Right to Protection.
- Right to Participation.

Right to Survival

This ensures rights to every child to enjoy the highest standard of health and medical care. The convention states that the State Parties shall recognize inherent right to life of every child. It also ensures to the maximum extent possible the survival and development of every child. As per the Convention, the State shall pursue full implementation of rights and shall:

- Take opportunity measures to diminish infant child and infant mortality.
- Ensure necessary medical assistance and health care for all children.
- Ensure appropriate pre-natal and post-natal care from mothers.
- Develop appropriate preventive health care, family planning, education and guidance.

Right to Development

- Every child has the right to a standard of living adequate for his or her physical, mental, spiritual, moral and social development.
- It is the primary responsibility of parents to ensure the adequate standard of living. And, it is the state's responsibility to oversee and ensure that this responsibility can be fulfilled.
- It is the State's responsibility to ensure that primary education is free and compulsory. It encourages state, based on their capacity to make arrangements for different forms of secondary education and improve access to higher education. And, education shall aim at developing child's personality, talents, mental and physical abilities to the fullest extent. Also, the children of minorities and indigenous population have the right to enjoy their own culture and religion.

Right to Protection

The State shall take appropriate legislative, administrative, social and educational measures to protect children from the following;

1. Any forms of maltreatment and abuse from parents and others.
2. Economic and sexual exploitation.
3. Substance abuse.
4. Sale, trafficking and abduction.
5. Torture and deprivation of liberty.

- With respect to adoption, the State shall encourage adoption for the best interest of the child and will develop systems for periodic review and evaluation and evaluation of the placement.
- The State shall provide special protection for refugee children and children deprived from family environment. It will ensure that the children with disability also have the right to special care, protection and rehabilitation so that they can enjoy a full and decent life of dignity.

Right to Participation

- Participation of children is a relatively new concept introduced in this convention. It says that a child has a right to freedom of expression, freedom to seek, receive and impart any kind of information aimed at the promotion of their mental, physical, social and spiritual development.
- Besides, the children have right to meet with others, join and form association. Also, they have the right to enjoy leisure, play and participate in cultural and artistic activities.

Administration of Juvenile Justice

Special focus has been given on administration of juvenile justice system. It articulates that a child in conflict with law has the right to treatment that promotes the child's sense of dignity and worth. It also guarantees the following to every child who is alleged as or accused of having infringed the penal law:

- To be presumed innocent until proven guilty according to law.
- To be informed promptly and directly of the charges against him or her and his or her guardian.

- To have legal and other assistance in preparation and presentation of his or her defence.
- To have matter determined without delay by a competent, independent and impartial authority of judicial body for fair hearing.

It also clarifies that a child cannot be compelled to give testimony, to confess guilty or to examine adverse witness. Privacy of the child should be fully respected at all stages of the proceedings (UNCRC, 1989).

Optional Protocol to the Convention on the Rights of the Child on the Sale of Children, Child Prostitution and Child Pornography

The UN General Assembly adopted the Optional Protocol in May 2000. It came into force in January 2002. The Articles 34 and 35 of the Convention on the Rights of the Child states that government should protect children from all forms of sexual exploitation and abuse. In addition, all possible measures must be taken to ensure that children are not abducted, sold or trafficked. The Convention's Optional Protocol on the sale of children, child prostitution and child pornography supplements the Convention by providing states with detailed requirements to end the sexual exploitation and abuse of children. It also protects children from being sold for non-sexual purposes, such as other forms of forced labour, illegal adoption and organ donation.

The protocol provides definitions for the offence of 'sale of children', 'child prostitution' and 'child pornography'. It also creates obligations on government to criminalize and punish the activities related to these offences. It requires punishment not only for those offering or delivering children for the purpose of sexual exploitation, transfer of organs or children for profit or forced labour, but also for anyone accepting the child for these activities.

The protocol also protects the rights and interests of victimized children. All governments must provide legal and other support services to such children. This obligation includes any considerations for the best interest of the child in any interactions with the criminal justice system. Children must also be supported with necessary medical, psychological, logistical and financial support to aid their rehabilitation and reintegration. As a compliment to the Convention on the Rights of the Child, interpretation of the Optional Protocol's text must always be guided by the principles of non-discrimination, priority in the best interest of the children and participation of children.

"The Standard Minimum Rules for the Administration of Juvenile Justice" is also an important child rights instrument which set the international standard for dealing with juvenile offenders. It expresses that efforts shall be made by all the countries to establish a set of laws, rules and provisions specifically applicable to juvenile offenders in each national jurisdiction. It emphasizes to establish institutions and bodies entrusted with the functions of the administration of juvenile justice. The treaty also indicates that the juvenile justice system shall accentuate on the well-being of the juvenile. The system must ensure that any reaction to juvenile offenders should always be in proportion to the circumstances of both the offenders and the offences. It clarifies that appropriate discretion should be allowed at all stages of proceedings and at the different levels of juvenile justice administration, keeping in view the special need of the juveniles as well as variety of measures available. Appropriate scope for discretion should also be allowed during investigation, prosecution, adjudication and the follow-up of dispositions.

SECTION 3.2

Approaches of Different Countries to Promote Child Rights

The children's rights movement promotes legal protections and safeguards for children, distinct from those of adults. After each world war, international legal instruments increasingly included protection for children across the globe. All the signatories of CRC treaty amended their own legislations according to their available resources to adhere to the universal set of standards set forth in the convention. Most of the developed countries and international agencies have adopted different approaches to promote child rights through local, governmental and non-governmental organizations.

This section tries to compare and contrast how children are treated among the different countries which have profound impact on the younger generations. An effort has been made in this section to glimpse through the approaches adopted by different countries to promote rights of children. Out of 177 countries, 6 countries, as listed below, among the top 30 were selected for review based on the Human Development Index (HDI) (2006). It is a comparative measure of life expectancy, literacy, education, and standard of living for countries world-wide. It is also a standard means of measuring well-being, especially child welfare. It is used to determine and indicate whether a country is a developed, developing, or underdeveloped and also to measure the impact of economic policies on quality of life.

Table 3.1: Countries Selected for Review based on the HDI

Region	*Country*	*HDI Ranking*
Europe	Norway	1
"	Sweden	5
"	United Kingdom	18
North America	Canada	6
Asia	Japan	7
Oceania	Australia	3

Source: Human Development Index 2006.

Measures Taken by Norway to Promote Child Rights

Norway ratified the Convention on CRC in 1991. Similarly, the Optional Protocol (OP) on the sale of children, child prostitution, and child pornography was ratified in 2001, whereas the OP on the involvement of children in armed conflict was adopted in 2003 (U.S., Department of State, February 25, 2000). The committee evaluated the State's progress in implementing the CRC in 2005 and noted that Norway had been one of the most active state parties in creating and implementing the CRC. The country's outstanding commitment to foreign aid and development (0.9% GDP) and the universal implementation of the CRC was acknowledged. It was also highlighted that certain legislative standards are higher than the CRC. The Government of Norway has not yet passed any separate legislation for children. All legislations were being harmonized with the CRC. An Independent Children's Ombudsman Office, within the Ministry of Children and Families, assures the protection of children law and its practices.

In Norway there is a focal point for children's rights' and there are other staff members available who specialize in children's rights. Norway as working on right based approach that welcomes child participation. These issues are strongly monitored by municipal corporations and other local authorities. Government shows high level of commitment for children's rights and welfare. It has amply funded systems of education and medical care, The government provides free education for the children through the post-secondary level. Education is compulsory up to the 10th grade and most children stay in school at least until the age of 18 years. It was found that there was no difference in the treatment of girls and boys in education or health care services. Besides, the key areas of intervention were education, health and nutrition, early childhood development and care, birth registration and civil rights, HIV/AIDs, child labour, trafficking and sexual abuse of children, and children affected by armed conflict. Due to abuse or neglect of various degrees, 23,500 children (2.1% of children up to the age of 17) were assisted by welfare services in 1998. The level of assistance ranged from protective custody, extra financial help, or simply guidance and support for their parents.

The Government examines all key aspects of the Norwegian legal and administrative system that are relevant to the protection of human rights in Norway. There are a large number of administrative, legislative, economic and educational measures that are implemented to improve the human rights situation in Norway. This applies particularly to matters related to the development of legislation, administrative procedures and control mechanisms, such as court and ombud schemes. The Government also examines the way in which information on human rights is disseminated in schools and other relevant sectors. The plan of action is developed to implement several measures for increasing the level of knowledge in these key areas. In view of the Government, it is also important that research forms part of the basis for building knowledge and expertise on human rights (Country Report on Human Right Practices; Norway, 1999).

Approaches of Sweden

Children and children's rights have formed an integral part of Swedish development policy for a number of years. In early 1990s, Sweden led the issue by focusing on the incorporation of issues related to the children in national development policies. At the multi-lateral level, the Swedish government works closely with UNICEF and was one of the major donors. It also had strong involvement with NGOs, particularly Save the Children, Sweden. Sweden also published a number of documents dealing specifically with child development and also carried out number of studies to find out how children and their rights can be incorporated into the development policies. At the same time, it was surprising to note that children and children's rights were not monitored in some of the official documents concerning Swedish development policy. There was specific focus on the girl child, both from a mainstreaming perspective (all activities should be built on a non-discriminatory perspective) and in terms of a number of special action towards girls. An evaluation of Sweden's policy towards children was undertaken by the Swedish Government in 2001, which resulted to the development of a programme containing 10 action points to continue the integration of a children's right perspective into developmental policy. Unlike other developed countries, Sweden had begun to explore and implement a child rights approach, which explicitly recognized children as rights holder and State as duty-bearers, putting the fulfilment of children's rights, as set out in the UNCRC, at the very core of development cooperation (Save the Children, 2003).

Approaches of United Kingdom

Realizing the paramount responsibility of child welfare, the Government of UK constituted Child Protection Unit (CPU) in different zones. Inter-agency groups with different social service departments were created and Metropolitan Police Service (MPS) joined with the group to provide counter measures to ensure safe environment for most vulnerable children. Prevention of abuse was kept high on the agenda of MPS. Standard professional procedures were identified, undertaken and documented by CPU. This initiative by the UK police broke the widely held perception that child protection was not in the priority of 'real police work'.

Primary role of the child protection unit was to make London a safer place for the children. It states that basic rights established by Human Rights Act, 1998 need to be considered in every case and the same applies equally to all children and adults. The Government of UK established a new operational command unit welding with 25 Child Protection Teams, 4 major investigation teams, and the paedophile unit. Partnership with other agencies was developed and guidelines were prepared. Another attempt was made with other agencies to provide counter measures to ensure safe environment for the most vulnerable citizen. The Internet Task Force for Child Protection was also formed to make the UK the best and safest place in the world for children to use the internet, and to help protect children all over the world from abuse fuelled by criminal misuse of new technologies (London Child Protection Procedures, 2007).

Approaches of Canada

The Canadian Government demonstrated its commitment to children's rights and welfare through well-funded systems of public education and medical care. Education was made free through grade 13 and was compulsory through the age of 15 or 16 years, depending on the province.

The UN Children's Fund reported that 100 per cent of elementary-age children attended school and high school was the highest level completed by most children. Federal and provincial regulations protect children from abuse, overwork, and discrimination. It also penalizes perpetrators of such offences. As a Canadian priority, the key element in efforts to improve human security was to strengthen respect for children's rights, particularly by eliminating exploitative child labour, sexual exploitation and the widespread use of child soldiers and their victimization in armed conflict. At the multilateral and bilateral levels, Canada was working in partnership with developing countries to protect children, strengthen their rights and assist victims of the sex trade (Bureau of Democracy, Human Rights and Labour, Canada 2007).

Canada adopted various child centred strategies to promote child rights and to make Canada fit for children. Besides, a number of child care and child centred family justice strategies, it funded community-based coalitions that established programmes and delivered services to meet the developmental needs of children living in risky condition. Long-term studies were undertaken by Canadian Government to track children's development and well-being from birth to early adulthood. Understanding the Early Years (UEY) was a national initiative that provided communities with information to enable them to make informed decisions about the best policies and most appropriate programmes for families with young children. In partnership with provinces and territories, Canada's Social Housing Programmes provide assistance to some 6,39,000 social housing units that benefit lower-income Canadians, including families with children, youth, people with disabilities, seniors and aboriginal people. Canada launched the three-year National Homelessness Initiative, Residential Rehabilitation Assistance Programmes and Shelter Enhancement Programmes to help prevent and alleviate homelessness in Canada. This included the Supporting Communities Partnership Initiative (SCPI) that provides funding for local community groups to offer supportive services and facilities for the homeless. Funding for a range of existing federal programmes was increased to address the needs of particularly vulnerable and/or over-represented groups within the homeless population, namely youth-at-risk, aboriginal people and victims of violence (Human Resources and Skills Development; Canada, A Canada Fit for Children, 2004).

In 1994, the UN Commission on Human Rights was concerned that international trafficking in children, sex tourism and child pornography were increasing. It created a working group to draft an optional protocol to the Convention on the Rights of the Child. Canada being a member of the said working group, it advocated and consolidated efforts to protect children in Canada as well as in other countries. Canada signed the Optional Protocol (OP) on November 10, 2001, indicating it would ratify the Optional Protocol at the earliest opportunity. Besides ratifying the OP, The Government of Canada was further protecting children from people who possess, produce or distribute child pornography and from other forms of sexual exploitation by increasing the severity of punishment of the guilty. It has also created a new offence of sexual exploitation to better protect young person's less than 18 years of age against those who would prey on their vulnerability. Criminal code amendments were introduced in other provinces and it was probably for the first time that all the provinces agreed to a common issue that required national level consistency.

Approaches of Japan

The first basic law having to do with children and their welfare was the Child Welfare Law (Jido Fukushi Ho), enacted in 1947. According to this law, 'children' were defined as young persons under the age of 18 years. Japan was a signatory of many international conventions which focused to protect the rights of children. There are various domestic laws and schemes to promote children's well-being, for example, all the children in Japan were covered by health care insurance and families with small children, who do not have a high income, were entitled to receive an allowance from the government. The local government supported by providing health and education services to the pregnant women, mothers and infants. Besides, the schools conducted health examinations of all students. In Japan, the parents were obliged to have their children attend primary and secondary schools for nine years. The government provides this mandatory education free of charge. There are three sub-categories: infants of less than one year of age, children aged one year or more who have not yet entered elementary school; and children from elementary school age through the age of 17 years. To ensure compliance with the laws, there are provisions which punish acts that harm children, both in special laws and in the criminal code. There is a juvenile justice system which was separated from the normal criminal justice system. In accordance with the Child Welfare Law, each of Japan's 47 prefectures operates several child guidance centers. Each of these centers employs a child welfare worker specialized in children's issues. They provide consultation on all sorts of matters concerning children in the areas under each center's jurisdiction. They make systematic enquiries and decisions from a specialist's viewpoint, give necessary guidance to children's guardians, and authorize arrangements for the temporary custody, if necessary. Such arrangements were made in close consultation with welfare offices and health centers. The city, town, and village governments employed commissioned child welfare volunteers to work closely with the child welfare workers and certified social workers, so that they could gain understanding of the living environment of the children, and new mothers requiring assistance. The public facilities for the special care of children include homes for infants, day nurseries, and hospital homes for children with severe mental and physical disabilities. The Child Welfare Law underwent large scale revision in 1997 to respond to changes in the living environment of children during the last 50 years. In the last five decades, the social scenario of Japan has changed a lot, whereby both husbands and wives started to work to maintain the family income. The trend toward nuclear families stunted the fertility rate among women to 1.23 in 2003, which resulted in decrease in the number of children. The revisions in the Child Welfare Laws enacted with emphasize of going beyond the concepts of protection and emergency relief to address the issue of supporting children in ways that will help them become socially, spiritually, and economically self-reliant by the time they grow as young adults. The revised law directed to establish support centers for households with children that requires services of the child guidance centers and could benefit from advice and guidance for proper care of the children. The functions of these facilities changed from the former custodial care to 'self-reliance' centres. 'Homes for fatherless families' renamed as 'livelihood support facilities for mothers and children'. These centers provide support to single-mother households, necessary measures, along with livelihood support. The Child Welfare Law, a 10 year agenda, officially named Basic Orientation to Assist Child-Raising and colloquially known as the Angel Plan, was joined put together in 1995 by the Education, Health and Welfare, Labour and Construction Ministries. The plan aims to build an environment that makes it possible for women to feel confident that they can raise children while holding jobs. Among the various measures promoted were the expansion of the capacity of day nurseries, extended hours of day nurseries, and a large increase in the number of child-rearing support centers throughout Japan. In 1999, this plan was revised to create the New Angle Plan, which covers 2000 to 2004 period with the provisions of promoting improvements in the corporate work environment. Now, the prevention of child abuse has become an increasingly prominent issue, with the number of reported cases growing rapidly in the past decade. The Child Abuse Prevention Law went into effect in 2000 and was revised in 2004. This revision expanded the criteria under which people were obligated to make a report to a child guidance centre, and it clarified the authority of centre personnel to make on-site investigations.

The Juvenile Law adopts special measures to the criminal cases of juveniles. For the criminal cases of juveniles, who are under 20 years of age, the juvenile law was applied, instead of Criminal Procedure Law. The Family Court has primarily jurisdiction over such cases. Children under 14 years of age, however, were handled primarily by the child guidance centre, as provided by the Child Welfare Law, when they have committed acts, which, if committed by a person aged 14 year or above, would constitute a crime. These children under 14 years of age under the jurisdiction of the family court only and in such case the governor of the prefecture or the chief of the child guidance centre refers them to the family court (Umenda Sayuri, Law Library of Congress, August 2007).

Approaches of Australia

Children hold special place in Australian society and Government has committed high levels of effort and resources to ensure rights of children. Australian Government ratified all significant international treaties that impact on children's rights. Government has created a separate Ministry for children and Youth affairs to ensure an integrated government approach across the spectrum of Federal Government policies and programmes for children. A new Federal Department of Family and Community Services has also been created in recognition of the need for leadership in issues relating to children and families. The rights and protection of children are governed by both Federal and State and Territory Laws.

Australian Government also defines children as individuals below the age of 18 years. Government recognizes children's access to free and compulsory education and right to access health care via Australia's universal health insurance programme. The age between which children must be educated varies across jurisdiction but is generally between the ages of 5 to 16 years. All jurisdictions have launched additional programmes to encourage children and young person's to seek medical care. It recognizes that children may be able to give consent to medical procedures where they are either over a statutory age (14 to 16 depending upon the jurisdiction), or, of sufficient maturity that they are able to comprehend the procedure and give informed consent.

Under the auspices of the Hague Convention, Government of Australia has amended its family law in respect to parental responsibility and measures for the protection of the "best interests of the child" is the court's paramount consideration when making orders regarding parenting, location and recovery orders. In some jurisdictions children's rights and the child's right to participate in decision-making have been specifically incorporated into legislation. In determining family law matters the Family Court considers the wishes of a child when determining what is "in the best interest of the child".

Children below the age of 10 years are unable to be changed with a criminal offence and children between the ages of 10 to 14 years have a refutable presumption that they are incapable of forming the necessary criminal intent for an offence.

When it comes to joining the armed forces, Australia does not allow children below the age of 17 years to volunteer to join.

Criminal laws are governed by both Federal and State and Territory law and recognizes the following acts as offence against children:

- Slavery.
- Sexual servitude.
- Trafficking (domestic or international) of children.
- Supply drugs (or other controlled substances) to children or to children for the purpose of trafficking.
- Obtain child pornography or child abuse material.
- Use a carriage service to procure or groom a child (below the age of 16 years).
- Forcibly transfer (i.e. by threats or coercion) children.
- Conscript or enlist children below the age of 15 years in war.
- Expose children (below the age of 14 years) to the unlawful manufacture of drugs, or to use a carriage service to possess, control, produce and supply.

To stop offence against children, government has amended strict punishment and penalty for the offender which varies from 7 to 25 years.

The standard age for criminal responsibility in all Australian Jurisdictions is to 10 years of age. For children between the ages of 10 to

14 years there is a refutable presumption that they are incapable of informing the criminal intent necessary to be guilty of a crime. There are separate laws, procedures and courts for children. Any statement, confession, admission, or information made by a child to police without the presence of their guardian, lawyer, or other responsible adult is presumptively not admissible as evidence unless the court is satisfied about the reason for the absence of the adult. Australian Government takes every step to rectify and rehabilitate child offender through alternative proceedings and any act is not considered as offence until court has explained to the child the nature of any allegations made against the child. To maintain confidentiality, criminal proceedings against a child are not open to the public and names are suppressed from publications. Generally, convictions of children of summary offences below the age of 16 years are not recorded and the court has discretion whether or not to record convictions.

Approaches of Other Countries

The Maekong sub-region countries have mostly included articles regulating penalties for violation of children's rights and have amended the articles over time to appropriately respond to current situations. Countries like Vietnam and Thailand have long history of having laws and regulations to promote and protect children's rights. In line with various international conventions, and declarations, the plan of action have been ratified, adapted, applied and enforced in different countries in the sub-region (Secure Care, Save the Children, 1999-2001).

Thailand has ratified the 1996 Prevention and Suppression of Prostitution Act, the 1997 Prevention and Suppression of Trafficking in Women and Children Act, the 1969 Immigration Act and empowered law enforcement bodies to implement National Legislation Relating to Child Labour. Lao PDR ratified the Convention on the Elimination of All Forms of Discrimination Against Women (CEDAW) and the Convention on the Right of Child. Domestic laws together with 1991 National Constitution, the Penal Code, Labour Law and Civil Codes have firmly placed children's and women's rights into the first comprehensive legal framework in the nation's history. The Government also signed the Declaration and Plan of Action of the World Summit for Children in 1991. Subsequently, the National Commission for Mothers and Children (NCMC) was established to draw up the first National Programme of Action for the Children (NPA).

Myanmar has ratified many conventions in relation to protect children from being abused. Subsequently, the Government has promulgated domestic legislations to follow the ratification. The Child Law, 1993 contains many provisions to protect children from exploitation, abuse, sale, etc. in order to ensure a full scale of child's development. The Penal Code, 1860 refers to offences against children such as procurement of girls, importation of girls from or to overseas, selling or buying of minors for purpose of prostitution. Under The Suppression of Prostitution Act, 1949 prostitution was discouraged and soliciting in public was considered a crime (SEAMEO Secretariat, June 2000).

In 1992, Cambodia signed the UN-Convention on the Rights of the Child reflecting the increased concern of the government in child welfare issues. Article 31, of the Constitution of Cambodia adopted in 1993 that explicitly stated that the government shall recognize and respect human rights as stipulated in the United Nation Charter, the universal declaration of human rights, and the convenience and conventions related to human rights, women's and children's right. Unlike any other states, it has also adopted law on Suppression of Kidnapping the Trafficking/Sales of Human Persons and Exploitation of Human Persons. The new labour code has also sets the minimum age of admission to employment at 15 years (Article 177). It is further stated that minors, whatever their sex, below the age of 18 and still under the responsibility of their partners or guardians cannot engage in any type of work or contract without their prior approval (Article 181).

Like many other countries and sub-regions, SAARC regions have also amended different legislations to adhere to the universal standard set forth in CRC. Nepal also ratified the UN Convention on the Rights of the Child. In fact, it was among the first batch of nations to ratify this convention to protect and safeguard children's rights. The ratification of the convention was followed by the adoption of the first children's law in the country — Child's Act which was enforced in 1992. The 'Children's Act, 1992' defines, "Child means every human being below the age of 16 years". It says, children below 10 years of age are not subject to any legal punishment and are pardoned for their acts against the law as they are innocent. But, in the case of children between ages of 14 to 16 years, they are subject to partial or half of the punishment to the adult criminals. Similarly, several articles were amended in the Labour Act, 1992, Nepal Citizenship Act, 1963, and Civil Code (Muluki Ain), 1963 to protect the best interest of the children (Gauri Pradhan, 2002).

Much of the legislations dealing with juvenile justice in the SAARC region are inadequate and inappropriate. It conforms to outdated concepts that criminalize poverty by making vagrancy, begging, and truancy, with harsh sentences for petty theft, substance abuse which particularly affect street children. Furthermore, there is often confusion in juvenile justice systems between children in conflict with the law and children in need of care and protection. Hence, a street child was liable to be arrested simply for being on the street without having committed any offence. It was essential that children in conflict with law, rehabilitation should be the focus instead of punishment. Efforts are also necessary to narrow down the existing gaps between different qualifying ages for juvenile offences in different countries. The laws of the land work in the best interest of the child. Juvenile laws, systems and personnel should be ensured to be child friendly. Thus, they have proposed to review or draft new child-friendly juvenile laws using participatory processes (including children), which will ensure transparency to the children while undertaking the process to enact a law. It was also emphasized to ensure minimum involvement of uniformed law enforcement officers in the administration of juvenile justice. Instead, probation officers, trained social workers and senior citizens should be given the responsibility for the same (UNESCO, Bangkok, 2003).

Existing Child Protection Mechanisms in India

India is the signatory of a number of international treaties pertaining to children and ratified the UN Convention on Child Rights in the year 1992. In 2005, The Government of India accepted the two Optional Protocols to the UNCRC, addressing the involvement of children in armed conflict, child prostitution and child pornography. To promote child rights within the country, various legislations, policies and schemes were amended to recognize children's rights as they were adopted in the convention. The Juvenile Justice (Care and Protection of Children) Act, 2000, is one of the legislative measures that adopted after the ratification of CRC and gave a new direction to the juvenile justice system of the country. A separate Ministry for Women and Child Development was formed in the year 2006 to emphasize the work on child welfare. A draft scheme on Integrated Child Protection was prepared (as on August 17th, 2006) to address the issue holistically. Further, a draft bill of the new 'Offence Against Children' Act was drawn up by the Women and Child Development Department, under the Ministry of Human Resource Development in the year 2006 to eliminate the violence against children. Special focus was given on child protection issues in the year 2006. As a result, Government of India included the Protection Rights of Children within the framework of Millennium Development Goals which India committed to achieve by 2015.

The following section briefly describes the key features of the Constitution, legislative measures, schemes and policies adopted by the Government of India to ensure the rights of the children. It will help us to understand the socio-legal scenario of the country in the purview of the child rights.

The Constitution of India

The Constitution of India recognizes the vulnerable position of children and their right to protection. Following the doctrine of protective discrimination, it guarantees in Article 15, special attention to children through necessary and special laws and policies that safeguard their rights. The right to equality, protection of life and personal liberty and the right against exploitation are enshrined in Articles 14, 15, 15(3), 19(1)(a), 21, 21(A), 23, 24, 39(e), 39(f) and reiterate India's commitment to the protection, safety, security and well-being of all its people including children. The Fundamental Rights and Directive Principles of the Indian Constitution provide the framework for child rights. Several laws and national policies have been framed to implement the commitment to child rights.

National Policies

The major policies and legislations formulated in the country to ensure child rights and improvement in their status include:

National Policy for Children, 1974.
National Policy on Education, 1986.
National Policy on Child Labour, 1987.
National Nutrition Policy, 1993.
Report of the Committee on Prostitution, Child Prostitutes and Children of Prostitutes and Plan of Action to Combat Trafficking and Commercial Sexual Exploitation of Women and Children, 1998.
National Health Policy, 2002.
National Charter for Children, 2004.
National Plan of Action for Children (NPAC), 2005.

Among these policies two recent policies which have had major impact on the country are:

National Charter for Children, 2004

Underlying the National Charter for Children 2004, was the intent to secure for every child the right to a healthy and happy childhood, to address the root causes that negate the healthy growth and development of children, and to awaken the conscience of the community in the wider social context to protect children from all forms of abuse, while strengthening the family, society and the nation. The Charter has the following sections on child protection:

- ★ Survival, life and liberty;
- ★ Protection of the girl child;
- ★ Protection from economic exploitation and all forms of abuse;
- ★ Care, protection, welfare of children of marginalized and disadvantaged communities; and
- ★ Ensuring child-friendly procedures;

National Plan of Action for Children (NPAC), 2005

The policy was formulated by the Department of Women and Children in the Year 2005. It gives emphasis on the following basic principles:

- ★ To regard the child as an asset and a person with human rights.
- ★ To address issues of discrimination emanating from biases of gender, class, caste, race, religion and legal status in order to ensure equality.
- ★ To accord utmost priority to the most disadvantaged, poorest of the poor and the least serves child in all policy and programme interventions.
- ★ To recognize the diverse stages and settings of childhoods, and to address the needs of each, provisions were made to entitle so that their rights and needs can be met in each situation.

The Action Plan aims at ensuring rights of all children up to the age of 18 years. It affirms the government's commitment towards ensuring all measures for the survival, growth, development and protection of all children. It also aims at creating an enabling environment to ensure protection of child rights. All the stages are encouraged to formulate State Plan of Action for Children in line with (NPAC).

National Legislations

- ★ Guardian and Wards Act, 1890.

- The Child Marriage and Restraint Act, 1929.
- Factories Act, 1954.
- Hindu Adoption and Maintenance Act, 1955.
- Probation of Offenders Act, 1958.
- Bombay Prevention and Begging Act, 1959.
- Orphanage and Other Charitable Homes (Supervision and Control) Act, 1960.
- Bonded Labour System (Abolition) Act, 1976.
- Immoral Traffic Prevention Act, 1976.
- Child Labour (Prohibition and Regulation) Act, 1986.
- Prevention of Illicit Traffic in Narcotic Drugs and Psychotropic Substances Act, 1987.
- Pre-natal Diagnostic Techniques (Regulation and Prevention of Misuse) Act, 1994.
- Persons with Disabilities (Equal Protection of Rights and Full Participation) Act, 2000.
- Juvenile Justice (Care and Protection of Children) Act (JJ Act), 2000.
- Prohibition of Child Marriage Act, 2006.
- Commission for Protection of the Rights of the Child Act, 2005.

The existing mechanisms for child protection in India primarily flow the provisions under the JJ Act, 2000 and National Plan of Action for Children 2005. Different Ministry and Departments address the child protection issues. Some of the schemes adopted by the Government of India are as follows:

Programme for Juvenile Justice

This programme has been designed for children in need if care and protection and children in conflict with law. The Government of India provides financial assistance to the State Governments/UT Administration to run institutional support system for children in need of care and protection and juveniles in conflict with law.

Childline Service — It is a 24 hours national toll fee emergency outreach support services for children with distress. Under this scheme children are provided with emergency referral services that includes rescue from abuse, shelter, medical services, counseling and repatriation.

Shishu Greh Scheme — This is the scheme for care and protection of orphans/abandoned/destitute infants or children up to 6 years and promotes in-country adoption for rehabilitating them.

An Integrated Programme for Street Children — Under this scheme, NGOs are supported to run 24 hours drop in shelters for the children with no family ties.

Rajiv Gandhi National Crèche Scheme — It is for the children of working mothers in the age group of 0-6 years. The scheme provides for comprehensive day-care services to the children of working mothers.

Scheme for Working with Children in need of Care and Protection — It is for children working as domestic help at roadside hotels, mechanic shops, etc. This scheme provides bridge education and vocational training to help children to come into the mainstream of life.

National Child Labour Project (NCLP) — It is for the rehabilitation of child labour and which has been designed to rehabilitate child labour through educational and vocational support services. Besides, Government has also formed separate Ministry of Women and Child Development and adopted various institutional support services to rescue and rehabilitate women and adolescent girls who are victim of sexual abuse and trafficking.

Integrated Child Protection Scheme (ICPS)

The Government of India in collaboration with other civil society organizations drafted (2006) the first ICPS for the country to reduce the vulnerability of children and to promote a child safety net in the society by adopting a community-based protection mechanism. ICPS aims to promote the best interest of the child and prevent violations of child rights through appropriate punitive measures against perpetrators of abuse. The proposed ICPS brings together multiple vertical schemes under one comprehensive child protection programme and integrates interventions for protecting children within the community set-up through integration of child protection with other community-based schemes. It puts emphasis to enhance the professional standard of the child protection services through improved infrastructural support, capacity building initiatives and monitoring mechanisms. It has also laid emphasis on crisis management systems through improved inter-sectoral linkages and networking and for rescue and rehabilitation of children in crisis.

Juvenile Justice (Care and Protection of Children) Act 2000

The JJ Act of 1986 was the first central legislation on juvenile justice passed by the Union Parliament providing a uniform law for the entire country. Prior to this Act each state had its own enactment on juvenile justice with there being differences in the ways juvenile were treated by different state legal system. The first uniform law on juvenile justice however did not result in any dramatic improvement in the treatment of juveniles. Juvenile Justice (Care and Protection of Children) Act 2000 gave a new dimension to the whole juvenile justice system of the country. An amendment bill was passed in 2006 to plug its loopholes.

Most of the acts now provide significance to the treatment, care, protection and developmental needs of children by adopting a child friendly approach in the adjudication and disposition of the matters for the best interest of the children. The Act also redefined children as an individual below the age of 18 years. It categorizes children as:

- ★ Children in need of care and protection.
- ★ Children in conflict with law.

Special emphasis has been given to protect the children from being abused by administration and justice authorities. Also emphasis was laid in the act to clarify the role and responsibilities of police. It instructs to set-up special police unit to deal with child related cases in each police station.

Role of Police

- ★ As soon as child in conflict with law is apprehended by police, the child shall be placed under Juvenile Police Unit or designated Child Welfare Officer.
- ★ The police should inform the parents or guardians of juvenile and the probation officer on such arrest.
- ★ In case of delay, details of the reasons to be recorded in police diary or general diary.
- ★ In case any voluntary organization takes the child to the board they should also inform the concerned police station.
- ★ The special Juvenile Police Unit or designated Child Welfare Officer shall produce the child before Magistrate or any other member of the board within 24 hours.
- ★ Prior to the production of the child before Juvenile Justice Board, the child may be placed under safe place within the police station (not in lock up) or in place of safety.

The Act also encourages children in need of care and protection to produce themselves before the juvenile committee in case violation of their basic rights. To protect children from being abused during trial the act emphasized that no juvenile shall be jointly charged with or jointly tried for any offence together with a person who is not a juvenile. The report regarding juvenile cases shall not be disclosed in any newspaper, magazine, or in any visual media regarding the inquiry, name and address of the child. Penalty extended to ₹ 1,000 will be imposed on the person who will be disclosing the matter to any form.

The Act also introduced the concept of shelter home for street or children in need of care and protection. Shelter home is a short stay home or drop in centre for children with minimum facilities of boarding, lodging, food, care and nutrition and other basic needs.

The Act also states that child can be rehabilitated or reintegrated into the mainstream society by:

- ★ Adoption.
- ★ Foster Care.
- ★ After Care Organization.

After the amendment of JJ Act, 2000, the Ministry of Home Affairs, Government of India constituted a committee to draft the Police Act which was supposed to be implemented from the year 2007. The Act has defined its role and functions; power and activities of police personnel according to their designation. It emphasized on empowering police constabulary and outlined policing patterns. The Act has emphasized also to improve the working and living conditions of police personnel and providing training for attitudinal change. It has redefined its administration and made police force accountable to their deeds/misdeeds. According to this Act, every police station should have a Women and Child Protection Desk, staffed by women personnel. A prominent display of all information required should be made public under the Right to Information Act. As per the Supreme Court guidelines, details of the persons arrested and held in lock-up should be displayed.

The Police Act, 2006, has been amended after the amendment of JJ Act, 2000. But still, no effort has been made to match the police system with the JJ Act, 2000. Thus, gaps in implementation of Juvenile Justice Administration will remain until Government made any effort to combine these two acts.

The JJ Act, 2000, provides significance on treatment, care, protection and developmental needs of children by adopting a child friendly approach. Focus has also been given on voice of children towards identification and solution of their own problems. But no effort has been made in the Police Act to incorporate this section.

Special emphasis has been made in the Juvenile Justice (Care and Protection) Act, 2000, to clarify the role and responsibilities of police. It recommends setting up of special police unit to deal with child related cases in each police station. The roles and responsibilities of police personnel designed to implement JJ Act, 2000, has not been included the Police Act. The JJ Act emphasizes to adopt child friendly approach in the adjudication and disposition of the matters for the best interest of the children. No guidelines have been designed to define the approach within the role of police personnel.

Analyzing these acts, it is felt that Government of India is still apathetic to implement juvenile justice system in proper fashion to ensure rights of the children.

SECTION 3.3

Violence Against Children — A Global Picture

Despite of new promises and universal ratification of the convention on the rights of the child, it was widely disregarded. Though no violence against children is justifiable, but it exists in every country of the world, cutting across culture, class, education, income and ethnic origin. In every region, in contradiction to human rights obligations and children's developmental needs, violence against children is socially approved, and is frequently legal and state authorized.

Many countries have failed to muster the political will to fulfil their legal obligations towards children. Children continue to suffer violence resulting in physical injury, psychological trauma and even death. Children are subject to arbitrary detention and abuse by police. Children in correctional or other institutions are beaten or tortured by staff; others are victims of arbitrary executions. In failure of law enforcement bodies to promptly and effectively investigate and prosecute cases of abuses allows these incidents to continue, The following statistics will help us to understand the range and scale of the problem:

- WHO estimated that 53,000 children died as a result of homicide and the incident was high among the age group of 15 years to 17 years (WHO, 2006).
- 80-90 per cent children suffer from third or more severe type of physical punishment in their home.
- Estimated 150 million girls and 70 million boys under 18 have experienced sexual intercourse and other forms of physical violence (UNO, 2005).

- It is estimated that in India, 20 per cent of all children under 14 years working as domestic labour (BBC News, 1st August, 2006).
- The ILO estimated the number of child workers as 44 million, while some NGO estimates show it as 55 million (ILO, 2006).
- According to ILO and UNICEF study (2000), children working in domestic service in other people's home in all developing regions of the world — Indonesia nearby 7,00,000; half a million in Brazil, 30,00,000 in Bangladesh and more than quarter million in Philippines, Haiti and Pakistan; 1,00,000 in Kenya, Peru and Sri Lanka.
- UNICEF estimates 3 million girls and women undergone some form of female genital mutilation and cutting in Sub-Saharan Africa, Egypt and Sudan. WHO estimates between 100 to 140 million women undergone some form of female genital mutilation cutting world-wide (UNICEF, 2005).
- Estimate from year 2,000 reflects that 1.8 million children were engaged in prostitution and 5.7 million in forced or bonded labour (ILO, 2006).
- The Global School-Based Student Health Survey carried out in developing countries reports that between 20 to 65 per cent school aged children are having been verbally and physically bullied in school. The situation was prevalent in industrialized countries as well (Global initiative to end all corporal punishment of children, 2006).
- ILO estimates that 126 million children out of 218 child labours in 2004 are engaged in hazardous work (ILO, 2006).

Settings Where Violence Occur

According to the UNO Report (2006) on violence against children found that children and youth experience violence generally in **four** different settings:

- Family and home.
- Community.
- Schools or educational settings.
- Institutions such as children's home, prisons and detention centres.

An attempt has been made here to narrate some of the happenings mentioned above, if not categorically but holistically, with some highlighting depiction.

Family and Home

Though the UN Convention ensures the legal and other protective measures before and after the birth against the family members and primary groups for ensuring protection of children against maltreatment, but violence within family set up was found commonly. Eliminating and responding to violence against children within family set up is perhaps the most challenging as it is considered as the most private and personal affairs. In most situation violence against children within family is not very fatal, but physical abuse, emotional neglect, rejection, insult are some common forms of abuse perpetrated by family members as a disciplinary measures have detrimental effect to child's development and well-being. Also, due to imbalance in sex-ratio and cultural practices, girls are more vulnerable to abuse than boys within family settings (WHO, 2006).

An overview of studies in 21 countries reflects that 7.36 per cent of women and 3.29 per cent of male reported sexual abuse within family during their childhood. Majority of the studies found that girls are 1.5 to 3 times more abused than boys within family circle (WHO, 2006). A study conducted by WHO in the same year reflected that 21 per cent of women reported to have been sexually abused before the age of 15 years. Some cultural and traditional practices also forced children to be abused within family that includes genital mutilation, forced marriage, emotional neglect, etc. According to WHO report, 82 million girls are forced to marry before 18 years world-wide and they in turn face high risk of physical and sexual violence in in-law's family (Finkelhor, 2005).

School and Educational Settings

Though violence against children in schools was not expected but children are also exposed to violence in educational settings. Although, it is not approved by educational authorities, various forms of abuse including corporal punishment, humiliating forms of punishment, sexual and gender-biased violence have been reported in most of the countries (United Nations General Assembly, 2006). The Global Initiative to End All Corporal Punishment of Children reports that 102 countries have banned corporal punishment, but enforcement was still uneven. Violence was also increasingly directed against lesbian, gay, bisexual and transgender young people in many countries.

Care and Justice System

World-wide 8 million children are in residential care, of which many are charged with petty crime. First time offenders are kept with other severe types of delinquent children and often with hard core adult criminals. In many countries children were also detained because of truancy, vagrancy or homelessness. It was not uncommon to find that children in detention were also subjected to various forms of corporal punishment and were at risk of physical sexual abuse by staff. It was also shocking to find that there were 77 countries which accepted corporal and other violent punishment as a part of legal disciplinary measure. Violence against child in conflict with law was identified as particularly widespread. Besides, violence in detention during pre-trial and post-trial was prevalent in almost all the countries, Physical and sexual violence and harassment against children by adult detainees, by staff/guards and by peers have also been reported in most of the countries. Arbitrary and prolonged detention, poor detention condition, physical torture including use of disciplinary measures as part of sentencing, ECT (Electro Convulsive Therapy) treatment and prolonged use of drugs were also found in some detention centres of a few countries. And most of these types of incidents were not recorded or disclosed.

Violence in Workplace

Though most of the countries have signed and ratified legislations to prohibit child labour, but it was still commonly found in most of the countries. Children were forced to work as child labours in the primary sector and secondary sectors. Pitiful and exploitative working conditions, excessive hours of work, physical abuse, hazardous work and unsafe working conditions were some of the special characteristics which show the victimization of children in various spheres of their life. In work places, violence was commonly inflicted by employers, co-workers, clients and customers. Sexual exploitation by criminal gangs and other workers have also been reported. Besides, child domestic workers were totally banned in many countries but still they are the world's invisible workers. They were made to stay alone in individual households, hidden from public scrutiny and their lives were controlled by their employers. Trapped between four walls, millions of children were toiling day and night as domestic servants in the homes of wealthier families (WHO, 2005). It was estimated that one million children are engaged in child pornography every year. In addition, bonded labour, child trafficking, kidnapping and other sexual violence were rampant in this sectors (ILO, 2002).

The study report published by UN in the General Assembly of the year 2006 reflects that violence against children takes a variety of forms and it is influenced by a wide range of factors from the personal characteristics of the victims and perpetrators to their cultural and physical environment. But much violence against children remains hidden, unreported and underreported for many reasons. Fear and stigma are among the few reasons. In many cases children and parents were afraid to report incidents of violence against them, if the perpetrator was from their own family or a powerful member of the society. Violence was also invisible because there were no safe or trusted ways for children or adults to report it. In some parts of the world, people do not trust police, social services or other authorities, particularly rural areas, where the accessibility was almost impossible. Even in many cases, reports were not recorded in a complete, transparent and consistent ways (UN, 2005).

Perception of Children Towards Police System

As the representative of the law and order machinery, police lay a very important role to safeguard the rights of children. Police is the first contact point in the whole justice machinery. In this section, we have attempted to reflect the perception of children towards police. The fundamental problem of any law enforcement administration depends upon how the implementation plan was tailored to meet the demand of the community. Most of the research studies indicate that the perception of children towards police influenced by a number of variables that includes race, socio-economic status and type of environment where the child resides (Benedict Wim & Reed and Brown Ben, 2004).

Several studies have been conducted internationally based on sub-cultural theories to know the attitude of children and young people towards authority figures which includes perception of children towards parents, teachers and police. Most of these studies were conducted with the school going children. The study conducted by Terry Nihart, Kim Michell Lersch, Christine S. Sellers and Tom Mieczkowski (2005) reveals that youth have generally positive attitude towards parents and teachers, but indifferent attitude towards police. The youth who reported more positive feeling towards parents and teachers have also reported positive feeling towards police. It also reveals that perception towards police depends upon lots of variables including age, gender, academic performance, social class, race, contact with police and likelihood of being caught or picked up by police. Feeling became more negative as the age of the children increased and the girls have reported me positive views than boys as because girls were less involved in delinquent activities as compared to the boys.

In another study, Amorso Ware (1983) found a positive correlation between attitude towards parents and police. But they discovered that attitude towards police are more positive than attitude towards parents.

Violence Against Children in India

The first National Study on Child Abuse was conducted in 2008 to cover 13 states with a sample size of 12,446 children by Minister for Women and Child Development. The study reported that 53 per cent of children faced some kind of abuse. The study found that boys were as much at risk as girls. The 'disturbing' fact was that 70 per cent of the children never reported the abuse. Compared to those in the age group 13-18, younger children (5-12 years) faced higher levels of abuse. According to the study, states like Andhra Pradesh, Assam, Bihar and Delhi reported high levels of abuse. An alarming trend revealed by the study was that the highest percentages of abusers were known people, friends and family, thereby dispelling the long-held notion of "safe families". In case of sexual abuse, more than half the child respondents (53.22%) reported of facing one or more forms of sexual abuse, either in the form of sexual assault or some kind of sexual advances. Almost 21 per cent respondents admitted to severe forms of sexual abuse — fondling of private parts, exhibiting private parts or being photographed nude. Of these, 65 reported to have been sexually assaulted.

Across different ages, the severest form of sexual abuse victims turned out to be children in the age group 11-16 while instances declined between age 16-18 years. About 73 per cent of sexual abuse victims were in the age group of 11-18 years. And 69 per cent of children said they had faced physical abuse by way of beating, burning, kicking or had been harmed otherwise. Almost 65 per cent of physical abuse victims were children in the age group 5-12 years. Almost, half the children in the country have suffered emotional abuse in the form of verbal, mental abuse or some kind of humiliation like girl-child neglect. In this case too, the largest victims of emotional abuse (47%) were children in the age group of 5-12 years. The study also highlighted that among different types of child groups, child in family, school children, child labours, street children and children in institutional care and street children were most vulnerable to sexual abuse. According to the study, about 62 per cent of children at work and about 55 per cent of street children faced some sort of sexual abuse (Ministry of Women and Child Development; Government of India, 2007).

SECTION 3.4

Street Children — A Global Scenario

Street children who spend most of the time outside the institutional set-up were more vulnerable than other children. The hostile environment contributes more to the potential violation of CRC. And street children were more vulnerable in respect to CRC because they were further exposed to extreme poverty and particularly vulnerability to the following — Violence (Art. 19), Disease (Art. 24), Discrimination (Art. 2), Sexual Abuse and Exploitation (Art. 34, 32), Substance Abuse (Art. 33), Emotional Deprivation (Art. 19, 31), Exploitative and Harmful Child Labour (Art. 32), Denial of Rights within the Juvenile Justice System (Art. 37, 40), Arbitrary Execution (Art. 6), Torture (Art. 37), Lack of Access to Education (Art. 28, 29), Healthcare (Art. 24) and Lack of Identity Documents (Art. 7) (UN Convention on the Rights of the Child, 1989).

There were lots of differences among the national and international agencies about the definition of street children but today the phenomenon of "street children" was universally accepted. A few decades ago, children wandering on the streets were identified by their occupation or by what they did to survive. "Rag pickers", "vendors", "shoe-shine boys", "porters", etc. were termed as street children. Today with increasing awareness among governmental and international agencies "street children" are seen as an especially vulnerable group worthy of special interest, attention and intervention. The term "Street Children" in a very narrow sense may suggest children such as those popularly known as '*rag pickers*' in India; '*parking boy*' in Kenya; '*peggy boys*' in Philippines; '*pivetes*' in Brazil; '*pajaro frutero*' in Peru and '*homeless youth*' or '*runaways*' in some developed countries. Agarwal (1999) and UNICEF (1988), described all children who send, live and earn their livelihood from the streets as "Children in Especially Difficult Circumstances" (CEDC). According to UNICEF, street children can be defined under these **three** broad heads:

- Street-Living.
- Street-Working.
- Street-Family.

Street Living Children — Children who cut ties with their families and live alone on the streets.

Children of Street Living Families — Children who live with their family on the streets.

Street Working Children — Children who spend all their time or most of their time working on the streets to provide income for their families or for themselves. These children have a home to return to and do not usually sleep on the streets.

Many studies tried to categories street children into different groups but found it to be difficult to differentiate. In this section below, efforts are made to understand the socio-economic profile and violence occurred against children who live with their families on the streets.

Socio-economic Profile of Children Living on Streets

Although there was no official statistics available to know the number of street children but still it is estimated that there are 150 million street children world-wide. This phenomenon is often attributed to multiple factors including economic stagnation, unequal distribution of wealth, lack of welfare and social services, AIDS, and civil war, natural disaster, unplanned rural-urban migration. The study conducted in Araaju, city in Brazil (2010) indicates clear gender imbalance in street children. It suggests that boys became independent from an earlier age and girls were taught to cope with poverty while staying at home. Families of street children had a median of six family members and lived in low cost housing on the outskirts of the main cities. Most houses had basic facilities as piped water and electricity but limited sanitary facilities. Majority of the families were single parent families, of which 46 per cent were single female headed and 7 per cent were single male headed households. Of the total only 40 per cent biological fathers lived with the family. Most parents were unemployed or earn low wage. Though illiteracy is a major problem among street kids but the study report shows that the enrolment rate in education was higher among younger street children (S. Abdelgalil, R.G. Gurgel, S. Theobald and L.E. Cuevas, 2004).

A Rapid Assessment Study (RAS) carried out in Cairo and Alexandria also found similar type of situation of street families. It reflected that the average family size of the street families was 5.94 and it ranges between 2 to 11 people at maximum. Demographic origin showed that the most (88%) of the families were from urban areas and only 12 per cent of the families have been migrated from rural areas. This study also shows that most of the children (62%) have dysfunctional families due to divorce, separation, imprisonment, death and sickness of parents or both. Because of the accessibility, the enrolment in primary schools were quite high (70%) among street kids. But it was reported that the dropout rate as also high, whereas only 30 per cent have never been to school. It was highlighted in the report that because of the abuse, neglect, exploitation within and outside the family and peer pressure, children left their families and preferred to stay alone on the streets (UNODCCP; Rapid Assessment Study, 1999).

Violence Against Street Children

The CRC sets out a framework for protection that emphasizes the family and community to bear the main responsibility for caring of children (Art. 5, 18). The role of the state was to support and enable families and communities to fulfil this role. However, it was an unfortunate fact that in many cases families and communities were not protective and nurturing.

Both the study in Brazil and RAS in Cairo and Alexandria showed that children living on the streets were forced to engage in economic activities from very early age to contribute to their family income. Children were also found to work as beggars, garage mechanics, hawkers, fruit sellers, rag pickers, in recycling factories and as prostitutes. Another study conducted in Araaju as mentioned earlier, identified mothers of most of the street children started working since their early adolescence; some were as young as 7 years, and by the age of 14 nearly all were working. Some girls were under pressure to work as sex workers and followed their mothers' and aunts' activities and received clients at home. The prevalence of adolescent pregnancy was also high, and 50 per cent had at least one child by 17 years of age.

Together with the high rate of family disintegration, children reported physical abuse as a major factor for pushing them away from home. It was highlighted in the RAS report that the prevalence of abuse was 82 per cent and neglect was 62 per cent which were the major contributing factors to push children on the streets. Parental drug and alcohol use among the fathers and stepfathers was considered precipitating factors for family disruption. Children also frequently used drugs, and said that drugs were easily obtained within the neighbourhood. Most parents had been street children themselves, often worrying about drugs, accidents, and murders. Parental fear for girls was mainly for rape and sexual harassment. But none of the parents perceived the negative impact of the street life could affect their children's psychological development, recreations, education, or school performance. In the background report of world of street children almost same situation was depicted. It described the problems faced by street children under three broad heads — *physical, psychological* and *social*. Under physical problems, emphasis was laid on the lack of adequate nutrition, and homelessness. Besides, children living on the streets were exposed to lots of psycho-social problems that include stressful past, transitory lifestyle which forced them to use psychoactive substances to sometimes unlearn behaviour. This, in turn, leads to medical problems, increase in the probability of accidents, violence and unprotected sex. Over time, it could lead to complications such as brain and liver damage and HIV/AIDS infections. Children living on the streets were also deprived from resources and opportunities. Moreover, exploitation within and outside the family and stigmatization in the society push them to added difficulties.

The UN Commission on Human Rights reported that the street children came from the poorest section of the society, and it was this initial socio-economic disadvantage that results into lack of protection, and made them so vulnerable to violence. The vast majority of street-living children were victims of domestic violence, and/or sexual and psychological abuse. Sexual abuse and exploitation of street children was common experience amongst boys and girls. However, street girls were the most vulnerable children in the world. Domestic violence, sexual abuse, neglect and rejection were some of the factors which pushed girls to violence and extreme vulnerability. Girls were particularly vulnerable to sexual violence. Because of their 'non-normative' sexual activity like sexual involvement with multiple partners, 'survival' sexing exchange for food, shelter and protection, and the difficulty in drawing boundaries between sexual abuse and commercial sexual exploitation, they suffer a perceived loss of rights over their bodies. This leads to manifestation of 'otherness' or dehumanization. Violence was also prevalent in gang culture. It was used to maintain discipline and asset authority within the hierarchy of the gang as well as taking the form in inter-gang violence. Violence can also be related to substance abuse. Involvement in the drug trade (often linked to gangs) carried a high risk of violence both against children and by children. Younger street children were involved as couriers and then became increasingly associated with the business of drug trafficking, as they get older. The average life expectancy of gang members in Rio was about 29 years.

UN Commission on Human Rights also reported that street children were particularly vulnerable to violence within juvenile justice system.

They were more likely to come into contact with the juvenile justice system in the first place, and were less able to defend themselves against violations of their rights within that system. Children were often detained by police without sufficient cause, and then subjected to brutal interrogations and torture in order to elicit confessions or information. Once placed in juvenile and criminal correctional institutions, children were frequently mistreated and abused, enduring severe corporal punishment, torture, forced labour, denial of food, isolation, restraints, sexual assaults, and harassment. In many instances, children were also detained with adults, leaving them at increased risk of physical and sexual abuse (Consortium for Street Children; April, 2001).

Delinquency Among Street Children and Justice System

In article 40, CRC articulates the minimum standard of juvenile justice system to be administered by all the signatories. It says that a child was presumed innocent until proven guilty according to law. Child in conflict with law has the right to treatment that promotes the child's sense of dignity and worth. The child and his guardian had the right to be informed of the charges against him or her and have the right to legal and other assistance in preparation and presentation of his/her defence. It also says that a child cannot be compelled to give testimony or to confess guilty, to examine adverse witness (UNCRC, 1989).

Looking at international perspective of juvenile crime, the policies of other countries provide some perspective on criminal justice. An international study of 15 countries — Australia, Austria, Belgium, Denmark, England and Wales, France, Germany, Hungary, Italy, Japan, Netherland, New Zeland, Russia, Sweden and Switzerland, notes that all have special provisions for young criminals in their justice systems, although some (Denmark, Russia and Sweden) have no special courts for juveniles (Nicolas MC Bala and Joseph, P. Harnick, 2001).

Research studies and case studies documented by different international, national agencies and individuals reflect that street children were denied of the right to treatment by justice authorities. Further, there were reports and case studies from few countries, which indicate that street children were abused by the justice system itself. Added to this, the exposure to poor environment, street children get involved in delinquent activities from an early age. The Rapid Situational Analysis Report demonstrates that 17,228 children were exposed to delinquent activities in Egypt in 5 years. Most of these children (86%) were involved in violence, which represented a major feature of their everyday life. And unfortunately, most of these children were at risk of violence by the authorities. Children on the street were beaten, tortured, sexually assaulted and sometimes killed. Several factors contribute to this phenomenon like perception of police towards street children as vagrants and criminals, widespread corruption and culture of police violence, the inadequacy and non-implementation of legal safeguards, and the level of impunity that officials enjoy. These street children were easy targets, as they are young, often with short stature, poor, ignorant of their rights, and generally without any responsible adult guardian to look after them. Police also have financial incentives to sort to violence against children. They beat children for their money or demand payment for protection, to avoid false charges, or to release from (often illegal) custody (UNODCCP, Rapid Assessment Study, 1999).

It is well known fact that children, who were abused in the past, later became the perpetrator of abuse. In Mongolia, 50 per cent of such street children turned to actually committing offence. A research conducted in Mongolia showed that children were being exploited sexually and were forced to work as labour as a result of intolerable home conditions. Within this context, it was estimated that 50 per cent of street children were abused, and many of these children have turned to petty crime, which constitutes the majority of offences committed by youth in Mongolia (Civil Society Forum for East and South East Asia on Promoting and Protecting Rights of Street Children. 2010).

In the Philippines, 80.9 per cent of children experienced some form of abuse and exploitation prior to their commissioning of the offence, mostly petty crimes. Unsupervised children were often confused with juvenile offenders due to lack of services, poor coordination between police and social workers and lack of proper documentations. In some countries, street children were at risk of being picked up by the police and placed in custody because they were regarded as 'unsupervised children' and the police cell became a sort of 'temporary shelter' (Marianne Murdoch-Verwijs Lim, 1990). In East and South East Asia, it was reported that street children face inhumane and degrading treatment, torture and abuse from police and other inmates. They were detained for lengthy period of time before trials. All these countries reported that limits set by the law was almost never respected. Over 50 per cent of accused children were detained at the pre-trial stage. Once the children came in contact with justice system, they were often treated as criminals and/or as adults.

The street children in Bulgaria were deprived of their basic rights and it was mostly by the police, the very people who were responsible to protect them. Human Rights Watch in Bulgaria reported that street children were often subjected to physical abuse and other mistreatment by the police, both on the street and in police lockups, and by skinhead gangs, who brutally attack the children because of their Roma (Gypsy) ethnic identiiy. Whereas, police often harass and abuse the children because they perceive them to be criminals. Once detained by the police, children became victim to gross procedural inadequacies in the juvenile justice system of Bulgaria (Human Rights Watch; Children of Bulgaria, 2005).

Verbal and physical abuse from the community and the police were some of the most common problems the street children face in their everyday life in Kenya as well. The police make arbitrary arrests of children for various reasons — loitering, carrying illegal weapons, refusing to give into sexual demands, or being rude to police officers. Once in police custody, the harassment of these children continues and sometimes worst. Abuse ranges from being insulted, beaten, kicked, and detained, to sexual abuse or rape. The detention centres were often so crowded that there was no separate cell for adults and children. The food served to these children was neither sufficient nor hygienic, and there was only one bucket at a toilet for everybody. At the police station, children were beaten badly and sometimes forced to make a false statement for a crime. Many children reported that they were scarce of police because they have heard from many other children, who had gone through very bad experiences while they were detained. Children were held in remand homes or detention centers before receiving a trial. If they are subsequently found guilty, they are sent to rehabilitation centres. Conditions at the remand homes were as bad as the police cells. But at the prison or borstal, the situation was far worse. In some cases, children were put together in the adult prison due to lack of space, or because they were assumed to be adults by the judge. There were reports of children being handcuffed to beds, stripped naked and beaten up. Sometimes children were not allowed to eat, or their food was withheld as a form of punishment. They were often subject to sexual abuse or sodomy by the guards or older youth (UN Office for the Humanitarian Affairs, 2007).

Thousands of children living in Guatemala's streets faced routine beatings, thefts and sexual assaults by the National Police and private security guards. During a Human Rights Watch investigation in the year

1996, nearly every child reported of assaults by police. These assaults occurred on busy streets of the city during the days, on quite streets in the middle of the nights, in alleys and deserted areas, and in police station. Often, common people on the street or other police officers witness such episodes. Children reported that the police bothered them almost every single day. They hit children and even steal their money, shoes, jackets and other belongings. If denied to give them what they want, they beat or arrest children arbitrarily. Girls on the street were additionally vulnerable to sexual attacks. A 16 years old girl reported of being raped by two police officers while a third kept the watch. The officers threatened to put her in prison for having *marijuana* if she made any noise. Like her, this has happened to many other girls living on the streets (Human Rights Watch; New York, 1997).

Compared to other countries in SAARC region, Nepal has less number of children in conflict with law. A few incidents highlighted in CWIN's (Child Workers in Nepal) reported would help us to understand the perception of justice system towards street children and the administration of Juvenile Justice System in Nepal. In the first week of August 1997, a group of 15 street based working children were arrested from the airport area and they were tried at the District Court instead of Juvenile Justice Court. They were also sent to Central Prison instead of any children's home. The children in the age group 10-15 were arrested on charge of creating public nuisance and prosecuted under the Public Nuisance Act. Their offence warranted a penalty of up to ₹ 2,500 and failing to pay so, they were imprisoned for at least 6 months. The children were just rounded up while working or walking on the street and were accused of creating nuisance in public place. After the arrest, they were kept in the custody for five days before they were sent to the Central Jail, where the seasoned adult criminals are kept. It was learnt that most of the imprisoned children migrated from the rural areas and did not have contact with their families. Only few children, whose parents/guardians resided in Kathmandu and periodically visited them. Of the total, 3 children were lucky to get free when their parents were able to pay for the bail. But for the rest, either homeless or runaways, who made a meagre living by rag picking or begging, were not able to pay the bail. As a result, they were languishing in prison along with the adult criminals (Gauri Pradhan, 2012).

Thus, we can conclude that street children were more likely to come into (actual or perceived) conflict with the law in the first place and in addition to that they were not sufficiently capable to defend themselves against violations of their rights once they fall into the trap. Usually, the street children came from the poorest section of the society and, from indigenous minority and/or low caste ethnic groups. These factors add up to a pattern of multiple handicaps which have serious implications for children's treatment in law, prison and in their access to justice. As victims of a society that criminalizes poverty with harsh sentence for petty (often 'survival') theft and amorphous 'vagrancy' laws. These street children were often at the mercy of state authorities, and unfortunately the same responsible officials contribute to the state's failure to protect and care for one of its most vulnerable group of citizens.

Street Children — The Indian Scenario

Until 1993, the term "street children" was not used in the "Official Vocabulary" of post-Independent India. Under pressure from the international agencies, NGOs and social activists, the Government of India agreed to set-up a "Scheme for Assistance to Street Children" under Ministry of Welfare, which was launched in February, 1993. The National Policy for Children declared in 1974 emphasized the provision of equal opportunities for the development to all children during their growing years. Policy stresses programme to maintain, educate, and train destitute to protect children against neglect, cruelty and exploitation, but it was practically only on the paper. There was absolutely no legislature that specifies the term 'street children' in the judiciary of India. The laws applicable under the Juvenile Justice (Care and Protection of Children) Act, 2000, relate quite strongly to the care of and rights of street children in general, without mentioning them in any specific terms, and were found at a national level without proper mechanism to implement and change the condition of the children in real life. In fact, many police officers/constables in the field do not know about the details of the Act. It was a well known fact that the street children constitute a marginalized group in most societies. But, India had the largest population of street children in the world. At least 18 million children live or work on the streets of urban India, labouring porters at bus or railway terminals; as mechanics in informal auto-repair shops; as vendors of food, tea, or handmade articles; as street tailors; or as rag pickers picking through garbage and selling usable materials to local buyers.

UNICEF estimates of 11 million street children in India in 1994 were considered to be conservative. It was estimated 1,00,000-1,25,000 street children each in Mumbai, Kolkata and Delhi, with 45,000 in Bengaluru (Civil Society Forum for South Asia, 2001). Centre for Communication and Development Studies also estimated that in urban areas alone there were 11 million children on the streets. Of them 4,20,000 street children live in the six metropolitan cities of the country. And a fraction of the total, i.e. 24,000 received some services under the scheme of 'Welfare of the Street Children'. It is estimated that in India, 90 per cent of street children were working children with regular family ties who live with their families, but were on the streets due to poverty and their parents' unemployment. The remaining 10 per cent are either working children with few family ties and considered the streets as their homes or they were abandoned and neglected children with no family ties (J. Health, Manag, 2009). Unfortunately, the harsh environment in which they dwell and their lifestyle, make the street children vulnerable to abuse. This threatens their mental, physical, social and spiritual health. Most of these children use alcohol and other drugs. Due to their experiences, they view health and social services with suspicion. Some aspects of street life such as extreme mobility, low knowledge of HIV, recreational sex, lack of adequate responsible adult protection and supervision compound the vulnerability of street children (Consortium for Street Children and Violence, 2001).

Unlike in many other countries, exploitation and abuse against children were also found to be a common phenomenon in India. With little or no protection and guidance from adults, street children were highly vulnerable to exploitation by adults. Living in unhygienic conditions, suffering from malnutrition, and lacking the basic amenities of safe drinking water, electricity and sanitation these children were at greater risk for poor health than their rural counterparts (Bhavnagri & Vaswani, 1999). Although findings were no consistent, the reports indicate that street children have twice as many health problems, including developmental delay, depression, anxiety, behavioural problems and social incompetence, when compared to other urban children (Rafferty & Shinn, 1991). As Le Roux and Smith (1998) noted, street children and children in labour were a reflection of broader systematic economical issues. Perceived as marginalized on one hand and as refugees on the other, these children were the subject of both pity and contempt. Given the enormity and complexity of the problem, it was a formidable challenge for India. The street children were often suspicious of adults, whom they view as responsible for their condition or as abusers.

UN Commission on Human Rights reported that street children come from the poorest sections of the society, and it was this initial socio-economic disadvantage, and the resulting lack of protection, that renders them to be so vulnerable to violence. Violence against street children in the public arena, to examine violence in the private arena was common and notoriously difficult area for human rights protection. The vast majority of street-living children were victims of domestic violence, sexual and psychological abuse. Sexual abuse and exploitation of street children was common amongst boys and girls. However, street girls were amongst the most vulnerable children in the world. Domestic violence, sexual abuse, neglect and rejection were just some of the factors pushing girls to extreme vulnerability. Girls were particularly vulnerable to sexual violence.

Human Rights Watch conducted a survey in India during February and March 1995 and December and January 1995-96. They spoke with more than one hundred street children, as well as representatives of non-governmental organizations, social workers, human rights activists, human right lawyers, and other individuals who worked with street children in metro-cities of India. Of the one hundred children interviewed, sixty complained of police abuse in the form of detention, beatings, extortion, or verbal abuse. All the children reported to be afraid of the police. Street children risk violence at the hands of the authorities much more frequently than other children. Children on the street were beaten, tortured, sexually assaulted, and sometimes killed. Several factors contribute to this phenomenon: perception of police that street children are vagrants and criminals, widespread corruption and a culture of police violence, the inadequacy and non-implementation of legal safeguards, and the level of impunity that officials enjoy. Street children were easy targets because they are young, often small, poor, ignorant of their rights, and frequently do not have responsible adults to look out for them. Police also have financial incentives to resort to violence against children (Human Rights Watch, Children's Rights in India, 2012).

Conclusion

However, it seems from the reviews that a change was taking place in the socio-legal systems of the world. Despite all the national and international instruments, the situations of street children were still the same in all developing and under-developed countries of the world. They were physically, mentally and sexually exploited within and outside their families. Forced labour, slavery, kidnapping, child trafficking were some of the crime perpetrated very frequently against children. It was very unfortunate that in many circumstances the judiciary systems also played the role of enabler in this whole game. They do not access the judiciary system because of fear and ignorance. Many times the representatives of the law enforcement bodies also act as the perpetrators of abuse. Therefore, this study was an attempt to identify types of abuse perpetrated against children within and outside their families, their self-protection mechanism, perception towards law and order machineries and their opinion towards a child friendly police system and its procedure. Information was also collected from their parents regarding perception towards child abuse and opinion towards creating child friendly law and order systems and its procedures.

4

METHODOLOGY

This methodology section describes the basic plan and steps adopted to enquire, comprehend and interpret problems and statements used in the research. After formulating the study objectives, the researchers made an attempt to define key terminologies used in the research to avoid ambiguity for the readers. This chapter describes the universe, sampling techniques used considering the research objectives and its feasibility. Different tools were used by us to recognize different forms of abuse that children of families living on the streets face and socio-economic conditions that build insecurities within the children and their families. The researchers have also made an attempt to understand the implementation of juvenile justice system for the protection of these children. To understand these factors, qualitative and quantitative tools were used to capture the holistic views of the children and their families towards their own rights; different abusive experiences that the children face; and various protective mechanisms that children along with their families adopt.

To achieve the **objectives** of the study, the following steps were used:

1. Review of secondary resources.
2. Direct observation of the situation of the street living families.
3. Discussion with children and their parents living on the streets.
4. Discussion with the personnel, government and social organizations working with street children.
5. Preparation of research design.
6. Identification of basic tools and pilot testing within the targeted respondents.
7. Finalization of tools.
8. Collection and cross validation of data.
9. Analysis of data.

Operational Definitions

For the purpose of the study, the researchers made an attempt to review and analyze definitions used by other international agencies. But, it was observed that there are wide discrepancies in the use of terminologies among different agencies. And this was done with the participation of the street children. Thus, the terminologies referred for this particular study have been operationally defined. And this was done with the participation of the street children.

Child

A child is defined as a person not having completed 18 years of age. The sample for this study constituted children in the age group of 12 to 16 years. Children were divided into two groups according to their gender.

Street Children

The street children are defined as children living with their families on the streets/pavements.

Parents

Parents in this study mean either the biological parents and/or the step parents, whosoever was staying with the child and had taken the responsibility of guardianship of the child.

Child Abuse

Child abuse refers to the intended, unintended and perceived maltreatment, whether habitual or not, of the child, including any one of the following:

- Any act, deed or word which degrades or demeans the intrinsic worth and dignity of a child as a human being.
- All forms of physical and/or emotional ill treatment, sexual abuse, neglect or negligent treatment or commercial or other exploitation, resulting in actual or potential harm to the child's health, survival, development or dignity in the context of a relationship of responsibility, trust or power (WHO,1999).

There are many forms of child abuse and they vary according to the cultural and geographical settings. The present study, however, focuses on the following **three** prominent forms of child abuse.

Physical abuse is a injury resulting from physical aggression. Even if the injury was not intended, the act is considered as physical abuse. It includes beating, slapping, shaking, kicking, pinching, biting, choking, hair-pulling, burning with cigarettes, scalding water, or other hot objects, severe physical punishment, or otherwise harming a child.

Sexual abuse refers to the use of a child for the sexual gratification of an older adolescent or adult and involves the exposure of a child to sexual contact, activity or behaviour. It is important to note that sexual abuse can occur between children. The key to defining an act as abusive is the difference in age and power between the victim and the offender. This may include the following:

(a) *Fondling:* touching or kissing a child's genitals; or making a child fondle an adult's genitals.
(b) *Volition of Bodily Privacy:* forcing the child to undress, spying on a child in the bathroom or bedroom.
(c) *Child Pornography:* using a child in the production of pornography, such as a film or magazine.
(d) Exposing Children to Pornography (movies, magazines, or websites) or enticing children to pornographic sites on the internet.
(e) Luring a child for sexual liaisons, through the internet or by any other means.
(f) *Sexual Acts with a Child:* penetration, intercourse, incest, rape, oral sex, sodomy, etc.
(g) Child prostitution or sexual exploitation (forcing or using a child to perform sex with others).
(h) Exposing children to adult sexuality in any form (showing sex organs to a child, forced observation of sexual acts, telling "dirty" stories, group sex).

Emotional abuse is also known as verbal abuse, mental abuse, and psychological maltreatment. It includes an act or failure to act by parents, caretakers, peers and others that have caused or could cause serious behavioural, cognitive, emotional or mental distress/trauma. It can range from a simple verbal insult to severe form of punishment. It includes ignoring, rejection, and lack of positive reinforcement, yelling or screaming, threatening, negative comparison to others, belittling, telling the child he or she is "no good", "worthless", "bad" or "a mistake", shaming, humiliating, or name-calling, habitual blaming, using extreme forms of punishment, such as confinement to a closet or dark room, trying to a chair for a long period of time or terrorizing a child; child exploitation — such as child labour, witnessing the physical abuse of others, use of abusive language and forcing the child to be involved in illegal activities.

Physical detachment/detention includes child kidnapping, parental child abduction, or child stealing, arrest by the police and being detained in the police station or detention in any institution.

Perpetrator of abuse The study defines perpetrators of abuse as any person involving directly or indirectly in the act of exploitation or abuse of the child. The perpetrators of abuse can be grouped as under:

- *Biological parents* or step parents with whom the child stays.
- *Relatives/family members* are persons having close association with the child.
- *Employer* is an individual or institution where the child works, ranging from few hours to months/years.
- *Service providers* are governmental or non-governmental agencies involved in the provision of services for the children and their families living on the streets.
- *Legal machinery* is a system developed by the government to maintain law and order in the society. This includes police officials, railway security forces, lawyers and officials of Child Welfare Committee (CWC) and members of Juvenile Justice Board.
- *Local leaders* include any influential person of the area. He/she may be involved in politics, labour union activities, leader of children's group or welfare activities in the area.
- *Stranger* is any person unknown to the child and it includes floating people and passer-by.

Offence is an act that is punishable under any law for the time being in force.

Child friendly approach in juvenile justice system — It is an approach that makes children comfortable to participate in the affairs of the justice system to protect their interest. For the purpose of the study, opinion of children was sought regarding legal procedures adopted by law and other machineries, behaviours of the personnel involved in the system, physical appearance and accessibility of the system, and processes adopted during negotiation and interrogation and time taken for the adjudication and disposition of cases.

Type of Research

This is mainly a combination of *diagnostic* and *exploratory* research. The diagnostic research is basically concerned with an existing social problem, its basic nature and forms. It also helps in discovering and testing certain variables with respect to their association or disassociation. A diagnostic study is also concerned with the case as well as with the treatment. Whereas, the exploratory research tries to discover the facts and gives insight of the issue studied. Exploratory research is necessary to be familiar with the subject and the scope and limit of the research study. It can help to clarify concepts and formulate the hypothesis.

This research study can be called as diagnostic research as it deals with abuse of children living on the streets, which is not a new phenomenon. It tries to find out the causal relationship between the socio-economic conditions of the street living families and various forms of abuse perpetrated against their children. The researchers also describes this study as an exploratory as it seeks to find out how people get along in the street life, what meaning they give to their actions, and what issues concern them. The goal is to learn "what is going on here?" and to investigate social phenomena without explicit expectations. The study intends to capture the practical experiences of children and parents regarding various forms of child abuse and protection mechanisms they adopt with their environment. It also tries to discover ideas and insights of children and their parents regarding child friendly approaches that legal machineries should adopt to protect the best interest of children. The study also intended to develop a working hypothesis from an operational point of view regarding the friendly way of dealing with children living on the streets by the law enforcement bodies, especially police personnel. This study identifies the views of children and their families regarding the operational protocols that police personnel should follow to help children to speak out their problems and to get required legal assistance for protection within their own environment.

Universe of the Study

Children of families living on the streets of Kolkata were selected as universe for the study. The population residing on the streets in the city was highly mobile and hence it was difficult to have a close estimate of the number of children living with their families on the streets of Kolkata. Both the Government and NGOs claimed to have programmes running for children and their families, but none of them had a comprehensive data of the beneficiaries. The study was designed with purposive sampling method covering 5 zones of Kolkata.

Sampling Design

1. *Selection of Zones*

For the purpose of the study, 5 administrative zones from the jurisdiction of Kolkata Police were selected — North, South, East, West and Central. From each of these zones, areas were selected where more than 10 families were residing in a cluster. Support was taken from local NGOs or CBOs to establish rapport with families living on the street.

2. *Designing an Empirical Map*

The areas where children lived with their families were identified through regular visits. Once the area was selected, it was plotted on the city map of Kolkata. The reference clusters were identified on the map and marked accordingly. During this process, NGO functionaries, taxi/auto drivers and local shop-owners were consulted. Transact walks were also conducted in the identified areas to get an idea of the selected zones.

3. *Selection of NGOs and CBOs*

Frequent and repeated visits were conducted in the identified localities to gain better understanding of the areas. During the study, 18 key locations were earmarked from 5 administrative zones, where a cluster of more than 10 families were living on the streets. To identify reputed NGOs and CBOs (Community Based Organizations), the local government authorities and international development agencies working in the area were contacted. The NGO directory published by UNICEF, in coordination with Government of West Bengal, was also very useful to identify NGOs working in those selected areas. Of all the NGOs and CBOs identified in the area, few active organizations were shortlisted based on the feedback received from the community. Finally, NGOs/CBOs were identified for the purpose of this study on the organization's willingness to participate in the study and their rapport with the children and their families living on the street of a specific locality. The following are some of the major NGOs and CBOs consulted during the span of the study.

Table 4.1: List of NGOs and CBOs

Zone	*Address*	*NGOs and CBOs*
North Kolkata	• Narkeldanga Main Road • Shobhabazar Metro	CINI Asha Zahid Sporting Club Madan Mohan Club
Central Kolkata	• Lebutala Park, Santosh Mitra Squar • Maulali Crossing • AJC Bose Road • Sealdah Railway Station • Taraltala	CINI Asha Saraswati Club
East Kolkata	• Kasba • Garihata flyover	DAS
West Kolkata	• Taratala flyover • Babu Ghat • Hastings	BLC
South Kolkata	• Netaji Subhas Road • Rash Behari Avenue	Children's Paradise (a religious organization)

Selection of Children and Parents

Number of families living on the streets in their coverage area was enumerated with the help of the team members of the NGO/CBO and or local leaders. About 920 children and their families were identified for the field visit. Of the total, 230 children in the age group of 12-16 years living with their families on the streets of 5 zones of Kolkata were shortlisted. From that list, only 40 children were selected from each zone through the process of purposive random sampling method and availability of children during the time of data collection. And of these 200 children, 50 parents living in and around the area for at least more than one year were selected for FGD (Focus Group Discussion). For the purpose of the study, equal number of boys and girls were selected from each zone.

Tools and Techniques for Data Collection

The tools were used for identification, cross verification and analysis of the information in the context of the set objectives of the research. Qualitative research methodologies were aimed at gaining a deep understanding of specific vulnerability factors, psycho social dynamics of the families living on the streets and their self-protection mechanisms. During the course of the study, the researchers intended not to impose the researcher's operational definitions on the participants but rather, tried to use different qualitative tools to explore ideas from the participants. The core intention behind the study was also to have a voice for children living with their families on the streets through ensuring their active participation to identify problems and its solutions. The concept of participation is still a subject to debate and practicability is further unevaluated. The researchers had made conscious efforts to ensure participation of children and their parents to foster open dialogue to amass information considering in their local context. Thus, the researchers also tried to maintain flexibility in using tools to adjust to the setting of the respondents, modified the use of existing tools to make them friendly and interesting for children.

Keeping in mind the sensitivity of the issue, child friendly tools and techniques were used to create an enabling environment for the children to respond with ease and share their experiences on different forms of abuse. The following tools and techniques were used:

I. *Interview with Children*

One-to-one interaction with the children living on the streets of Kolkata was conducted using the structured interview schedule which is given in the annexure at the end. This was conducted to elicit specific information from them and was conducted on the basis of guidelines developed for this study. Before designing the interview schedule, a series of group discussions were conducted with children to understand the field situation. Based on that, an interview schedule was designed and field tested. Accordingly, necessary modifications were made. The researchers interacted with individual children and gathered their responses on the items given in the questionnaire through a child friendly dialogue. The responses of the street children were jotted down by the researchers on individual interview schedule of each child respondent separately. The interaction with the children was conducted in Bengali and Hindi language.

II. *Critical Incident Techniques*

Critical incident technique was helpful used to examine a number of issues pertinent to a particular problem. It allows respondents to understand the dimensions of their role and their interactions in different social setting to narrate their experiences of abuse. Critical incident techniques were used during one-to-one interview to facilitate children to narrate their experiences of abuse. The researchers narrated some stories that facilitated children to relate and recall their experiences of abuse that they had faced in the recent past. This enabled the researchers to understand and relate different experiences of children with most frequently occurred forms of abuse and their reaction.

III. *Focus Group Discussion*

Focus group discussion technique was used to produce good conversation on a given topic. A group was formed with typically 7 to 10 volunteers who met with some specific demographic needs. The purpose of focus groups was to gain information and insight as to how the target audience would react to the topic of discussion. The purpose of focus groups was to find information about how specific demographic group feels about a particular issue. It also allowed direct interaction and clarification as well as facilitate those who may not be able to communicate in written form. This was less expensive than conducting individual interviews.

It was important to note that obtaining information regarding sexual abuse was difficult as it was a very sensitive issue and there was a social stigma attached to it. For this reason, the quantitative data may not reflect the actual incidence of sexual abuse of the children living on the streets. We gave more emphasized on qualitative tools to supplement and complement the data revealed from one-to-one interview method. We used these techniques to quickly identify types of abuse perpetrated against children, perpetrators of abuse and the self-defense mechanisms.

Other Participatory Exercises

Ranking and Scoring Exercises

Ranking and scoring techniques was one of the acknowledged tools for participatory appraisal. It helps to activate respondents to undertake ranking exercise and leave more room for discussion as to what should be ranked/scored. Therefore, ranking exercises are relevant for participatory identification of indicators.

It is important to note that obtaining information regarding sexual abuse was difficult as it was a very sensitive issue and there was a social stigma attached to it. For this reason, the quantitative data may not reflect the actual incidence of sexual abuse of the children living on the streets. For this reason, the researchers used the qualitative tools to supplement and complement the data revealed from one-to-one interview method. They used this technique to quickly indentify types of abuse perpetrated against children, perpetrators of abuse and the self-defense mechanism. From this exercise, they tried to find out most commonly occurred abuse and their perpetrators. The children were provided with assistance, if needed to enlist the types of abuses other children or their friends usually face in similar living environment. It was conducted separately with both the boys and girls and the findings were grouped as per the gender. Based on this group work, children identified themselves 37 forms of maltreatment or abuse that were perpetrated against them. Further, the types of maltreatment and abuses faced by the children were grouped in five different categories with the help of children's inputs. The categories were — physical, mental or emotional, sexual abuse, economic exploitation and legal abuse. Similarly, they identified the perpetrators according to the social settings and stated their self-defense mechanisms.

Case Studies and Stories

Case study, as name indicates concentrates on special case. The case study places more importance over the full analysis of the limited social unit in depth. The objective of this method was to locate the factors that account for the behavioural pattern of the given unit as an integrated totality.

For the purpose of the study, researchers identified the children during one-to-one interview for case study. Against each type of abuse, one child from each gender was selected for the purpose of the case study. Those children were studied intensively to gain a holistic understanding of the problem. The researchers tried to understand the complex of factors that were operative within the street living environment and the reaction of those children to those stimulants.

Venn Diagram

A Venn diagram is an illustration of the relationships between and among sets, or groups of objects that share something in common. This was used in *Participatory Research Exercises*, also called as *Chapatti Diagram* (Indian pan caked shaped bread). The respondents place circles of different shapes of bread in a symbolic relationship with each other. This technique was used with children to sense relations among different support groups or institutions within the social settings of the respondents. Children drew circles of different sizes to depict their reliability on different social groups and institutions or services. Children were also facilitated figure out their ideas and thoughts in the form of colourful circles. Children identified various institutions like local youth groups, local party people, and police stations as machineries available for their protection and ranked them with size as per their scope to access those items.

Key Principles

(a) To ensure confidentiality, we did not maintain the original name and address of any child. With the children and their parents were mutually agreed.

(b) Time of data collection and interaction with the children and their parents were mutually agreed.

(c) Creating enabling environment by use of different tools to foster participation of children in the study.

(d) We spent considerable time with the children to earn their trust. It was mutually agreed with children that the researchers will maintain secrecy and not disclose or discuss their personal issues with their parents and other members in their community.

(e) We made conscious effort not to impose our opinion on children during the facilitation process and maintained a non-judgemental and unbiased attitude.

(f) Prior to the interaction, the researchers obtained consents from the children who were interested to participate in the study. We sensitized them about the objective of the study and obtained permission from their parents and the local community leaders.

(g) We used professional use of value based, ethical standards and principles of social work during exploration, data collection and documentation. Though, participation of children was still tentative and relatively unevaluated but, we strongly felt that given an opportunity, children can equally participate in problem identification and decision-making process. Thus, we made purposeful effort to engage children as partners in the whole initiative and tried to have their understanding and views as they themselves described.

Data Analysis and Report Writing

After the required and relevant data was collected, the same was coded into the computer using an excel worksheet. The data was complex and multi-dimensional, which was later converted into frequency tables and charts/graphs to undertake the analysis and interpretation of data.

Limitations/Challenges of the Study

- This study was unique and had little information base to build upon especially for developing countries. The universal definition of child abuse in the Indian context was lacking. The scanty understanding of the extent of different forms of abuse was only available. The study had difficulty also in defining some of the terms due to lack of well defined indicators.
- Only few studies were available on abuse of street children and implementation of Juvenile Justice Act. Also, it was difficult to find out any comprehensive research documentation on the same issue.
- The researchers also faced problems while having one-to-one interview and undergoing FGD process because of the curiosity of local community people and other passers-by. This was really a great impediment and interruption to carry out the process.
- Though the researchers used different tools to establish communication with children regarding abuse and law enforcement systems; still they experienced limitations in explaining various terminologies related to legislative aspects to children.
- The researchers felt after completing the study that a lower number of sample and more in-depth qualitative study without giving much emphasis on quantitative aspect would have been a better approach for this type of exploration.
- Interaction and informal interviews and discussions with police personnel in the presence of affected children to record the perception of police towards those children would have been more effective to design a better strategy of child friendly police system.
- For further studies, researchers found that there was a scope to work on the gaps in implementation of Juvenile Justice System in the State of West Bengal.
- Because of the environmental distractions and other allurements, it was difficult to attract children for a long time. Normally, the attention span of those children was found to be very low. So, it

was extremely difficult to complete whole set of questionnaire at a stretch.

- Because of the sensitivity and nature of the research topic, the researchers used various qualitative tools to establish rapport and collect their opinion. This entire process took longer time than it was expected. The researchers had to make repeated visits to complete the data collection process.
- Collection of data during day time was very difficult as the street living families do not return to their place of stay before the evening hours. Thus, the researchers had to collect data during the evening time.
- It was very difficult to apply the random sampling method because of the mobility of the population.
- It was observed during the data collection phase that though many of the organizations were working for street children but none of them had retrieved a comprehensive data base of children living on the streets.
- The definition of street children was not uniform. Different agencies use their own definitions to describe street children. There were some studies conducted by a few agencies which gave an idea of the problems of street children but did not provide any segregated data on children living with their families on the streets.
- Obtaining data regarding sexual abuse was little embarrassing because this was a very sensitive and stigmatized issue. The researchers facilitated one-to-one interview session and conducted FGDs to get some idea of personnel life experiences of those children who all have had such traumatic episode of life. A few children narrated some of those incidences of sexual abuse. Those experiences have been narrated in the form of case study. Thus, the quantitative data will not reflect the actual incidence of sexual abuse of children.

5

URBAN POVERTY AND VULNERABILITY OF STREET CHILDREN

Urban poverty is a multi-dimensional phenomenon. The urban poor live with many deprivations. The daily challenges may include:

- Limited access to employment opportunities and income.
- Inadequate and insecure housing and services.
- Violent and unhealthy environments.
- Little or no social protection mechanisms.
- Limited access to adequate health and education opportunities.

But urban poverty is not just a collection of characteristics; it is also a dynamic condition of vulnerability or susceptibility to risks In order to provide a richer understanding of urban poverty, it is important to highlight two analytical frameworks: (1) a dynamic framework of poverty (vulnerability and asset ownership); and (2) the multiple characteristics of poverty and its cumulative impacts.

More than half the world's people live in cities. Over 90 per cent of urban growth is occurring in the developing world, adding an estimated 70 million new residents to urban areas each year. During the next two decades, the urban population of the world's two poorest regions — South Asia and Sub-Sahara Africa is expected to double.

The urban growth is attributed to both natural population growth, and rural to urban migration. Urbanization contributes to sustained economic growth which is critical to poverty reduction. The economies of scale and agglomeration in cities attract investors and entrepreneurs which is good for overall economic growth. Cities also provide opportunities for many, particularly the poor who are attracted by greater job prospects, the availability of services, and for some, an escape from constraining social and cultural traditions in rural villages. Yet city life can also present conditions of overcrowded living, congestion, unemployment, lack of social and community networks, stark inequalities, and crippling social problems such as crime and violence.

Many of those who migrate will benefit from the opportunities in urban areas, while others, often those with low skill levels, may be left behind and find themselves struggling with the day-to-day challenges of city life. Many of the problems of urban poverty are rooted in a complex of resources and capacity constraints, inadequate government policies at both the Central and local level, and lack of planning for urban growth and management. Given the high growth projections for most cities in developing countries, the challenges of urban poverty and more broadly of city management will only worsen in many places if not addressed more aggressively.

Food Insecurity in Urban India

World Food Programme (WFP) indicates that more than 38 per cent of children under the age of 3 years in Indian cities and towns are underweight and more than 35 per cent of children in urban areas are stunted. The report states that the poor [population in India's burgeoning urban areas do not get the requisite amount of calories or nutrients specified by indian Council of Medical Research (ICMR)] norms also suggests that absorption and assimilation of food by the urban poor was further impaired by non-food factors such as inadequate sanitation, facilities, insufficient housing and woeful poor access to clean drinking water.

Settlement Pattern of Urban Poor in Kolkata

Kolkata is the second largest city of India having 45,80,544 people residing in 187.33 square km area. It is the home for five Nobel Laureate and is the nerve centre of intellect and human values, where many modern movements began in are, cinema and theatre, science and industry. India's quest for freedom also began in this city. Still the city is concerned as the gateway, commercial and communication hub for the North-East Indian States. The cultural and commercial values of Kolkata attract people from diversified caste and religions not only from different parts of West Bengal and India but from other neighbouring countries as well. With urbanization and shrinkage opportunities in gainful employment in rural areas and on the other hand economic pull in the city accelerated the migration of a large number of poor people in the city.

A very large section of Kolkata's population lives in abject poverty in slums and squatter colonies all over the city. About one third of the population of the Kolkata Metropolitan Corporation (KMC) lives in the slums. The estimated slum population in Kolkata was 14,90,811 according to 2011 census. It was one of the densely populated cities with a population of 24,429 per square km. In terms of number of total slum population; it was second largest in India. According to the Lakdawala Committee (2007), the poverty level was estimated more than 89 per cent in the slums of Kolkata which was higher than Bengaluru (73%) and Chennai (77.2%). Most of these people were generally engaged in low wage sectors. They were found to be settled in low cost settlements near the railway station, bus stands, markets, big colonies and also on the pavements and railway platforms because of the employment opportunities and easy connectivity with other parts of the city.

According to the official record of KMC (Kolkata Metropolitan Corporation Initiative, 2003), there are about 2,011 registered and 3,500 unregistered slums within 141 municipal wards. Kolkata has also a floating population of 60,00,000 who commute to the city daily from the nearby districts for work. The population of Kolkata is growing over the years with a steady increase in slum population.

The settlement pattern of Kolkata's poor population was categorized as under **two** broad heads:

- People settled in authorized slums.
- People settled in unauthorized slums and squatters.

Authorized Slums

The authorized slums can be classified into **two** broad categories:

- Tenant slums are owned by landowners or huts built by the middlemen and are rented out to the poor migrant families.
- Refugee Resettlement Colonies are settlements constructed on the land leased out for 99 years to the refugees from Bangladesh by the Government at nominal rents.

The slums located in the heart of the city are as old as 150 years and was developed during the pre-industrial area. The relatively recent slums were located in the outskirts of the city. In these authorized slums, people are recognized as legal residents and were entitled to basic amenities such as portable water, electricity and road. People pay a fixed monthly rental for their house and electricity. The Government of

West Bengal had enacted Thika Tenancy Act, 1981, which protects tenants from eviction. The families settled in these types of settlements were also entitled to enjoy benefits of different welfare schemes.

Unauthorized Slums

People settled in unauthorized areas were considered as illegitimate dwellers and government does not provide any facilities. These families were generally settled in sub-rental groups living on the slum edges, urban periphery that has not been legalized, vacant government land and encroachments on the roadside. These families are comparatively new to the cities, dislocated from the city itself or retrenched from their work place or displaced due to increase in family size. These groups are among the poorest families and are routinely omitted from the official figures. If all these groups are accounted for, then the estimates of urban poverty would be much higher.

Kolkata Municipal Corporation from time-to-time reviews their official records and recognizes some of the slums considering the legalities of the land on which the families have settled. The families who are settled on the encroachments of the road or pavements are most vulnerable in terms of their settlement pattern. Authorities conduct routine eviction drives to drive the families away from pavements.

Walking down the streets of Kolkata, the most visible section of the society is the families on the streets with their children. The number of street living families in Kolkata has steadily increased over the years because of urbanization. These families have migrated from poverty stricken districts and states and immigrated to the city in search of a suitable livelihood options. Though this section is visible on the streets they are invisible in the official records. No official figures are available about the actual number of families living on the pavements without any shelter and other amenities of life. In the year 2008, Action Aid (NGO) conducted a rapid assessment study to estimate actual figure. According to their survey report an estimated 58,997 homeless persons are living in the city. Among these homeless population, children constitute about half of the population. These population are not included in the census figure as they do not live in "Census Houses". Thus, the question of any resource allocation does not arise. Rather, they are being seen as illegal residents in the city who have no claim over the State's resources (Action Aid, 2008).

Government of India recognizes that the urban population play a vital role in the socio-economic transformation and contribute to 50-55 per cent of the total GDP of the country. To create economically productive, efficient, equitable responsive cities, Government of India had launched Jawaharlal Nehru Rural and Urban Renewal Mission in the year 2008. The broad objectives are as follows:

- Integrated development of urban infrastructure.
- Structural reformation and efficiency of urban governance.
- Provision of basic services to urban poor through integrated development of slums that includes housing and development of infrastructure in slum settlements.

Thus, the scheme aims to provide the inner environment of the city through a collaborative effort of urban development and poverty alleviation departments and also encourages public private partnership in the whole endeavour. Instead of this policy the families living on the street of Kolkata will be deprived as they do not have any legal identity and basic entitlements. Thus, though this scheme created a ray of hope for the urban poor, but their families living on authorized land and has land entitlements will only be benefitted through the scheme. A number of developmental organizations, academic institutes are working on the loopholes of the scheme and advocating with government to uphold the entitlement rights of homeless population.

Looking at Children in Urban Areas — A Scenario

Most of the world's urban children — over 80 per cent of them — live in Africa, Asia and Latin America, and their numbers are growing fast. Africa, one of the least urbanized regions, already has more than twice as many urban children as North America.

Urban children are generally considered to be better off than rural children; healthier, better housed, better educated and with access to a wider range of services and opportunities. Cities can indeed offer these advantages, but the reality is that hundreds of millions of urban children live in deep poverty, their rights neglected, and their needs unmet, their prospects damaged by conditions that threaten their health and undermine their development. The following example is a condition in a squatter settlement in Johannesburg, but many urban children around the world live in similar condition including India.

Canaansland, a squatter camp in a busy part of Johannesburg, is a community of 350 families living on a little over an acre (approx. 0.5 hectares) of land with no toilets, no electricity and one water point. It was one of the research sites for an international research programme on "Growing up in Cities" which explored children's understanding of their own urban environment with a view to improving these based on children's recommendations. The children, aged 10 to 14, who made up the Canaansland group, had clear views on the community's problems: "it is not a good place", said one child, "There is a lot of fighting. The roads are too busy and people drive very fast. It smiles very badly when there is a wind and when it rains".

All the children spoke of the lack of facilities. The single water tap served over 1000 people, and most of the children regularly had to wait to fill heavy containers for their families. The only available toilets were in commercial locations across busy streets, and many people used a nearby vacant lot, and the children were revolted at the stench that surrounded them. They were also bothered by the general filth of the camp, where rubbish was cleaned up and removed only at irregular intervals.

Children's homes were small and crowded, and often did not keep out the wind and rain. It was difficult to deal with the cold in winter-heating was possible only by using open braziers, and children were aware of the danger of toxic fumes, and the ease with which fire might spread through their crowded camp. The lack of electricity meant that doing homework was almost impossible, and even during the day there was not enough light in their homes for reading or writing.

The violence and quarrels in the community upset all the children. They spoke of adult drinking problem, of frequent brawls, gun shots at night, high noise levels, and difficulty in sleeping. Most adults paid little attention to the frequent violence, but the children found it frightening.

Because of their identity as squatters, children felt stigmatized and humiliated by the surrounding community. They were accused of dirtying shopping areas and public toilets, and when they window-shopped; they were treated like potential thieves and forbidden access to stores. Girls spoke of being kicked, slapped and verbally abused by-passers-by when they played on the pavement at the edge of the camp, and it was common for traffic to speed up when they played on the street, scattering children and their possessions.

The children came up with a range of practical suggestions for improving life in the camp; but when they met with the Mayor to present their work, they focused on their four most significant issues: (1) improved housing that would keep out inclement weather; (2) the urgent need for sanitation; (3) a place to call their own where they could do their homework; and (4) the need for people from settled homes in the vicinity to treat them with greater respect.

Characteristics of Urban Areas which Generally Distinguish them from Rural areas in Low and Middle-income Nations

Higher concentrations of people, enterprises, vehicles, and their wastes mean greater health risks in urban areas if provision for infrastructure, services and waste management is absent. However, there is also a greater capacity for management of health problems when there is competent local government. This is because of proximity and economies of scale in provision of basic infrastructure and services, and higher capacity to pay by households and enterprises.

A different range of occupational health and safety risks — for example, levels of exposure to industrial chemicals and wastes, dust, dangerous machinery, excessive heat. Specific groups, such as waste pickers, face particularly high risks.

Greater vulnerability to 'natural' disasters — for many urban dwellers because the only land to which they have access for housing is at high risk from floods, landslides, earthquakes, etc.

Greater reliance on cash income — for food, fuel, water, housing (or land on which it can be built), building materials, transport and waste disposal, especially in the larger or more economically successful cities. Less reliance on access to natural resources for subsistence or livelihood.

Greater potential impact of 'good' local government — because of economies of scale and proximity with respect to the provision of infrastructure and basic services, and more highly developed communication networks. This in turn provides a firm foundation for the promotion of democratic participation.

More diverse and more transient population — in many cities or particular city districts, which can weaken the basis for co-operative action, especially in areas with cheap rental accommodation, but greater scope for joint action, community mobilization and negotiation with government for infrastructure and services, especially within democratic structure.

Greater reliance on illegal solution — a higher proportion of households live on illegally occupied land, or illegal sub-divisions, tapping piped water and electricity networks illegally. Consequently, they run a greater risk of eviction.

Greater reliance on housing as an economic resource — in terms of location (poor groups often live on dangerous sites because these provide better or cheaper access to employment or income-earning opportunities); as an asset (for owners, even if ownership is uncertain); as an income earner (renting rooms, space for household enterprise).

Of course, none of the above is exclusively urban, since many rural areas have some of these characteristics — for instance many poor rural dwellers are at risk from eviction and face serious occupational health and safety risks from farm equipment and agricultural chemicals. Nor does every urban area have all the above-many urban dwellers work on farms or engage in urban agriculture for example. Many households also have both rural and urban components to their livelihoods or survival strategies.

Children's Rights and Good Governance

In any context, urban or rural, good governance and the full enjoyment of human rights are mutually reinforcing; human rights inform the principles of good governance and, in turn a key characteristic of good governance of these rights.

Principles of Good Governance

Good governance has **eight** major characteristics:

★ It promotes and encourages **participation**, including that of children.
★ It requires **respect for the rule of the law**, and the full protection of human rights.
★ It is **responsive**, implementing decisions and meeting needs within a reasonable time frame.
★ It involves **transparency** in decision-making, and information is freely available and easily understandable to all.
★ It promotes **equity and inclusiveness**, such that all members of society feel that they have a stake in that society.
★ It is founded upon **accountability**, not only of governmental institutions, but also of the private sector and civil society organizations.
★ It means that processes and institutions produce **effective** results that meet the needs of society, while making the most **efficient** use of resources and promoting sustainability.

- ★ It is **consensus-oriented**, involving the meditation of different interests in society and sensitivity towards influence of different actors, including the poorest and most marginalized.

The world's urban settlements provide particularly fertile ground for the establishment and development of systems of good local governance guided by human rights principles and, in particular, for application of the general principles and other provisions of the 1989 Convention on the Rights of the Child (CRC). While all provisions of the CRC apply to all children in every situation, some articles are particularly salient in the urban context: Articles 16, 18, 24, 27, 28, 31, and 32.

The explicit right of every child to enjoy adequate living conditions, a safe environment and access to housing and basic social services, including education and health, is also underlined in other human rights standards. Article 25 of the 1948 Universal Declaration of Human Rights states that, "everyone has the right to a standard of living adequate for the health and well-being of himself and his family, including food, clothing, housing and medical care and necessary social services". These or similar principles are included in other important instruments:

- ★ Article 21 of the 1951 International Convention Relating to the Status of Refugees;
- ★ Principle 2 of the 1961 International Labour Organization Recommendation No. 115, on Worker's Housing;
- ★ Article 5 of the 1965 International Convention on the Elimination of all Forms of Racial Discrimination;
- ★ Article 11 of the 1966 International Convent on Economic, Social and Cultural Rights; and
- ★ Article 43 of the 1990 International Convention on the Protection of the Rights of All Migrant Workers and Members of their Families.

Formal declarations from high level international encounters help to re-emphasize periodically the importance of promoting specific initiatives for urban dwellers including transparent accountable governance, fair distribution of income, provision for health services and free education, adequate shelter and nutrition, promotion of employment opportunities, and a constant attention to the special needs of women and children. Notable in this regard are the Declaration on Human Settlements adopted by the UN Conference on Human Settlement

(Habitat) in 1976 in Vancouver, the Declaration on Social Development adopted at the 1995 World Summit for Social Development in Copenhagen, and the Declaration on Human Settlements adopted in 1966 by the UN Conference on Human Settlements (Habitat II) in Istambul.

In addition, ***A World Fit For the Children***, the outcome documents from the UN General Assembly Special Session on Children held in May 2002, emphasizes the role of local governments and authorities to strengthen partnership at all levels and ensure that children are at the centre of agenda for development. The same document also draws to the importance of promoting national and sub-national policies for children, and to developing capacity and particularly community capacity — for monitoring and assessment.

Global Trends in Urban Development

Today, most of the world's urban population is to be found in Asia, Latin America and Africa. Indeed, one quarter of the world's urban population lives in only two countries — China and India. Europe too has a sizeable share of the urban population — one fifth of the world's 3 billion urban dwellers. During the twentieth century, the world's urban population grew more than tenfold and the average size of the 100 largest cities increased more than eightfold. The proportion of people living in urban areas grew from less than 15 per cent in 1900 to an estimated 48 per cent by 2002. This change has been fuelled by expansion in the world's economy, most of which has taken place in industrial and service enterprises located in urban areas. Since, most economic growth continues to be in urban-based enterprises, the trend towards ever larger urban population is likely to continue.

Many of the largest and fastest growing cities in all regions are those that have been most successful in increasing their role within the globalizing economy. Some of these cities, such as Dhaka and Bangkok, and their nations' capital and largest city. Others such as Shenzen in China and Bengaluru in India, are changing the urban geography of their nation as they grow to challenge older and larger cities.

Despite the growing influence of globalization, local, political and demographic contexts continue to shape the form that urbanization takes. A significant part of urban explosion in many African nations around independence was simply women and children joining their husbands and fathers, once colonial restrictions had been removed. In addition, in many parts of Africa, urban change has also been profoundly influenced by civil wars and the sheer number of refugees seeking new bases for their livelihoods. HIV/AIDS has also had a significant impact on rural-urban population movements, as children who have lost their parents to this disease (and who may have been unable to inherit their parents' land because they do not have a birth certificate to prove their parentage) are drawn to urban centres in search of a livelihood.

Factors Contributing to Urban Poverty

1. *The Quality of Local and National Governance*

Shifting attention to the causes that underpin poverty and exclusion among urban children requires a new focus on two of the most complex and politically controversial issues within nations — the distribution of power. Authority and resources among different level of government, and the quality of 'governance' in terms of its responsiveness, accountability, transparency and quality of engagement with civil society. Almost all policies, programmes and decisions by governments (and international agencies) have implications for urban children. Urban areas, by their nature, are points of concentration for, and connection to, the monetary economy. The stability of urban households with children is tied to the underlying and basic causes of economic change in urban areas, and the well-being of urban children (as well as) is tied to good economic performance nationally, and to fair distribution of the benefits of economic growth — through a commitment to pro-poor growth, stable incomes, unexploitative working practices. education and training programmes.

The size of inter-governmental transfers from Central Government to regional and local authorities is highly relevant for children because most responsibility for basic infrastructure and services lies with local government agencies, and most urban government in Africa, Asia and Latin America lack the fiscal base to meet their multiple responsibilities for child health and development. There are huge differentials between high and low income nations in the revenue per person controlled by local authorities (varying by factors of 100 or more), and even larger differentials in their capital investment capacity per person. In high income nations, the web of local institutions that serve, support and protect children (and parents) is taken for granted. Coverage for some services may be sub-standard, and some groups are ill-served or excluded, but the vast majority of the urban population is served.

2. *Growing Inequality Within Nations*

Much child deprivation is linked to inequality within nations — including nations with good economic performance. According to available data, income inequality has increased in most nations, especially in Latin America and countries previously in the Soviet Bloc (which tend to be among the most urbanized of low and middle income nations).

Rising average urban incomes do not necessarily mean falling child poverty; in the United States child poverty rates have increased 31 per cent in urban areas and 50 per cent in sub-urban areas since 1970s, despite the fact that real per capita incomes are much higher today than they were in 1970s. Even falling unemployment may not mean a reduction in child deprivation; in the UK, the proportion of households with children with no income earner grew between 1985 and 1996, even though unemployment levels fell.

An analysis of child poverty in rich nations shows the importance of government policies and redistributive taxes as a means of reducing levels or preventing them from rising too much during periods of economic difficulty; it indicates, too, that the withdrawal of state support for the unemployed or those on low income can increase child poverty even during periods of economic prosperity. There is no evidence that measures to keep down child poverty have an adverse effect on economic growth. Many of the world's wealthiest nations also have the lowest levels of child poverty and the highest levels of inter-governmental transfer. It is worth noting the emphasis among many nations with the lowest levels of child poverty on getting the unemployed back to work.

In this rapid development process, children especially girls, become vulnerable to and, often, victims of neglect, abuse and exploitation. The serious impacts on children of the macro-economic reforms promoted by the World Bank and IMF in the early 1980s came as a surprise to most of their proponents, who had assumed that the resulting economic growth would more than compensate for short-term losses. Rarely was provision made to protect the social expenditures with most importance for child development. This is still the cases of many nations. Public expenditure on health is very low and stagnating in low income nations and falling marginally in middle income nations.

3. *The Effects of the Global Economy*

The very poor economic performance of the world's low income nations and the economic deterioration in many middle income nations underlies much child deprivation. It also underpins the very large debt burdens that so many nations face. A globalizing global economy creates winners and losers and growing inequality between nations presents particular challenges for children.

Many nations have faced significant declines in per capita incomes in recent years. The situation in Eastern Europe, Central Asia and most of Sub-Sahara Africa during the 1990s has been particularly extreme. Sharp rises in un-employment, reductions in wages and often, increase in the price of basic goods have had serious impacts upon larger sections of the urban (and rural) population. In Tajikistan, for example, by 1996 real GDP had fallen to 40 per cent of its 1990 level, while government expenditure dropped from 65 per cent of GDP in 1992 to 16 per cent in 1998.

It is difficult to protect children from lower income households in the face of both falling incomes and declining government expenditure, Urban populations may be more vulnerable to these changes because of their dependence on the monetary economy for their livelihoods (just as larger sections of the urban population may benefit more from economic growth), but in most locations there are so many linkages between rural and urban areas that is difficult to discuss these separately. For instance, in Accra, Ghana's largest city, the proportion of the population living in poverty increased rapidly between 1987 and 1993, whereas it increased in both rural and other urban areas. But growing poverty in Accra may have serious impacts, including fewer job opportunities for rural dwellers, less remittance flows to rural (or other urban) areas, less urban demand for rural products, and more urban to rural migration, which in-turn increases dependency burdens in rural areas.

Conditions for Children in Urban Areas

Physical Infrastructure

Environmental conditions are generally particularly poor (and risky) in low income urban districts. Wherever there is high concentration of people and of waste, the potential for contamination, contagious diseases are great. When this potential is not countered by effective provision, health costs are very high and infants and young children are disproportionately affected. Millions of urban infants and children died each year, and many more suffer from illness or injuries that and should be prevented. Age-related risk factors include immature immune systems, higher exposure to pathogens, greater susceptibility to particular chemicals and inadequate understanding to avoid hazards.

The information base for a precise identification of the relative importance of different causes or risk factors is limited: there is a clear need for better data if the dynamics and effects of urban poverty are to be understood and effective action is to be taken.

Water and Sanitation

Diarrhoeal diseases are still a primary cause of infant and child death for large sections of the world's urban population. Human excreta are the primary source of diarrhoeal disease pathogens. When provision for water and sanitation is poor, diarrhoeal diseases and other diseases linked to contaminated water (such as typhoid) or contaminated food and water (such as cholera and hepatitis A) are among the most serious health problems within urban neighbourhoods — or whole cities. The impact of diarrhoeal disease can be considerably underestimated since, when combined with mal-nutrition, they can so weaken the body's defenses that diseases such as measles and pneumonia become major causes of child death.

An essential factor in ensuring children's health is the availability of safe, sufficient water supplies and provision for sanitation — something frequently absent in poor urban settlements in low and middle income countries. Too little water is a critical problem, making it impossible to maintain the sanitary conditions essential for preventing endemic disease that contributes so heavily to the death and repeated illness of many children.

The impact of inadequate water provision is compounded by the effects of poor sanitation. Only a small proportion of poor urban residents have adequate provision for sanitation, and here too, the problems are not confined to informal settlements.

The use of public latrines is particularly problematic for young children. Taking a small child any distance to a toilet is impractical, and the darkness, smell and large pit openings in most latrines make their use unpleasant or even frightening for young children, Evidence from a number of urban settlements indicates that hardly any children under six use these latrines and that in most cases their excrement ends up being thrown into yards, drains or streets, creating a potent source of contamination.

The absence of drainage and garbage collection contributes further to the likelihood of contamination and disease. The impacts of inadequate water, sanitation, drainage and waste removal are not limited to diarrhoeal diseases. Many case studies in low-income settlements have shown the high proportion of children who have debilitating intestinal worm infections. The prevalence among children of various skin and eye infections such a scabies and trachoma that are associated with a lack of water supplies for washing is also particularly high among those living in poor quality homes and neighbourhoods. Moreover, malaria, which is often considered a rural disease, is now among the main causes of illness and death among children in many urban areas. The occurrence of malaria is often related to poorly drained locations as the ***Anopheles*** mosquitoes breed on standing water.

Chemical Pollution

Although they do not present the same health burden as biological pathogens, toxins and pollutants in water supplies and food, in the air and in unprotected dumps, are a world-wide concern. This is especially the case in urban areas and, disproportionately, in areas inhabited by the poor. Children are particularly vulnerable to harm from exposure because of their rapid growth and immaturity, both physiologically and metabolically. Lead ingestion is a particular problem for urban children, especially in countries where leaded fuel and paint are still used.

Children are also at risk due to exposure to harmful chemicals, indeed, pesticides are increasingly becoming a source of concern in some inner city areas, where they are used to control roaches, rats and other vermin.

The single most significant form of chemical pollutant in terms of children's health in low and middle income countries is indoor air pollution resulting from the use of coal or biomass fuels, poor quality stoves and inadequate ventilation. This is a problem in both rural and urban areas, but one form which children are less likely to have relief outdoors in towns and cities, given the poor quality of the outside air. All the same, indoor concentration of pollutants can be many times higher than even the most polluted outdoor air, and infants and young children are often heavily exposed because they remain with their mothers as they cook or undertake other tasks within the home. The effect of these pollutants, combined with malnutrition, may retard growth and increase the incidence of acute respiratory infections.

In many cities, the concentration and mix of ambient air pollutants is already high enough to cause illness and premature death for more susceptible individuals. World-wide, 1.5 billion urban dwellers are exposed to ambient air pollution levels that exceed WHO standard —

and in many cities; the concentration of pollutants is far above these standards.

Accidental poisonings are common, especially for one to three years old, most often from kerosene, household products (for instance bleach) and medications. The risk of poisoning is greater in poor quality, overcrowded dwellings where there is no storage space to keep these substances out of reach of children, and where the demands on parents mean that children are not always supervised. Urban children are also at risk through their mothers' exposed to chemical pollutants, some of which can cause or birth defects in the foetus or even kill it. Chemicals that are known to harm the foetus by transfer through the placenta include lead, methyl, mercury, and certain pesticides. In most low income settlements, however, the developing foetus is more at risk from the mothers' nutritional deficiencies or from the impact of parents and malaria on her health.

Physical Hazards

Millions of urban children around the world are killed every year as results of preventable injuries that occur within their homes and neighbourhoods, and tens of millions more are seriously injured. Heavy traffic, unprotected stairways and heights, unfinished houses, dangerous house sites, piles of debris and a scarcity of safe play space all expose children to high levels of risk. The danger of injuries increases when tired, over-worked caregivers are unable to provide adequate supervision. In countries where infections and parasitic disease are well controlled, unintentional injury ranks as the leading cause of death for children, accounting for almost 40 per cent of deaths in one to 14 age group. In countries where disease and nutritional problems still kill many children, the percentage of injury related deaths is lower, but the number of injuries per person is considerably higher especially in the poorest urban communities.

In urban and rural areas alike, falls are the single most common cause of injury, especially for younger children. Burns are common for children under four-from hot water or other hot fluids, and from accidents with open fires, stoves or kerosene appliances. High levels of overcrowding increase the likelihood of these events. A study in a Brazilian squatter settlement focused on 600 children under five, drawing on interviews with mothers. The mothers reported that in the two weeks prior to interview, 30 per cent of the children had had at least one accident and 12 per cent of these were serious enough to have required care in a clinic or hospital. Falls accounted for 53 per cent of the accidents, followed by cuts (17%) and burns (10%). Many of the falls were linked to the rough terrain of the settlement. The age of the child was an important determinant of accidents and peaks in accidents are in the second or fifth years of life.

Road accidents are among the most common cause of injury in cities in both high and low income countries. But the rapid growth of road traffic in many low income and most middle income nations, along with poorly maintained roads, multiple use of roadways and an absence of side-walks and safe crossing has contributed to death and injury rates that are much higher than those in Europe or the USA, per vehicle or passenger-mile.

Housing

Many children's rights are rooted in the fundamental human right to decent, secure, affordable housing. Survival, health and optimal development are related to the quality of housing and its surroundings; access to livelihood, schooling and other services are determined by its location; emotional security, family stability and even the quality of community relations are tied to security of tenure. But the urban poor struggle with housing-getting it, keeping it and coping with its inadequacies.

In most cities in low and middle income nations, between 25 and 50 per cent of the population live in illegally built settlements. The quality of housing in these settlements is generally poor and often wretched, made of wood and plastic scavenged from dumps. This is a result not only of low incomes, but also of the reluctance of households to invest because of the uncertainty that they will be permitted to stay.

An unknown number — but certainly tens of millions-of the world's urban children and adults are actually homeless and sleep in public places (pavements, stations, parks, graveyards) or construction sites and work places. In Central Mumbai, India, more than a hundred thousand people live on pavements, half of them children, because incomes are insufficient to allow them to live even in cheap peripherial areas.

Homelessness is predominantly an urban phenomenon, in part because of the commercialization of land and housing markets in the world's cities. Even in high income countries, research confirms that homelessness among families with children is increasing despite the recent years of affluence. The experience results in anxiety and depression for both children and parents, and can lead to the breakup of families, as children are placed in foster care. In New York City, 60 per cent of residents in shelters for adults had children who could not be with them.

Access to Play

Urban safety hazards and health risks have a significant effect on the play opportunities available to children. The availability of stimulating, diverse environments that allow them to pretend, experiment and lean are central to optimal development, and have been related to resilience and improved outcomes in high-risk children. Where homes are overcrowded, children may have little choice, but to pass much of the day outside, and they can be extraordinarily resourceful in finding opportunities for play within even the most deprived environments — indeed many poor environments are rich in challenge and diversity. But they can also expose children to serious risk, and caregivers often respond by restricting play.

As children become more mobile, safety becomes an increasing concern. In conditions of urban poverty, excreta, broken glass, plastic bags, rotted food and burning materials are common hazards.

As children begin to move further from home their range of action and the number of risk factors that they face also increase — traffic in particular, but also stray dogs, standing water, open drains and debris — filled lots.

Opportunities for play are also restricted in high-income nations countries, where spaces for recreation in urban areas are often limited or, increasingly, involve a financial cost; while motor vehicles make streets hazardous for play and open areas are used for parking. Moreover, parents' working partners the distance between home and school and growing use of the car mean that, outside school hours, many children are isolated in their homes and separated from their peers. This isolation may be heightened by parents' concern for the safety of their children in urban areas.

Evictions

Millions of urban dwellers around the world live in fear of eviction. In the case of illegal settlements even those on undesirable land at risk. The impact of eviction upon children can be particularly devastating. Evictions usually lead to homelessness and almost always to major economic upheaval. Possessions may be destroyed, family stability jeopardized, livelihoods and schooling threatened and social networks undermined.

Children involved describe the violence, panic and confusion of the evictions and the experience of sleeping rough afterwards and being separated from friends. They also face the difficulties in re-establishing a stable life and frequent breaking downs in family relations as a consequence of the stress and economic difficulties.

Evictions or displacement also arise armed conflict, political violence, natural disasters and other emergencies that affect millions of adults and children each year, and often result in children.

Being separated from their family. This can mean streams of refugees or displaced rural dwellers flooding into cities where housing is already at a premium. These displaced people are often resented by other urban dwellers. This is especially so if they are undocumented immigrants who often live in constant fear of discovery and forced repatriation. Children from 'illegal' or 'unwelcome' communities are highly vulnerable to prejudice, harassment, attack and incarceration, especially when they are forced to work for survival.

Housing Quality and Conditions

Even when poor urban families are securely housed, their housing is seldom adequate to support their children's survival, development and the highest attainable standard of health. Numerous hazards are posed by flimsy shelters on disaster-prone land. Accidental fires are common in areas with highly inflammable building materials, and are rendered still more serious by the lack of inadequacy of emergency services. In other cases, fires can be deliberately set to drive households off the land they have occupied. In high-income countries, fires are also related to poor housing conditions, but more often to faulty wiring, defective heating equipment and the absence of smoke alarms. There are also numerous health risks associated with poor quality housing construction and materials. Lack of screens exposes children to flies and mosquitoes, and porous walls and roofing harbor rodents and insect pests. Hard to clean floors increase contact with pathogens — the agents that cause disease especially for babies and young children.

Poor living environments, including noise and crowding, have long been recognized to generate stress, to undertake coping strategies, interfere with social relationships and contribute to physical and mental illness.

Poor quality, overcrowded housing also favours transmission of acute respiratory infections, which are the single largest cause of infant and child death in most low and middle income nations. Although these infections are no means an urban phenomenon, they tend to be more prevalent in urban areas, as the frequency of contact, the density of the population and the concentration and proximity of both infectious and susceptible people promote disease transmission. And, with limited health and financial resources, a child who contracts bronchitis or pneumonia in low and middle income nations is 50 times more likely to die than a child in Europe or North America. Overcrowding is also a risk factor for the transmission of many other diseases and affects children, including diarrhea and tuberculosis.

The Quality of Care

Inevitably, challenging living conditions undermine the capacity to provide optimal care for children. Overburdened caregivers are far more likely to have to leave children unsupervised or to cut corners in the many procedures that are necessary for healthy living-managing water supplies, keeping children clean, preparing and storing food hygienically and dealing with waste and excreta in the absence of adequate services. For example, reduced cooking times are thought to be connected with the retention of toxicity in boiled cassava meal, a staple food in many parts of Africa, especially when combined with a protein-deficient diet.

Even high levels of parental knowledge about health, hygiene and safety cannot guarantee that children will be well provided for in very poor conditions. Heavy demands on caregivers in combination with long distance to work and the absence of viable alternatives an mean that there is no good source of care for many young children for long hours every day. Often the burden of care in households falls upon girls, who are left to look after their siblings while parents work. The psychological stress imposed by living in poor urban conditions also takes their toll. Caregivers in crowded and chaotic conditions have been found to be less responsive to their, and more restrictive, controlling and punitive. Under the many pressures of poverty this can escalate to abuse and neglect.

When resources are scarce and mothers or child careers are faced with a heavy domestic workload or are forced to work long hours outside the home, one result be malnutrition. This condition contributes to more than half of all child deaths, to chronic illness and to a slowing of development on all fronts. It also undermines children's immune defenses and increases their vulnerability to disease.

The difficulty of providing adequate care for children in poor households can be exacerbated in urban areas by break down of family units and frequent lack of social support. Many observers have pointed to the relatively high numbers of urban households headed by single mothers around the world as a factor explaining poor outcomes of children. There is no question that female-headed households are disproportionately poor, or that it takes more effect on the part of a single adult to provide high quality care for children. However, there is also evidence that women are more likely to invest their limited resources in children's well-being and long-term success, and that many children do better in female-headed households.

Urban Neighbourhoods

Many poor urban children live in run-down inner cities, peripheral squatter communities or barren suburbs where their social, cultural and recreational needs receive little attention.

Neighbourhood quality, accessibility and opportunity for children and adolescents are determined to some degree by the level of formal municipal provision. But local community institutions like churches, cultural centres and recreational clubs also play a significant role, and they depend on the level of social organizations and commitment within a community. Many African-American churches in the major cities of US have taken initiatives to mobilize community members to plan and manage their own neighbourhoods, but research in the USA has also indicated that this kind of neighbourhood resource base tends to be weaker where there are high concentrations of poverty, joblessness and residential mobility.

Children and adolescents may not only victims of violence, but also contribute to it. Bullying by peers is a problem for many children, and vandalism, drug use and gang-related crime by young people are the cause of fear and concern in communities around the world. These activities may, in turn, bring children into contact with law enforcement officials. In certain cases where the juvenile justice system is weak or non-existent, children become subject to arbitrary treatment by the police or to other rights abuse. In part at least, phenomena such as vandalism can be related to boredom and the lack of opportunity and hope. In many communities the provision of recreational facilities, job training and options for constructive involvement has resulted in dramatic reductions in crime and gang violence.

Schooling and Work

Schooling, like most other basic services, tends to be more readily available to urban children than their rural counterparts. But school remains either inaccessible or unaffordable for many poor urban children. Moreover, the general quality of schools in poor urban areas can be extremely low, and this constitutes yet another disincentive for parents and children. Especially in illegal settlements, governments may overlook their obligation to provide education or, indeed, any other services.

Many children are denied their right to education in order to undertake household or domestic chores, or to care for younger siblings. This is a true for rural areas as it is for urban ones, but the lack of public utilities and services in many poor urban communities contributes to inappropriate burdens for millions of children, especially girls.

Other children may be withdrawn from school to contribute to household income. A survey in Kolkata 'slum' revealed that 84 per cent of school age children not attending school, and that of these 49 per cent were working outside the home — as rag-pickers, domestic helpers, leather workers or battery breakers. Child labour not only impacts upon educational opportunities, it can also take dangerous and degrading forms. There is probably no city in the world where there are not some children exposed to hazardous work, but the proportion of children in this position is particularly high in many low and middle income nations where, for instance, they make a living picking through waste or working with dangerous machinery, heat, toxic chemicals and dust. Domestic labour in the homes of others is especially prevalent in urban areas, often involving children sent from rural areas, and entailing long hours, little or no pay, little relief from isolation and, frequently, abusive treatment and sexual violence.

A recent estimate from UNICEF in India indicates that there are more than 1,00,000 child prostitutes in that country's five major cities. This in turn, exposes these children to violence, exploitation and sexually transmitted diseases, including HIV/AIDS.

Children on the Street

The phenomenon of children living on the street is a peculiarly urban one, although many of the children involved may originate from rural areas. The demands of work for some urban children push them onto city streets for many hours a day, and in some of these cases links with home can become tenuous. In other cases, work may be secondary, and children may have left home because of abuse, a desire for excitement or relief from oppressive home conditions. At night, these children become particularly vulnerable to all forms of abuse. During winter, cold can be a deadly enemy; in Moscow, where there are estimated to be 50,000 homeless children, many sleep on air, tents for the metro system to escape the freezing temperatures, or even risk disease in the city's sewers in order to find relative warmth.

A large proportion of children on the street engage in hazardous work-dodging traffic as they sell goods to passing motorists for instance. Many are involved in legitimate work; others choose or are pushed into illegal activity, engaging in petty crime and theft, working in the commercial sex or drug trade or becoming drawn into organized begging or rag-picking rackets. Whether or not they are breaking the law, these children are among the most stigmatized urban dwellers, constantly facing abuse from other citizens and harassment by the police. Often children are arrested for crimes or simply for vagrancy, and can be trapped for long months in the slow moving bureaucracy of the justice system, detained in conditions that violate their basic rights.

Taking Action

Promoting the Role of Children

The CRC offers urban authorities a framework within which to make real progress towards realizing children's rights. On a practical level, and within an urban context, a commitment to the CRC can be translated through, among other things:

- The development of city-wide children's rights strategies, providing the framework for policy action, promoting the coordination of activities among relevant actors and identifying concrete goals and targets to promote and monitor progress and encourage the broad engagement of civil society.
- The establishment of local government structures that mainstream child's interests in local plans and policies.
- The incorporation of children's concerns, and particularly those of children belonging to the most vulnerable groups, in local budgets.
- The development of periodic state of the city's children reports to review progress and advance the cause of children.

Promoting children's rights in an urban context challenges local governments to be flexible and to adapt their organizational structure to meet local needs, and there are already many examples of cities in which the challenge is being met. In Croatia, the Towns and Districts

Friends of Children initiative launched in 1999 sees local authorities and civil society, children's institutions, parents and children working together to make their towns and districts more child friendly and to monitor achievements through a sophisticated set of indicators based on children's rights.

Child Participation in Local Governance

One of the characteristics of good local governance for children is founded on the rights of children to express their views freely, and to seek, receive and impart information (Articles 12 and 13 of the CRC). Participation is a process in which children and youth engage with other people around issues that concern their individual and collective life conditions. In this process, the child experiences him or herself as playing a useful role in the community. Participants interact in ways that respect each other's dignity, with the intention of achieving a shared goal. Formal processes of participation deliberately create structures for children's engagement in constructing meaning and sharing decision-making.

The Child Friendly Cities Movement

The potential for action by urban government on children's rights and for children to participate in and contribute to the decisions that affect their life has led to the development of the Child-Friendly Cities. While there is no single definition of a Child-Friendly City, the unifying principles is that a city considered friendly when it is able to assume the rights of its children. A Child-Friendly City legislates and enforces ordinances consistent with the CRC, and gives priority to children, especially in the provision of basic services and the allocation of resources. The goal of the initiative is to reach all urban children, not least those who are poor and excluded, and to promote new ways of doing this, including the participation of children. To achieve this, The Child-Friendly City initiative encourages national governments and supports urban authorities to provide the necessary legal policy and institutional framework.

The Child-Friendly concept has taken root in urban areas around the world. In Malaysia, for example, a Charter on Making Urban Areas Child-Friendly was developed after a national conference on children's rights; its 'ten strategic actions' are aimed specifically at urban local authorities. This has been complemented by a child friendly survey instrument that involves the participation of children in assessing their own urban environment and compilations of a book on action-oriented activities.

In South Africa, the city of Johannesburg is the first major urban centre to make a commitment to implementing the CRC at the local level. The Johannesburg initiative will be used as a pilot project for this process, which will unfold throughout the country between 2002 and 2006.

Enhancing Data Collection

In addition to structures that promote children's participation, effective action for and with children on the availability of current and accurate data. Government and agencies, whether at the local, national or international level, cannot address the needs of deprived or excluded children if they lack information on who these children are, where they live and in what conditions. Interesting initiatives in this area include the establishment of a local information system for monitoring children's rights. This system produces information on demography, employment, family income, migration, health, nutrition, breastfeeding, education, child development and water and sanitation. The data are gathered through the active participation of the National Census and Statistic Institutes with support from local communities. Dhaka City Corporation uses a geographic information system to map urban basic service delivery, and in Moscow, the City Government has given its support to the establishment of a city database on street children, who had previously been invisible in urban statistics.

Other new and relevant approaches for understanding urban conditions include city-wide mapping of housing conditions and health outcomes, and accurate detailed 'slum' and 'shack' censuses undertaken by organizations of the urban poor (these provide not only detailed information, but also a powerful tool with which low-income groups can negotiate with local agencies). There are also many examples of neighbourhood or district maps developed by and with children that have provided local governments and other local agencies with the means to address children's needs and promote respect for their rights.

An example that successfully demonstrates how the elements discussed in this section can be combined to ensure that children are put first in urban governance is provided by the experience in Ceara State in Brazil. Here, we find national and regional structures developing power to local authorities, cross-sectoral and inter-authority cooperation, innovative legislative change in favour of children, democratic structures for community participation, community-based data collection of local indicators, and effective support from international organizations. Together these elements enable real progress to be made in promoting children's rights at the local level.

Improving Physical and Social Conditions

Safer, healthier, more secure housing and neighbourhoods are key to meeting children's rights such as those to education, health care, protection and an adequate standard of living. Perhaps the most significant innovation of the last 30 to 40 years has been the acceptance by most governments of the need for upgrading initiatives to improve housing and ensure basic infrastructure and services in illegal or informal settlements or slums. Most upgrading programmes include improved provision for piped water, sanitation, drainage, roads and paths; some include schools, health care facilities and day-care centres. Some programmes also provide support to households to improve the quality of their homes and for micro-enterprises. Although success has been varied, these programmes are underpinned by two critical principles. The first is that the inhabitants have the right to infrastructure and services even if they live in illegal or informal settlements. The second is that the slums or squatter settlements have value. Before upgrading programmes become common, official housing policies usually viewed these settlements simply as targets for demolition, and the populations were displaced. It has increasingly come to be understood that recognizing title and security of tenure enhances both the economic prospects of the poor, and benefits the national economy.

Key Elements for a Child-Friendly City

In every region of the world, a city that respects children's rights is a city that requires:

- Good access for all children to affordable, quality basic health education services, clean water, adequate sanitation and solid waste removal.
- Local authorities to ensure that policies, resource allocation and all initiatives and actions emerging from governance structures are made in a manner in the best interests of the children in their constituencies.

- Non-discrimination based on gender, ethnic background or social or economic status.
- That special attention is given to disadvantaged children, such as those who are living or working on the streets, sexually exploited, living with disabilities or without adequate family support.
- A sustainable future under equitable social and economic conditions, and protection from the effects of environmental hazards and natural disasters.
- Safe environment and conditions that nurture the development of children of all ages with opportunities for recreation, learning, social interaction, psycho-social development and cultural expression.
- Those children have the right to participate in making decisions that affect third lives and are offered opportunities to express their opinions.

The present study had been conducted among the children of families who are settled on the streets of Kolkata. These populations are considered as illegitimate section of the city because of the settlement pattern. Broadly speaking the growth of street families are the consequence of vicious poverty cycle, out migration from the rural areas due to rural landlessness, unemployment and lack of coordination between rural and urban policy-makers. Children of these families live in appalling and inhuman conditions and are the victims of this social, economic and political complicacy. Living on the fringe of society and disadvantaged by the pressure of poverty and insecurities, these children are exposed to various forms of physical, economical and sexual exploitation. Their basic minimum rights are grossly violated and they are debarred from the mainstream of the society.

6

DISCUSSION AND INTERPRETATION

As one of the signatories of the CRC, the Government of India recognizes that every child has the right to minimum standard of living that includes conducive environment for his or her physical, mental, spiritual, moral and social development. Though, the primary responsibility of the children lies with the parents to provide adequate support for holistic development, but still the State has the responsibility to oversee and ensure that such duties by the parents are fulfilled. It is also recognized that children suffer from various forms of abuse and neglect and they need to be protected from such devastating incidence of life. The Government of India is committed to take all necessary and appropriate legislative, administrative, social and educational measures to protect children from any form of maltreatment or abuse from any sources including their own parents. The Government is also committed to stop economic and sexual exploitation against children and to take required protective and rehabilitative measures to enable such children to enjoy a decent life with love and dignity. Especially in the case of children living with their families on the street, the dysfunctional family environment added to lack of appropriate adoptive and protective skills exposes the children to various forms of abuse and exploitation from both internal and external environment.

Child abuse is not a societal issue, but it has its roots within the problems at the family level. During the analysis of the study, it was observed that the acute poverty was one of the key factors for maltreatment and abuse of children. It gets more escalated by conditions such as environmental insecurities, marital strife, alcoholism, drug abuse, illiteracy and lack of knowledge on law and other machinery. All these conditions caused a critical stress situation, precipitating a crisis that frequently results in child abuse and neglect.

Here, the collected qualitative and quantitative data have been analyzed to understand the socio-economic profile of the street children, types of abuse perpetrated against children in different settings and perception of children and parents regarding existing law enforcement machinery. Efforts were also made to seek opinion of the children and their parents regarding effective law enforcement machineries.

Since, the objectives of the study are manifold, this chapter has been divided into several categories to see the findings of the study which are given below:

Section 6.1 Socio-economic Profile of the Respondents.
Section 6.2 Abuse and Perpetrators-perception of Children.
Section 6.3 Abuse and Perpetrators-perception of Parents.
Section 6.4 Self-protection Mechanisms.
Section 6.5 Child-Rights-perception of Children and their Parents.
Section 6.6 Perception of Police Regarding Street Children and Child Protection.
Section 6.7 Opinion of Children and Parents Towards Law Enforcement Mechanism.

SECTION 6.1

The Socio-Economic Profile of the Respondents

Here, we describe the socio-economic profile of the children and their families living on the streets. It also explains their migration and settlement patterns in the urban pockets of Kolkata and their struggle to access the basic services.

Child Respondents and Gender

For the purpose of the study, the researcher identified 200 children, of both genders, of the age group 12-16 years, who lived on the streets of Kolkata. As per the methodology adopted for this study, equal number of male and female children were selected for the study, using the random purposive sampling (details in the methodology chapter) technique. Thus, the total 40 children include equal numbers of both genders, who were selected from different zones of Kolkata city.

Based on the field experience of the researchers and literature review, it was found that the age group of 12-16 years was much more vulnerable as compared to 17-18 years. Besides, the children younger than 12 years of age were not able to express their problems and opinion sufficiently. Thus, the researchers purposively selected the age group of 12-16 years.

Table 6.1: Gender-age-wise Distribution of the Child Respondents

	12 Years	*13 Years*	*14 Years*	*15 Years*	*16 Years*	*Total*
Male	32	28	18	12	10	100
Female	34	30	21	11	4	100
Total	**66 (33%)**	**58 (29%)**	**39 (19.5%)**	**23 (11.5%)**	**14 (7%)**	**200**

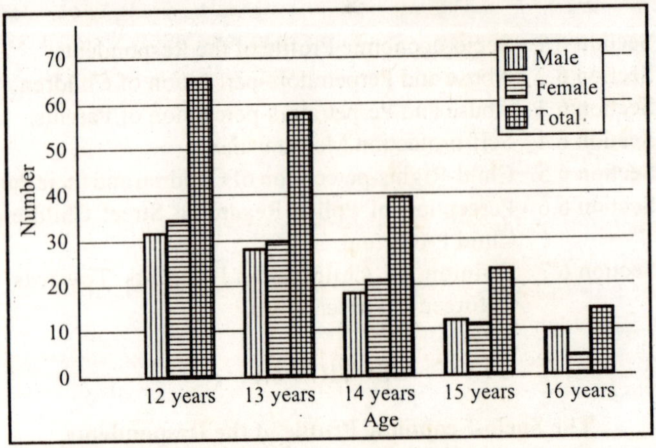

Figure 6.1: Gender-age-wise Distribution of the Child Respondents

Educational Status of the Respondents

Table 6.2 indicates the educational status of the children living on the streets. It was found that only 66 (33%) children were enrolled in the formal system and 110 (55%) were drop outs. It was interesting to observe that the participation of girls in the formal educational system was comparatively higher than the boys. It implies that there were more boys, who never went to school or who left the school half way through.

Table 6.2: Educational Status of Children

	Formal School	*Drop-out*	*Never Been to School*	*Total*
Male	27	60	13	100
Female	39	50	11	100
Total	**66 (33%)**	**110 (55%)**	**24 (12%)**	**200 (100%)**

It has been found that 45 per cent children attended more than one type of school (Government and Non-formal NGO run school). During the field visits, the researchers enquired the family for the reasons of sending children to different schools. It was realized that the parents felt safe to send their children to school instead of having them play on the streets, especially, for the girls, as the parents felt more secure to have them go to school to avoid any type of maltreatment. But from the conversation, we got an idea that the family did not think that education for the girls were an important aspect for their development. The schools run by the philanthropic organizations were felt to be the safest place for their children, especially the girl child, when the parents were away for work. It was also reflected that the family allowed their male children to attend far away formal schools and the distance was not the major concern. But for the girl child, both the distance and safety were an issue for which parents preferred to send them to the nearest NGO or Government run schools.

Religion and Language Spoken

Of the total 200 children, there were 100 (50%) who followed Hindu religion, 96 (48%) were Muslim and 4 (2%) believed in Christianity. It was evident from the field visit that the families with similar religious background tend to shelter in a cluster.

Bengali was the first language for 190 (95%) children, whereas the remaining 10 (5%) children spoke dialects of Hindi language in their family. It was found that the most of the children were able to converse in Bengali as there were 176 (88%) children who had the experience of going to the school at least once. But when it comes to reading and writing, only 46 (23%) children were able to read and write in Bengali. The researchers also observed that only 22 (11%) children were able to write their names in English, though none of them were able to speak or read English. And for this reason, the focus group discussions and questionnaire for the purpose of data collection was prepared in Bengali.

Migration to Kolkata

Table 6.3 indicates the pattern of migration across different zones of Kolkata. The settlement varies in these zones based on the development and job opportunities available in the area. Of the total 200 children. 80 (40%) migrated from other parts of West Bengal; 75 (37.5%) migrated from Bihar and remaining 45 (22.5%) came from Jharkhand, the neighbouring State of West Bengal.

Of the total 80 children migrated from other parts of West Bengal State, 40 (50%) lived on the streets of South Zone, 24 (30%) in East Zone and 16 (20%) in North Zone. It was identified that no children from West Bengal State lived on the streets of Central and West Zone of Kolkata. The researchers found that most of the children who migrated with their families came from South 24 Pargana District of West Bengal. And to maintain the proximity with the area of origin, majority (50%) of the children were found to have settled in the South Zone of Kolkata. The most common areas of South 24 Pargana from where these families and their children migrated were Laxmikantapur, Canning, Joynagar, Kakdip, Mograhat and Diamond Habour. And from the North 24 Pargana area, Habra, Gobordanga and Bashirhat were the areas where families migrated in a large number. Also, there were families who came from Howrah District, Ranaghat and Nabadwip area.

Besides West Bengal, children were found to have migrated from Bihar and Jharkhand along with their families to settle in Kolkata. It was observed from the data that there were no children migrated from Jharkhand to the South and East Zone. The preferred location for settlement of children with their families migrated from Bihar and Jharkhand was West and Central Zone. Of the total children respondents migrated from Bihar 25 (33.3) lived on the streets of West Zone whereas 22 (29.3%) settled in Central Zone. Similarly, of the total children migrated from Jharkhand 15 (33.3%) settled in West Zone and 18 (40%) in Central Zone.

Table 6.3: Pattern of Migration

	West Bengal	*Bihar*	*Jharkhand*	*Total*
North	16	12	12	40
Central	0	22	18	40
East	24	16	0	40
West	0	25	15	40
South	40	0	0	40
Total	**80 (40%)**	**75 (37.5%)**	**45 (22.5%)**	**200**

Reasons for Migration

The most common push factor among the migrant families of West Bengal, who live with their children on streets, was the lack of employment in their native village. Most of them were from agrarian community and had very small land holdings in their villages and were highly dependent on the rainfed irrigation. And, due to the irregularity of monsoon and failure of crops due to pests, the earning from agriculture was not sufficient to meet the expenses of their large joint families. Similarly, the families who migrated from Jharkhand and Bihar were also pushed out of villages to search for employment for their survival. Many families did not possess cultivable land for many generations they worked as agricultural labourer. Due to the seasonal variation, it was not a reliable source of income for them. This left no option for them, but to migrate to the cities in search of better employment opportunities. During the focus group discussions with children, many shared their dream of living in a rented house or at some point of time, get some lease (*patta*) land from government on the outskirts of Kolkata. This dream was cultivated amongst children, as they have witnessed other families who received such benefits through their political connections. These children wished to get similar benefits for their families as they have experienced the pain and struggle to live on the streets.

Length of Settlement of Families

It was common to find the families migrated to seek employment at the local market in rural areas, from where they migrated, was not stable for work. It was safe to assume that the uncontrolled population growth over the years has reduced the per capita cultivable land, and created overcrowding and high rate of disguised unemployment in the agricultural sector. These circumstances of livelihood pushed people out from the village to large cities. It was usually the young male worker and his family who took the responsibility to go in search of daily wage employment in any unskilled vocation. Hence, we find that daily age work was central to the livelihood of such migrant families living on the streets of Kolkata.

Table 6.4: Length of Settlement of Families

	Less than 5 Years	*5-10 Years*	*More than 10 Years*	*Total*
North	12	23	5	40
Central	9	19	12	40
East	12	14	14	40
West	8	20	12	40
South	4	20	16	40
Total	**45 (22.5%)**	**96 (48%)**	**59 (29.5%)**	**200**

It was observed (Table 6.4) that the families who have recently migrated to Kolkata, preferred to settle in North and East Zone. During the interview process, the researchers identified that most of the migrant families (48%) livings on the streets were in the group of 5-10 years. Besides, there were some exceptional circumstances narrated by the families. 'Kajal' was one such lady, who came in contact with us during the field visit and it was worth mentioning her life experience in brief, which pushed her to live on the street.

> Kajal, at the age of 9 years along with few other girls were brought to Kolkata from a small village in South 24 Pargana District of West Bengal. She came to work as a domestic help and was entrusted to one of her distant relative to care for her. She did not enjoy working, as her employer used to overload her with work. At her workplace, people did not behave nicely with her and even after working for 4 months, she was not given any remuneration. She felt very lonely in the big city like Kolkata and had no one close to her from her family or relatives. After dragging the work for few months, she got frustrated and ran away from her employer's place. She roamed on the streets of Kolkata, not knowing what to do next. Fortunately, she got in touch with an elderly woman who stayed by herself on the pavements. She identified Kajal roaming on the street and happily extended support to her. Kajal was given shelter by the woman on the pavement and promised to send her home once she was able to recall her parents' address or contact details. The elderly lady also arranged for work as a maid in one of the families known to her. Kajal started working as a part-time help for about 4 hours everyday. Over a period of time, Kajal got adjusted to the life on the streets and grew up with the old lady till she got married to a hawker, who lived on the same pavement. After a few years Kajal's husband helped her to locate her patents. Interestingly, now Kajal does not want to stay in the village, where her parents lived. For more than 2 days in a row, as she was not able to adjust rural life without electricity and other entertainment means.

Strategic Settlement Options

During the mapping exercise, it was identified that most of the families lived in strategic location of the city like areas near the bus/train terminal, business centres and other important road junctions. They happen to choose such locations that provide better transportation connectivity to the work place and back. Also, it was easy to find petty jobs in the busy locations of the city. In addition, they earn higher wages by working in the core of the city as compared to the wages in the outskirts for similar work. Besides the economic advantages, the downtown of Kolkata offers non-threatening locations to stay, like the places under the flyover or bridges, premises near government offices and public places like parks, railway station and bus terminal. Such areas are less prone to the eviction drive by the authorities.

Living Condition

As commonly seen in the rural parts of India, the families living with their children on the streets were also conscious about the caste system. It was observed that the families belonging to the same caste happen to stay together in the area. And, sometimes the barriers of caste were an issue, if the families perceived advantages of living close to other families from their native village or home state. Such settlements enabled them to develop better understanding and support system between families while they continue to face the challenges of living on the streets of Kolkata.

The living conditions (Table 6.5) especially the place of shelter taken by the children at night determined the degree of vulnerability. Of the total 200 respondents, it was found that 97 (48.5%) used to sleep under a plastic sheet at night and 54 (27%) preferred to sleep in the open space. Only few children were fortunate enough to sleep inside the room. Thus, majority of the children (93%) took shelter in unprotected places. Besides, their vulnerability to get sexually abused at night, they were also exposed to severe cold of winter and mosquito bites throughout the year. It was a nightmare for such children when it rains heavily at night during monsoons. It was not uncommon to find the families with their children standing under the flyover or shed for the whole night, as it was nearly impossible to find dry place to sleep.

Table 6.5: Places for Night Shelter

Shelter	*No. of Children*	*Percentage*
Inside a room	14	7.0
Under a plastic cover	97	48.5
Under a shed	35	17.5
Open space	54	27.0
Total	**200**	**100**

Every morning, the children and their families pack up their belongings before they go away for work. The heap of their belongings, which includes utensils, cloths, bedding and other household goods are stacked and covered with a plastic sheet during the daytime. At night, when they return back, they roam on the street and wait till late evening before they are allowed to unpack their belongings and cook the meals.

And most of the evenings, children remain hungry for long hours as their parents wait for the pavements to be cleared from public traffic, so that they can convert it into an improvised kitchen. With all these challenges and limited supply of water, it was extremely difficult for the families to maintain proper hygiene for preparing their food. By the time they feed themselves and their children, it was too late in the night and many children were found sleeping on the street without bedding. Later, the family members work together to make temporary shelters on the pavements with help of plastic sheets. This gives them some space for privacy and eliminates the reflection of lights from the vehicles moving on the street. And for those families, for whom making of temporary shelter was not possible, they would try to hide and protect themselves as well as the children by covering with a plastic sheet on the pavements. Children are also found to sleep under a tree or in open space on the pavement. Again, they are to re-pack their belongings before morning. Illness also does not prevent them from this daily routine.

Family Size and Type

The researchers observed that most of the families living with their children on the streets were nuclear in nature. It was followed by the second largest category of joint families. Usually, the number of members in each nuclear family varied from 6-8 people, whereas in the joint and extended family, it was found to exceed more than 10 members.

Water and Sanitation Facilities

During the field visit, it was visualized that except for the children and their families living on the streets of West Zone, the street dwellers of the remaining four zones had access to the roadside 'pay and use' toilets facilities up to 11 p.m. And due to lack of such services in West Zone, the families resorted to the use of open spaces for defecation. It was also observed that families tried to save on the expenditure for using toilets by limiting the use of toilets for teenage girls and adult women. The rest of the family members, which includes the male members and children preferred to use the open canals, riverside, parks and roadside drains. It was not perceived to be a problem as the families followed similar use of open fields for defecation in the rural areas. Though, the open spaces in the city did not allow sufficient privacy, but still the migrant population was found to get accustomed with the new city environment. Hence, it was not an issue for the families living on the street to use spaces for toilet.

Most of the families living on the streets of all Zones in Kolkata were using roadside taps for supply of portable water. This service was made available by the *Kolkata Municipal Corporation*, but, there were no facilities available for the bathing. Men and women were commonly found to be taking bath in the open spaces with clothes on. In such circumstances, it is safe to assume that people living on the streets were not able to maintain proper personal hygiene. And this may be an important reason for acquiring many diseases.

Economic Conditions of the Pavement Dwellers

Based on the data analysis, the families living on the streets can be categorized based on their frequency of pay. It was found that the families had daily, weekly or monthly wages depending upon their profession. It was 59 per cent of the earning members of the family were daily wage earners and 28 per cent earned through a job that paid them on a weekly basis. Whereas, 13 per cent had regular part time or full time jobs, which paid on monthly basis. It was noted during the study that the respondents were not comfortable to share the exact amount of their income. And for almost all the families, the source of income was not stable and so it was not possible to categorize them based on the amount of their income.

It was identified that 57 per cent male and 88 per cent female earning members of the family received pay below the minimum wages fixed by the government. And, it was commonly found that the male earners had better chances of employment and they tend to receive higher wages. Men were commonly engaged to work as labourers, rickshaw pullers, artisans, loaders, hawkers and rag-pickers; whereas the females generally work as domestic help, vegetable sellers, unskilled daily labour, rag-pickers and beggars. It was unfortunate to identify that the poverty of the family also forced children to engage in some form of work at a very early age. Commonly, the male children were found to start earning as early as 8 years of age whereas female children usually start at the age of 10 years.

Most of the boys followed their father or other men in the community and tend to shift from one profession to other. While these youngsters struggle to stabilize themselves in the competitive job market, it was easy for them to fall prey of anti-social groups. They were lured or pressurized to get involved in illegal activities like drug trafficking, stealing, pick-pocketing and violence. Whereas, the girl children usually were engaged as domestic help or help their mother at home. They often become the care-taker of their siblings when their mothers are away for work. This indeed was a means of child-labour in disguise and prevented the girl children from attending the school or play.

Income and Expenditure

Most of the pavement dwellers possess limited economic skills, which limit or restrict their access to better paying jobs. They were usually found to be engaged in the informal sector, where the wages were exceptionally low. With the day long struggle, they just earn money to pay for their food. And in case of emergency, they were forced to borrow money from other people at a reasonably high rate of interest. It was observed that for most of the families, living in a house was a dream, but was not fulfilled due to lack of steady income or their income was not sufficient.

Based on the estimated income and expenditure of the families, they were categorized into **three** major groups:

- The first being a high income group, where the expenditure per family ranges from ₹ 2000-3000 per month. Of the total number of parents interviewed, 40 per cent were estimated to belong such large families with about 10-12 members. In these families, there were more than 5 earning members including the children.
- The second group consists of families having moderate income and spends on an average of ₹ 1500-2000 per month and their family size was usually of 8-10 members.
- The third group of families, who had an average family size of 5-6 members and were found to be spending approximately ₹ 1000-1500 per month. Naturally, as the family size increases, the earning of family members also increases. And unfortunately, the poor ignorant street dwellers fall in the trap and produce more number of children without realizing the hidden costs involved in the upbringing and development of the children.

Based on the analysis of the data, it was realized that most of the families spend 68 per cent of their income on the food, 22 per cent to seek pleasure from substance abuse, 5 per cent on recreational activities and rest 5 per cent on buying assets or utensils for the family. During the interview with the children, most of them revealed that they gave the earnings to their parents and kept aside ₹ 5-10 everyday for their own use. It was identified that the daily expenses for recreational and substance abuse was relatively higher among boys than girls. It was also found that girls spend ₹ 3-4 on substance abuse whereas the boys of similar age spend about ₹ 7-10. It was not uncommon to find the younger boys involved in consumption of alcohol and frequent participation in gambling to earn extra money. Instead the girls showed more responsible behaviour with respect to spending money. Most of the girls worked as a domestic help and got paid on monthly basis. So, they were less tempted to increase their daily expenses on entertainment and were found to be more cautious and prepared for an unexpected emergency situation within the family; demanding high expenditure. Many girls who worked as maid reported that they try to save money from the money given by the employer to meet the daily expenses of rations and cooking. They further reported that on an average they were able to save about ₹ 3-4 per day. And, there were some interesting stories when the girls came forward to rescue their family from eviction or illness by using their savings of many years.

The saving habits of families living on the streets were found to be very poor. For most, a portion of the wages was kept with their employer as they did not have access to bank nor they have homes to keep the money safely. It was found during the data collection that only 20 (10%) families invested in private saving policies like Sahara. Due to such poor saving habits, the families had no other sources to access money at the time of emergency. In such crisis, they are forced to take loan from *Mahajans* (moneylenders), who charge an exorbitant rate of interest, which may be as high as 25-35 per cent per year. Some families were also found to have taken loans or advance wages from their employer. This was slightly safer way for the families as they were not required to pay the higher rate of interest, as in the case with moneylenders.

It was revealed that the families preferred to take loan from their neighbours in case of emergency. In most of the cases, the neighbours belong to the same caste or they happen to have migrated from the same native area or home state. And for some of the unplanned expenses, which may vary from ₹ 30-50, the families borrowed from the money lenders and repay within 203 days without any interest. But when they require borrowing larger amount like ₹ 100-500, they resorted to employers. And in most of the cases, the employers did not hesitate to extend such support with the condition of adjust the amount payable with their next remuneration. It was only in some unexceptional circumstances, the families went to the moneylenders for borrowing amount greater than ₹ 1000. Such a situation mainly arose when some of the family members were hospitalized and there was a dire need to meet the medical expenses or they were evicted/arrested for petty reasons. It was very unfortunate that this population, who silently struggle to earn their living, do not have access to bank or its services due to lack of any legal document to prove their place of residence or identity, which was mandatory for opening a bank account or borrowing money from the bank. Thus, they become victims of the moneylenders, who charge high rate of interest and exploit them for their ignorance, innocence and crisis.

It was reflected that families approached moneylenders for various reasons during their life on the streets. Of the total 200, 179 (89.5%) children's family borrowed money to meet the emergency medical needs and 140 (70%) borrowed during festivals or social ceremony like marriage. Whereas, 107 (53.5%) families borrowed to meet the daily needs. Moneylenders were easily accessible to the families as they open throughout the day. Due to convenience and informal understanding with the moneylenders, most of the families approach them, in spite of the high rate of interest on the capital. It was also noted during the study that all families knew that they had to pay a high rate of interest for the money. But, when they were asked by the researchers, as to how much was the rate of interest or how much more they have to pay, most of them, i.e. 69 per cent children's family were unaware. The respondents informed that they repay the loan in small installments like ₹ 50 every few days. But interestingly, none of the respondents maintained records of how much money that have already repaid so far or how much is the remaining balance that they have to pay.

Basic Entitlements

Almost all the families living on the streets did not have any residential proof and so they remain deprived from some of the basic entitlements like other citizens of India.

Voter Identification Card

The right to have a voter identity card was one of the key entitlements of every citizen of India. Except 12 per cent of the families, none had the voter card or any other legal identity proof. Among these, who had voter cards, 10 per cent were found to be living in Kolkata for more than 20 years or have recently migrated and have received the voter identity card in their native village. The families who have settled for more than 20 years narrated experience of local counsellors, who helped them to get enlisted in voting list prepared by the government. They also narrated that as they do not have any settlement address they had to enlist their name as the resident of their relative's home in the nearby slums. Another respondent spoke that they do not have any voter identity card registered in Kolkata but have got the same from their native village.

Below Poverty Line (BPL) Card

Though the State Government had promised BPL cards to all families living below the poverty line (as defined by the government), the ground reality among the urban poor was very different. Among the respondents only 190 families (5%) had received their BPL cards. The Draft Report published by Kolkata Municipal Corporation (KMC) in February, 2008 stated that 1,27,000 people came under the BPL category. But ironically, the list did not include those thousands of homeless people living on the streets of the city.

Public Distribution System (PDS) of Foodgrain

The families living on the streets were considered as 'illegal migrants' in the city as they do not have any sort of residential proof. Thus, none of the member of families living on the streets have ration card and they failed to receive the benefits of PDS system. It was also true that the State Government was hesitant to issue ration cards to homeless people as there was a security concern and a legal notice was issued by the Ministry of Home Affairs. The said circular clearly instructed to avoid issuance of ration cards unless it was established that the person was a resident of the new address. The, Ministry argues that "illegal Migrants" use the ration cards to acquire citizenship status in India.

Children's Perception about the Environment

Detailed survey and focus group discussions were conducted to know the perceptions of children about the environment. The findings are shown in Table 6.6.

Table 6.6: Common Areas of Concern

Concern of Children	*Male*	*Female*	*Total*	*Percentage of Children*
To take food at roadside	10	0	10	5.0
No place to study at home	5	20	25	12.5
Can not cook food before evening	0	34	34	17.0
Lack of safety	0	42	42	21.0
No bathing facilities for female	0	50	50	25.0
Constant noise of vehicles	31	23	54	27.0
Constant threat of eviction	21	34	55	27.5
No place to sleep during rainy season	27	29	56	28.0
Late night raids by police and administration	31	34	65	32.5
Filthy environment	28	37	65	32.5
No safe place to keep belongings	30	41	71	35.5
Lack of privacy	43	45	88	44.0
No safe place to sleep at night	32	78	110	55.0

- The utmost important concern of children was lack of safe place to sleep at night. Of the total 200 children, 110 (55%) reported the same.
- Lack of privacy was an important concern for a significant number of children. Among the children 44 per cent reported that they do not have any privacy in whatsoever ways. They were always remained exposed to public. It makes them feel very odd when people passing by on the streets observe them with curiosity.
- The children and the families who lived on the pavements of busy roads reported that they were not allowed to cook the food during the day time. So, they are to eat unhygienic food available on the street while they waited for the meals to cook at night. Also, due to lack of any storage facilities, the food prepared at night was not appropriate to be used on the next day.
- Other than those, constant noise of vehicles, filthy environment, taking food at the road side and lack of place to study were also some of the concerns raised by children of both the gender.
- Getting a shelter during rainy season is a problem for all the street living children across all the zones. In Kolkata, water logging is a common phenomenon. In such circumstances, the children and their families were forced to take shelter under a shed, where they stand for the whole night as the ground remains wet or waterlogged.

- Further, 35.5 per cent children felt that lack of safe place to keep their belongings is a major concern of the pavement dwellers which included money and other important personal assets.
- Frequent raids by the police at night were also a major concern for the children. Authorities conduct raids (Hallagiri as they call it) on the slum dwellers at night without prior notice. The families including the children get forcefully evicted from their temporary shelter. They snatch all their personal belongings including utensils, money and other assets.
- During the group discussions it was revealed that the girls were more insecure and unsafe than the boys. Girls felt that they require more privacy than boys. They did not have, not even, private place for bathing. They have to take bath on the streets.
- Girls felt the threat of being sexually assaulted at night by unknown people on the streets. Many had experienced that sometimes; unknown drunk persons enter into the temporary sheds and try to touch their private parts. Thus, they feel very unsafe to sleep in open spaces.

Families settled on the pavements face risk of evictions, exploited by the authorities and political leaders. In spite being a citizen of the country these families are treated 'illegitimate dwellers' in the city because of unplanned urbanization and lack of coordination between administration of the place of origin and home state. Though, it is legal obligation of state parties to promote equitable, humane and lawful conditions to its every citizen but the street families are denied from their rights to participate in the mainstream society. Without the legal status, families become the natural target of social and economic exploitations. They rarely can seek justice because of their ignorance and access to legal instruments. Therefore, government should take steps to protect the legal identity of its citizen and take rehabilitative measures to protect rights of their children at large.

SECTION 6.2

Abuse and the Perpetrators — Perception of Children

As discussed in the earlier chapter that the children living with their families on the streets were exposed to a number of risk factors because of their socio-cultural, environmental and lack of legal support. During the time of data collection, the researchers were told by the children that they get exposed to various types of violence in different settings. The way it was expressed, it appeared that they have got habituated to undergo different types of trauma in their young life. It was not easy for the researchers to identify the incidence in these children's life as they did not disclose due to fear of punishment. Ethically also, the researchers never probed the children to narrate their horrified personal experience if they were not interested to disclose. Also, the parents tried to keep such incidence private within their family members as it could lead to isolation of the family and the child due to the social stigma attached to it. Here, efforts are made to understand the perception of the children about abuse and perpetrator within different settings, where children interact on a usual basis.

Children's Perception of Abuse and Abusers

The researchers used different qualitative and quantitative methods to ensure participation of the children to understand their perception about the incidence of abuse and abuser.

Ranking Exercise

One of the key tools used by the researchers in this study was the ranking exercise. This was used to help the children to priorities the types of abuse or various forms of maltreatment which they encounter at some point of time. The children were also encouraged to enlist the types of abuses other children or their friends faced in similar living environment. The exercise was conducted separately with both the boys and girls and the findings were grouped gender-wise. Based on this group work, children identified 37 forms of maltreatment or abuse that were perpetrated against them or other children living on the streets. Further, the types of maltreatment and abuses faced by the children were grouped in the following five categories with the help of children's inputs. The categories were:

- physical abuse,
- mental or emotional abuse,
- sexual abuse,
- economic abuse, and
- legal abuse.

From the data analysis, it was revealed that there were some types of abuses which were common to both the genders. Also, it was common to find that children of both the genders had some experience of abuse in their life, but their perception of safety in the same environment varied widely. Some of the common reasons identified were the structure, status and culture of the family. It was important to note that obtaining information regarding sexual abuse was difficult as it was a very sensitive issue and there was a social stigma attached to it. For this reason, the quantitative data may not reflect the actual incidence of sexual abuse of the children living on the streets. Instead, the researchers had used methods to elicit qualitative information through the case studies. And this was done by facilitating interviews and FGDs with some case studies., which helped the children to associate it with their own life. In this process, there were few children, who narrated some of their experiences of sexual abuse. These real life incidences were reflected in this study in form of case studies.

Table 6.7 describes various indicators used by the children to indicate the experience of abuses and also the same were categorized in five different sub-groups.

Table 6.7: Indicators of Abuses as Described by Children

Types of Abuses	*Indicators*
(1)	(2)
Physical Abuse	• Hard work • Beating, inflicted physical pain, burns and injuries
Mental/Emotional	• Eviction • Humiliation, emotional torture and harassment • Harsh treatment by the family members • Curiosity of unknown people on the street or passer-by • Family members don't allow to play and force them to work • Fear of accident • Fear of being alone due to separation or death of parents • Unknown person enter into their plastic shed and so they can not sleep peacefully • Comparison with other children • Use of abusive language • Bullying • Social stigma
Sexual	• Use of offensive words • Unknown person enter into the plastic shed for mal-intention • Known/unknown person lure children with money and gift • Touching and hugging of children with wrong intention • Making the child fondle others body parts • Touching of private body parts of children

(*Contd.*)

Table 6.7 (*Contd.*)

(1)	(2)
	• Establishing physical relationship with children • Sexual harassment by senior group members • Observing children with wrong intention • Exhibiting parts to children • Showing pornographic films/pictures
Economic	• Do not get proper remuneration • Forced to extra work and overtime without extra payment • Snatching of money and personal belongings
Legal	• Detention at police station for without reason • Forceful eviction at night • Forcefully snatching of belongings by law enforcement personnel • Taking financial loans • Non-cooperation during lodging of complaints

In this study, the researchers used the questionnaires as well as conducted FGDs to understand from the children about the common abuses that they face. Besides, critical incident technique was also used during one to one interview to facilitate children to narrate their experiences of getting abuse. In order to facilitate the response from the children, the researchers narrated some stories that helped them to recall their experiences of abuse faced by them in recent past. The entire process of data collection was helpful for the researchers to understand and relate different experiences of children with the frequency of the occurrence of these abuses. For the purpose of data collection, the information about their experiences in the last 6 months was included.

Table 6.8: Perception of Children Towards Commonly Occurred Abuses

Types of Abuses	*Male*	*Female*	*Total No.*	*Percentage*
Physical	48	40	88	44.0
Emotional	98	100	198	99.0
Sexual	11	73	84	42.0
Economic	30	39	69	34.5
Legal	85	41	126	63.0

From the data as shown in Table 6.8, it was clear that the children living on the streets were vulnerable to all the types of abuses. Though the purpose of the study was not to estimate of the scale of child abuse, but the above table gives the estimation of different types of abuses.

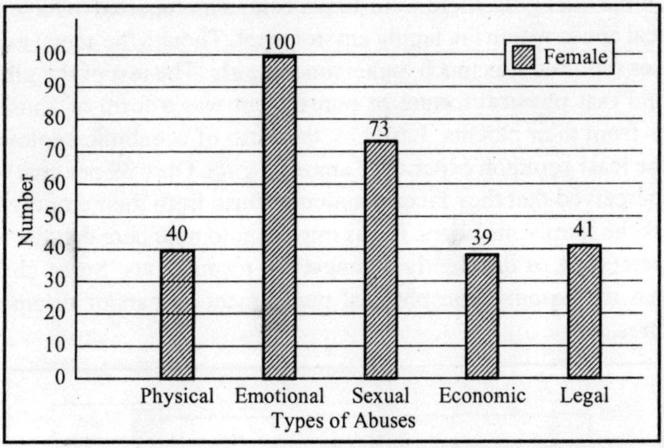

Figure 6.2: Perception of Girls Towards Abuse

It was quite evident from Figure 6.2 that all the girls were found to be very sensitive towards emotional abuse and they all were able to remember their experience of it. It was the most frequently occurring type of abuse amongst girls and all the girls were able to narrate their exposure to emotional abuse.

The second most commonly occurring abuse amongst girls was to get sexually abused. They reported during the data collection that they always felt the threat of getting sexually abused on the streets where they lived as the environment was open and unsafe. They were always on their guard as they do not have any safe place to live and maintain their privacy. Their life was open to everybody passing on the streets and they frequently encounter threat of sexual abuse from known as well as unknown people on the streets. It was shocking to note that of the total girls, there were 73 per cent who reported of having faced situations in which they get sexually abused at some point of time in their life.

It was shameful to see that the third common type of source of abuse faced by these children were from the authorities who were meant to serve people and protect them. The official of the legal system, which includes the police, municipal authorities and traffic controllers, was found to be the third most sources of abuses faced by the girls. The authorities instead of protecting them as they belong to a vulnerable group threaten them with sudden eviction and exposed them to sudden raid by the police. It was found that 41 per cent of the girls had some incidences of legal abuse within last six months.

Of the total girls, there were 40 per cent, who reported to have faced physical abuse within the family environment. Though the actual number of cases reported was much higher among girls. The rest of the girls did not find that physical torture or punishment was a form of abuse if it comes from their parents. Lastly, in the form of economic exploitation was the least common experience amongst girls. Only 39 per cent of the girls perceived that they faced economic abuse from their employers as well as the family members. It was important to note here that the abuse was perceived so differently amongst the respondents. Some children felt that the parents give physical punishment as part of disciplinary measures.

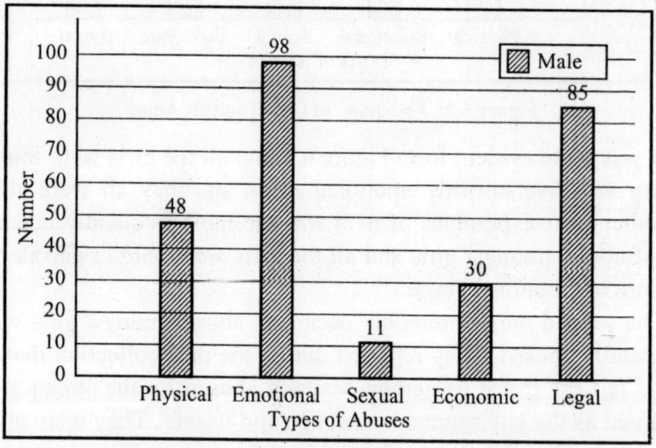

Figure 6.3: Perception of Boys Towards Abuse

From Figure 6.3, it was evident that the boys were also found to be sensitive to emotional abuse as 98 per cent of the boys reported to incidence which caused them emotional trauma in the recent past. Most commonly, they faced such emotional abuse at the work place, in their community and within the family. The second most common type was the abuse in the form of harassment by the legal and administrative authorities in the area. Of the total boys, there were 85 per cent, who reported to have faced such incidences. On priority, the third most common type of abuse was the physical abuse. There were 48 per cent boys, who reported to have faced several physical assaults by the employers, police officials, neighbours and from their own family members, including their parents.

It was common amongst the boys to go out and earn money to support the income of the family. Most commonly, they were subjected to hard and unsafe work and due to their dependency; they were not able to refuse to work in such unhealthy environment. There were about 30 per cent of the boys, who reported to have faced economic exploitations by the employers, shop owners and family members. When it came to sexual abuse, it was not perceived to be a threat amongst boys. As they lived on the streets, they were aware of sexual abuse that can occur to them but they did not feel afraid of it and had their own mechanism to avoid it. But, there were 11 per cent of the boys who reported that sexual abuse was a threat for them as girls.

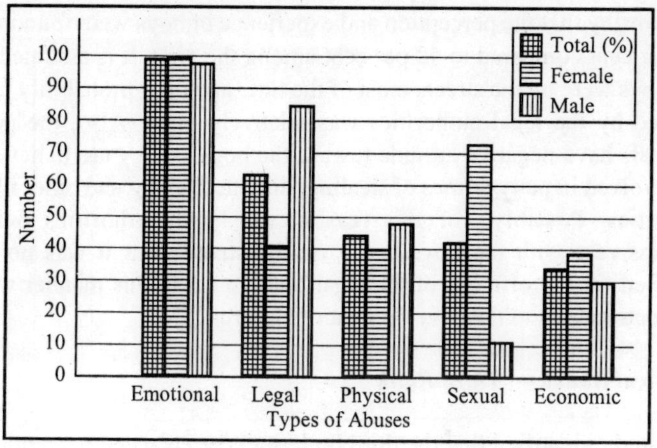

Figure 6.4: A Comparative Analysis of Abuses as Perceived by Both the Genders

Emotional Abuse — First Rank

It can be clearly seen from the comparative chart that emotional abuse was the most frequently occurred abuse among children living on the streets. Of the total children, there was almost everyone (99%) who recalled their recent experience of chronic verbal aggression. Though the incidence of emotional abuse was notably high but many children did not feel that all those incidences could be labeled as abuse. It was found that all the girls and 98 per cent boys were able to identify at least one incidence of last six months, which caused them emotional trauma. During the process of data collection, it was felt by the researchers that the girls were sensitive towards emotional abuse compared to the boys. While stating this, it was quite possible that the boys also felt equally painful on being emotionally abused but they did not open up to express the same as it might affect their image amongst their friends or peers.

Abuse by Legal Authorities — Second Rank

The study identified that the second most common abuses experienced and perceived by the children living on the street was to get abused by the legal authorities, which includes the police personnel, municipal officials, traffic controllers, etc. Of the total respondents, there were 126 (3%) children, had experience of abusive behaviour from the officials of law and order machinery. This was something contradictory to their role of being a public servant, who was entrusted and responsible to provide necessary support to all the residents and citizens of this country. It was noteworthy that the perception and experience of boys were found to be 85 per cent compared to 42 per cent among the girls. It is assumed that the boys were on the streets most of the time and their probability to get abused by the legal authorities was relatively more. Also, the police officials have negative attitude toward the boys as they are believed to be involved in petty crimes of stealing, drug trafficking and other illegal activities. Possibly, for this reason, the legal authorities behave aggressively with the boys living on the streets. But it was no way justified for the officials of the legal body to act in this manner which was detrimental to the development of children.

Physical Abuse — Third Rank

The study identified that the third highest experience and perception of abuse amongst children of both gender was to get physically abused. There were 48 per cent boys and 40 per cent girls, who expressed their recent experience of physical abuse, where they felt humiliated. Though the actual incidences of physical abuse were high among both the genders but only 44 per cent of children perceived that those incidences were abusive. Among girls, most of the physical abuse occurred within the family set-up. As the abusers were their own parents or close relatives, children were not so free to disclose their experiences.

Sexual Abuse — Fourth Rank

The researchers found that the boys were hesitant to discuss about the experience of sexual abuse in their life. Instead, it was found that the girls were much more open to talk about their trauma that they had undergone due to sexual abuse. Unlike the general perception, girls were more open to narrate their perception and experience of sexual harassment compared to the boys. On the other hand, boys wanted to keep their abusive sexual experiences to themselves and it was identified during the focus group discussion that many boys were sexually active by the age of 13 years. Of the total, there were 73 per cent girls who shared their experiences of sexual harassment on the streets, which was also common with other girls like them living on the streets. But in the case of boys there were only 11 per cent who opened up and articulated abusive sexual experience that occurred to them or other boys of their age who lived on the streets. It was evident from the data that 42 per cent of the total children taken as samples were victimized due to sexual exploitation and rest were hesitant to disclose or share their experience about it.

Economic Abuse — Fifth Rank

With reference to the economic exploitations, there were about 34 per cent children who described their experiences of abuse in the recent past. The perception of economic abuse was found to be stronger among girls (39%) than the boys (30%). And most commonly, the boys got exploited by their employers and only few expressed their frustration due to the pressure from the family members to earn and supplement the family income. Commonly, the family members, including parents took away the entire earning of the children and still they were not perceived as perpetrators of economic exploitations by the children.

Children's Experience of Abuse in Different Settings

Similar to the ranking exercise for the types of abuse, the researchers also conducted the same exercise for the perpetrators with the help of

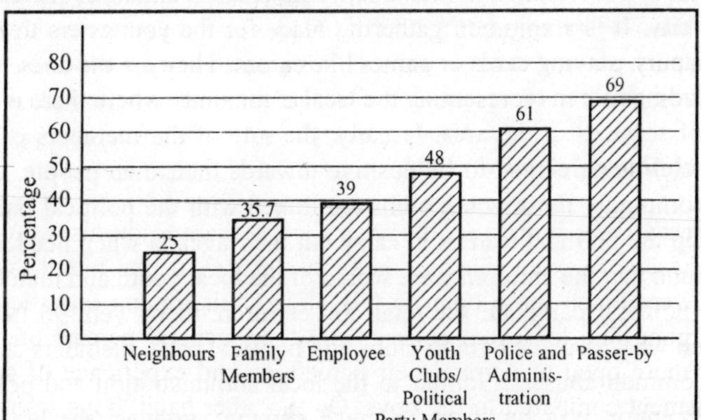

Figure 6.5: Perception of Children Towards Perpetrators of Abuse

children living on the streets. The findings of the same are described as under:

Passers-by — First Rank

On the top of the list, in case of setting where abuse is perpetrated, as perceived by the children was the unknown people passing on the streets. The children perceived them as the most common abusers in their life on the streets. Of the total 200 children, 138 (69%) felt threatened by the unknown people on the streets. And the feeling of insecurity and fear of abuse with reference to the passers-by was found to be much stronger among the girls as compared to the boys.

Local Administration and Police — Second Rank

The law and order machinery was meant to protect and provide necessary support to the public. But during the study, it was shocking to find that the officials of local administration and police department, instead of ensuring protection to children, were the second most common perpetrators of abuse. It was found that of the total respondents, there were 122 (61%) who perceived threat from the government authorities like police, municipal corporation and traffic controllers. And this perception was much stronger amongst the boys (86%) compared to the girls. The boys were the one who were the common targets for abuse and threats from these authorities.

Youth Clubs and Political Party Members — Third Rank

In Kolkata, it is common to find local youth clubs in almost every streets of the city. It is a common gathering place for the youngsters to read newspapers, playing cards or games like carom. They are the ones, who take leading role in representing the local community where there is any issue of services in the area. Usually, the role of the members of the youth club is perceived to be positive towards their own people. And most commonly these youth clubs are linked with the political parties and help the political leaders to carry out their agenda when needed. It was found that the children were scared of the local youth and members of the political party. Of the total 200 children, there were 96 (48%) children who perceived youth clubs and political party members as the third common abusers. Similar to the local administration and police, the perception was found to be much stronger amongst the boys as compared to the girls.

Employers — Fourth Rank

Due to the pressing needs of the family, the children were forced by their parents to get involved in some sort of economic activities. And being a vulnerable and innocent group, they were pushed by their employers to work in unhealthy and hazardous conditions. It was not uncommon to find that these children are made to work overtime without any extra remuneration. Besides, they were subjected to abuse when they commit mistakes or their attention gets diverted to other fun loving or play activities. Of the total 200 respondents, there were 78 (39%) children who reported to have got abused by their employers. Again, this feeling was found to be much stronger among the boys as compared to the girls.

Family Members — Fifth Rank

It was very common for the children to get punished by the family members. However, when the researchers looked at the perception of the children, many did not perceive that the punishment in form of slapping, scolding or use of obnoxious language was a type of abuse. Many children felt that it was acceptable for the parents to punish their children when they commit mistakes. During the study, it was observed that the environment in which the children live was highly insecure. And the children have no other option but to depend on their parents for their needs, care and protection. In return, the children were accepting some of the inhumane behaviour of the parents and did not report the same to the researchers. Of total 200 children as respondents, there were only 35.7 per cent children who perceived that their parents and other members of the family were the abusers. And of these who reported, the feeling was more common among the boys than girls.

Neighbours — Sixth Rank

It was observed that there was interdependence between the neighbours and the families living on the streets. There was a feeling of trust to protect each other's interest especially to overcome the environmental threats. For example, when the parents go for work at night, the neighbours working in the day shift keep a watch on others family and belongings. In such circumstances, the neighbours act as the guardians of the children when their parents are busy at work. Taking advantage of such a situation, there are incidences, where the neighbours abuse the children. It was found that there were 50 (25%) children who perceived neighbours as the abuser and the feeling of being unsafe was felt more commonly among the girls compared to the boys, while talking about the neighbours.

It was evident from the above described ranking exercise that the children who lived on the streets were vulnerable to abuse by almost everyone around them. There was absolutely no one other than their own self upon whom they can trust. Unfortunately, many of them also did not feel safe with their own family members, and it was unimaginable for them to be protected and cared by the others around them, including, the neighbours, law enforcing authorities as well as the common people on the street. These findings mirror the unhealthy portion of our own society where the children living on the streets are abused for some petty reasons. Due to their poor economic and socio-cultural environment in which they are brought up, they tend to have low self-esteem and are easily accustomed with the abuses. They start accepting such incidences and trauma of life as normal part of their daily life. For the girls, it was easy to suspect anyone on the street to be their next abuser, whereas, boys were exposed to harsh external environment. Due to their socio-cultural environment, the boys were exposed to more forms of abuse than the girls, except for the sexual abuses. Therefore, their responses were found to be much stronger towards perpetrators, other than sexual abusers, compared to the girls.

Abuse and Neglect Occurring in Different Settings

The children were victims of violence or abuse in various settings due to different socio-cultural and physical environment. Besides, the behavioural pattern of the perpetrator remains the key factor for an abuse to occur. Here, the researchers made an attempt to understand the perception of children about the prevalence of abuses occurring to the children living on the streets. Some of the identified common areas selected are as under:

- Abuse within family set-up.
- Abuse within educational set-up.
- Abuse at work place.
- Abuse within immediate community.
- Abuse by legal authorities.
- Abuse by peer group and deviant behaviours of the street children.

Family Set-up

The CRC has a fundamental assumption that the family is the natural environment for the growth and well-being of all its members, and particularly for children. Thereby, it recognizes that the family has the greatest potential to protect the children and provide necessary physical and emotional support for their holistic development. In our society, the privacy and autonomy of the family is highly valued. Every individual has the right to have a life within the family and to keep private to its members. We being a social animal, such correspondence are also guaranteed within the international human rights instruments. And, through the interaction and observation with this family environment, the children tried to acquire skills for protection, survival and development. This naturally influences the way the children grow up and develop the personality. Hence, parents and members of the immediate community and their cultural values become an important source of children to learn and adapt to the existing value system. In this section, the researchers tried to understand the environmental and socio-cultural factors that influence the developmental process of children, while they live on the streets. Also, the same are correlated with the child neglect and abuse occurring in similar environment.

It was observed that the prevalence of violence and neglect of the street children was quite common by the family members and their relatives. It was evident that there was a strong relationship between the abuse or neglect and the environment of the children. The physical standard of the children was not conducive for the physical, mental and emotional growth. One of these factors was the nature of settlement of these families. They used to live on the encroached land or pavements, which is always called for eviction by the local authorities. As a result, these families were not recognized by the local authorities for the purpose of benefits provided by the government.

Additionally, the poor economic condition to meet the basic requirements of life made the children more vulnerable to abuse. It was common for children living on the street to lack proper shelter and clothing. They struggle to enjoy regular and healthy meals and were always under the threat of expulsion from their temporary shelter. Due to lack of basic amenities, they were exposed to filthy environment, poor hygiene and remained denied to access to basic healthcare. Hence, these children were found to seek material support and security outside their family environment. And in the struggle to do so, they got subjected to severe physical and emotional neglect leading to poor development, malnourishment, serious illness, physical injuries, low self-esteem and develop feeling of insecurity. It was also common to find that the parents of such children usually failed to provide required affection, emotional support, supervision and control that were required for proper psycho-social development of a child. Instead, the children were exposed to the domestic violence, problematic behaviour, unnatural pressure and addictive behaviour of their parents. As a result, children develop poor self-image, easily become a prey of substance abuse and develop destructive pattern of behaviour. And in almost all cases, the parents themselves lack knowledge as to what they are going through and what would be the implication of the same on their children. Due to the pressing needs of the day-to-day life, most parents develop short sighted reactive behaviour without any understanding of what it could lead to in the lives of their children.

Parental Love and Support

On further investigation, it was found interestingly that out of such dismal picture and total number of respondents, 39 children got positive support from their parents within the family. Such as:

- Total number of siblings was less than three.
- All the children in the family were enrolled in the school.
- Father was not addicted in any form.
- Parents did not force them to earn money.
- Both the parents had experience of schooling in their early age.
- Children used to sleep peacefully with their parents.

The general characteristics of the families where children are severely abused are:

- Like their parents, the children do not go to school.
- Domestic violence and addiction was common within the family.
- Children were forced to go to work at an early age.
- Parents were not physically or mentally prepared for parenting.
- Large number of children with poor spacing and nuclear structure of family.
- Poor management and inadequate source of income.

Due to some above mentioned factors, the children were plunged into a traumatic life without any support and care by the family members. It was common to find that the parents believed in large families as they felt that having more children would help them to earn more money.

Also, they had no idea of the use of contraceptives leading to poor family planning. All these factors were culminated to a vicious cycle of poverty, pain and trauma in the life of the children. Though, the researchers found that the parents, especially mothers felt that they would have been a better position, if they were little more aware of managing the basics of their life. They realized that their day-to-day struggle was so much demanding that they were not able to extend any support to their children in spite if their best efforts. But, they sounded to be committed to avoid the detrimental effects of poverty from the lives of their children as much as possible. And as all parents, they wished to provide a good future to their children.

Feelings of Denial from Parents

The feeling of denial from parents was very strong among the children. Out of 200 children, 64 (32%) complained that their parents did not pay individual attention and not got the opportunity to express themselves to their parents when they were in emotional stress. They also felt that they did not get the attention especially when they needed the most. They replied that because of their parent's involvement in economic and other social responsibilities they could not give individual attention to them. It was also observed that interpersonal relationship and support within the family was very week.

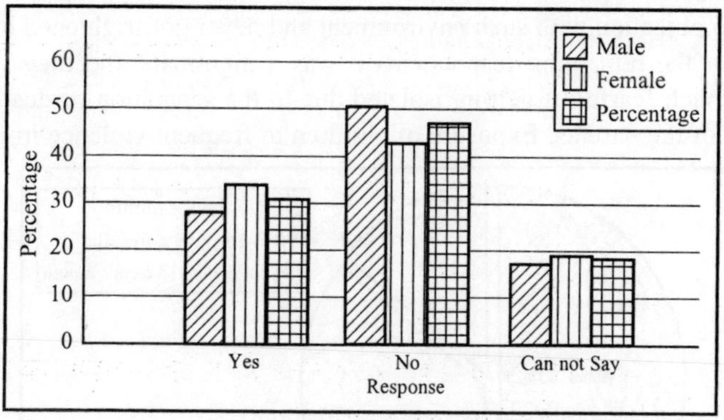

Figure 6.6: Feelings of Denial

Children do not get time and opportunity within the open environment to interact and share their emotional problems to their parents. Children feel threatened to interact with their fathers regarding their problems. In most of the cases, the mothers tried to support their children to address their psychosocial needs and children were much more open to mothers than their parents. But, still children were not satisfied with the emotional support they got from the family.

The size of the family had positive correlation with the emotional deprivation of children. It was evident from the data that emotional deprivation was more common among large families. They found it much more difficult to interact with parents and used to get less individual attention. Parental control and support was also less than other small families.

Family Violence

Based on the interview, it was revealed that the children were exposed to violence and constant chaos within the family environment. Out of the total respondents, 98 (49%) reported that violence within the family occurred more than half of the days of a month; whereas 74 (37%) reported to have such incidence in the family for 7-15 days in a month. There were only 28 (14%) children who informed that such occurrence was not experienced for more than 7 days a month. In most of the cases, these types of violence occurred when their father or other elder members of the family got intoxicated by drug or alcohol. It was common for these children to get exposed to physical torture against them and their mother, with constant screaming and high pitched argumentation. It was so common within the family that the children (87%) got used to it and had no objection with such environment and never got frightened by it. But for the remaining respondents it was a nightmare and they were very much fearful of getting isolated due to the separation or death of either of the parents. Exposure of children to frequent violence in their

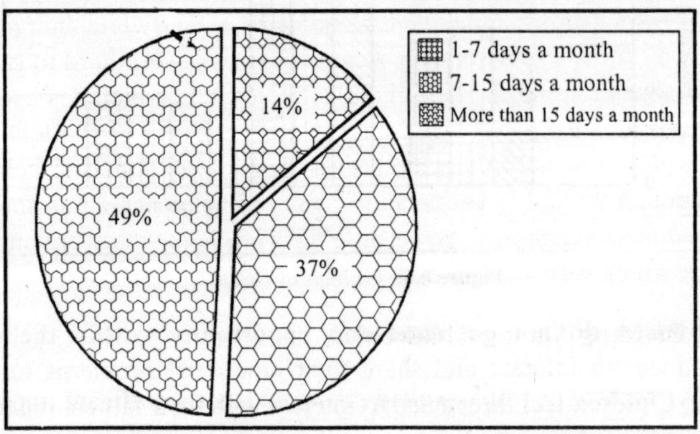

Figure 6.7: Children's Experience of Family Violence

homes severely affected a child's well-being, personality development and social interaction in their childhood and adulthood.

Expectation of Family Members

There were 72.5 per cent children expressed their limitations in satisfying the expectations of their family members. Boys complained that their parents always try to pressurize them to earn more money from an early age and forced them to contribute as much money as possible to support the expenditure of the family. Thus, it was an silent and unrealistic pressure on the part of the boys. The girls also were subject to the various social pressure in the family.

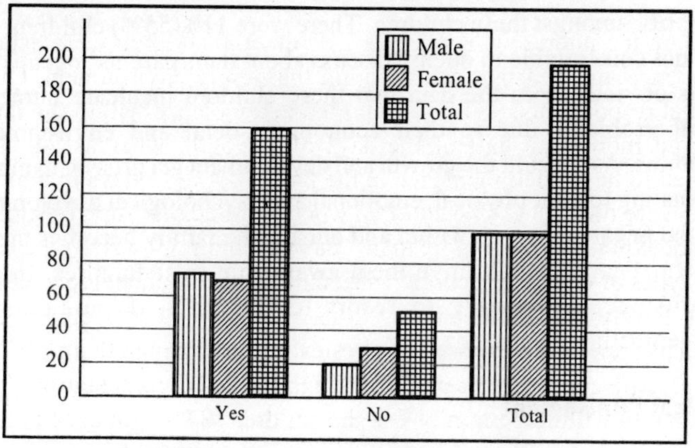

Figure 6.8: Expectation of Family Members

From an early age, children were restricted by their parents to go out and play with other peers of their age. Rather they were burdened with the responsibility of taking care of their siblings, while their parents were away for work. Also, they were expected to work hard to support their mother in doing the household activities which includes cooking, cleaning and washing. It was found that 50 per cent of the total girls were expected to help their mother in their job as domestic help and would not receive any remuneration by the home owner. Thus, they felt deprived of the economic power like their brothers who were engaged in work which were paid in cash.

Image Building Among Children

The environment in which a child grows up has a significant impact on the personality of the child. For the children living with their families on the streets, they were usually exposed to demoralizing conditions leading to development of inferiority complex and low self-esteem. Among the children 81 per cent reported that they felt uncomfortable to live on the streets as their deprivation was exposed to outsiders. They did not want others to know as to what kind of life they were undergoing. Similarly, children reported that they felt embarrassed for their fathers' behaviour under the influence of alcohol or intoxicated substance. It was also found that there were 136 (68%) children, who felt guilty due to their poor economic conditions and 112 (56%) felt ashamed for their physical appearance, which includes their clothing. The type of occupation of the family members was another factor, which induced the feeling of inferiority amongst these children. There were 110 (55%) children, who were not comfortable to openly discuss about their parents' occupation. It was obvious from the data that these children inculcate numerous mental problems due to their economic, social and environmental conditions. As a result, the growth and development get grossly hampered culminating to poor physical, emotional and psychological development. And the negative factors within and outside the family becomes the key repellent factors which drive them away from their families. In such circumstances, they try to resort to the help of outsiders for complementing their needs.

Physical Punishment

In India, it is socially acceptable for parents to use corporal punishment in child rearing. This phenomenon is not only observed within the families living on the streets, but it remains widely accepted across social strata. It is considered to be normal for the parents to take necessary disciplinary measures in order to control their children and at times, punish them for their misdeeds. But, in the case of street children they tend to become subject for the frustration of their parents. It is common to observe that the family tensions and insecure situation leads to poor capability of the family members to adopt methods and approaches for parental control and disciplining. Occasionally, for some minor mischief, the children were subjected to unpredictable responses or sudden emotional outbursts from their parents. From children's perspective, in about one third of the cases their parents behaved harshly with them, which could not be justified with the severity of mistakes they committed. It was common to observe that the parents adopted faulty system of reward and punishment for the desirable and undesirable conducts of their children.

More than 88 per cent children of both sexes reported to have faced severe forms of physical punishment from their fathers which includes slapping, beating up and hurting them when their fathers were drunked The study also showed that the children were also physically punished by their mothers using some cooking utensils. The girls were subjected to punishment especially when they expressed their desire for food or money. And it was difficult for these innocent children to comprehend their parents' behaviour for some simple things. It was observed during the study that in most of the cases barring a few exceptions, the stress in the family and other forms of insecurity faced by their parents' were translated into cruel forms of disciplinary actions towards their own children. It was quite evident that the types of disciplinary approaches adopted by parents, who were struggling to cope with the stress and frustration of life, were unable to provide conducive environment within the family for the psychological growth and development of their children.

Aggressive Verbal Assault

Usually, it was seen that the children were called by their nick names. Many a times, nick names were given out of love by parents or the neighbours. But on the other hand, it was also very common to find that the children were called by odd and unusual names describing their physical appearance, disability and colour. For example, it is very common to find a child with spectacles to be called as '*chasmis*' or '*kana*' (Blind). During the study. The researchers found that parents used aggressive words often and on to call, accuse, blame, order or threaten their own children, labelling the same as a mechanism to rear their children. It was seen that the fathers adopted physical abuse as a means to release their own frustration on their children, whereas the mothers used verbal assault and aggressive language. For the boys, the most common cause of aggression was due to lack of sufficient monetary contribution to the family. Also, it was used by the parents when the boys demanded some special food or material things like toys or clothing. And in the case of girls, they were subjected to aggressive verbal behaviour when they showed unwillingness to support their mothers in domestic chores or for not paying proper attention to their siblings.

Perception of Children Towards Abuse within the Family

During this study, it was found that the incidence of physical abuse within the family setting was alarmingly high. Added to this, the occurrence is in the open environment of the streets, which depresses the self-esteem of the children. The families live with their children in clusters in the open space and so the rude behaviour of the parents towards their children was commonly observed by the neighbours. In India, the children are considered to be the property of their parents and usually no one interferes when such incidences occur. It was unfortunate that historically there was a cultural approval to inflict physical punishment in the name of disciplinary measures for children. And, it was not only accepted by the parents but also by the children. This could be observed from the data that only 63 (74%) boys out of the total 85, who reported heavy physical punishment from their family members. The condition among the girls was seen much more as compared to the boys. On further investigation, it was found that feeling was common amongst the girls as they lacked any source of support within the society other than their own parents. Thus, the girls did not perceive the cruel behaviour of their parents as a form of abuse as they were the only ones who would protect them from the outsiders, when the need arises.

While working with the children living on the streets, it was realized that the female children were much more vulnerable than the male within the family set-up. Usually, they were considered as a 'responsibility;' or 'property' and were not viewed as individuals, who may have specific needs and freedom to enjoy rights. It was expected from the girls to accept and act as per the orders of their parents and they were not allowed to participate in the process of decision-making within the family. And when it comes to matter concerning their lives, decision were taken by the dominant member of the family, usually the father, without any prior consultation. The common goal of the parents was to arrange for their marriage at an early age. They were not given any opportunity to interact with the groom and most commonly the marriage takes place at a short notice of time without the study of background of the groom and his family. Many a times, it results into a frustrated marriage life with high risk of domestic violence against the girl or trafficking in the name of marriage. Often, they were sold off to the brothels after their marriage, where they lead a life of impoverishment and neglect.

After analyzing the socio-economic profile of the families living on the streets of Kolkata, it was found that most of them had migrated to

Kolkata from remote village of neighbouring districts. Usually, people belonging to similar caste and religion preferred to stay close to each other and form a cluster. Similar clusters were formed by the people who migrated from the same districts. Such settlement helps them to develop distinctive reciprocal relationship with each other in order to protect themselves from outsiders in the new city. Though, there are some inheriting similarities in social and cultural values due to their common background but it was observed that they did not possess strong bond and solidarity amongst each other.

Due to poverty and insecure life on the streets, the families have lot of dependency on neighbours. They take help of each other for small things in their day-to-day life, which includes supervision of their children. The members of one cluster seem to have frequent interaction with its members. Also, they come in contact with different types of culture and economic strata while they were at work. Female members working as domestic members come in contact with the culture, values and practices of families of different caste and class. Similarly, for the male members, they get exposed to the life of the city. Initially, the change was a cultural shock for the children and their families hailing from remote rural parts. But the younger generation of the migrant population, which includes the children, adapts to some of these cultural values and practices of their social and economic strata. Their expectations from life are very different due to the exposure and they start simultaneously dreaming of material possessions like travelling in a taxi, dinning in a restaurant, and owning a house. Many children and family members set some of these as their goals and work towards uplifting the standards of their living.

Moreover, due to their nature of being a floating population, they lack support from social organization. Therefore, the people and children living on the streets do not have the experience of primary relationship within the group. The children usually grow up in such an environment, which lacks of parental love and care, social control and supervision. From an early age, they get exposed to predominance of individualism, lack of community feeling and a mechanical way of living life on the streets. Such socio-cultural environment creates devastating effects on the personality of the child, which prohibits them from achieving personal accommodation and usually induces insanity, delinquency and other deviant behaviour among children. It was evident from the study that the environment on the streets was absolutely not appropriate for the growth and development of the children. It lacked almost all elements which were essential for the development of the child to become socially and emotionally a normal citizen. Moreover, unnatural demands of the community and the feeling of inferiority when compared with children of higher economic strata depress their self-esteem and they develop a defiant attitude towards the existing socio-cultural and legal system of the country. As a result, the children are deprived of their rights and they fail to develop a sense of responsibilities towards themselves and the society at large.

Street Children in Educational Setting

CRC recognized that the responsibility for the education of the children lies with their respective State. It is the duty of the State Government to ensure free and compulsory primary education to be available to all children irrespective of their family or socio-economic background. Further, the State should also encourage different forms of secondary education and make higher education available to all, based on their affordability. The right of every child to receive education was recognized by the Government of India and necessary revision was made in "The National Policy of Education, 1992" in which indicated **three** thrust areas in elementary education:

1. Universal access and enrolment;
2. Universal retention of children up to the age of 14 years; and
3. Substantial improvement in the quality of education to enable all children to achieve the essential levels of learning.

Sarva Shiksha Abhiyan (SSA)

It is the Government of India's flagship programme, which was launched to achieve *Universal Elementary Education* (UEE) in a time bound manner. As per the 86th amendment of the Constitution of India, the education was recognized as the fundamental right of the child and amended the Right to Education Act. The elementary education was made free and compulsory for the children of age group 6-14 years. In addition, a supplementary scheme of mid-day mea' was launched to enhance the attendance at school and to improve the nutritional status of the children, The strategy proved to be very successful in improving the enrolment ratio of children in the school and decreased the dropout rate from the school. It was also a boon in disguise to protect the children during the school hours from any sort of abuse.

National Child Labour Project (NCLP)

It was launched in India and was operational in the city of Kolkata in collaboration with the various non-governmental organizations to rehabilitate child workers by placing them in special schools with the following facilities:

- Non-formal/formal education.
- Skilled/craft training.
- Supplementary nutrition @ ₹ 5 per child per day.
- Stipend @ ₹ 100 per child per month.
- Health care services through a doctor appointed for a group of 20 schools.

Besides, the Government of West Bengal also launched an alternative system of education called "Shikshalaya Prakalpa" along with the NCLP. This was done to improve the accessibility of the schools to the deprived urban children in West Bengal. In addition, number of non-governmental organizations started education centres in different wards of Kolkata city to provide educational opportunities for the unprivileged children, improve the enrolment ratio of the formal schools and to support children so that they are able to retain in the formal school system. Because of these initiatives, the primary schools became easily accessible to the children in Kolkata. As a result, there was a shift in parents' attitude towards the education of their children. Unlike in the past, the parents were now more interested and aware of the importance of their children's education. The researchers were told by many parents during the data collection process that they find the schools to be the safe place for children, when they are away for work during the day. Further, the parents also realized that due to lack of safety in home environment and poor support system within the family, they prefer to send their young children to the schools when they out for work. As a result, the enrolment in primary education was found to be quite high (88%) among the respondents. Apart from the government affiliated schools, the children were also attending non-formal schools and education centers run by the non-governmental organizations.

In spite of all the above said advantage available for the children to receive education, it was found that the dropout rate among the children living on the streets was quite high. Due to easy access to education, most of the children were enroled in the school at some point of time, but they were not able to retain themselves in the school for variety of reasons. Of the total children, there were 67 per cent who dropped out of the school. Thus, a significant number of children remained deprived of their fundamental right to education. Though, the exact data was not available, but based on the interaction with the children and their families. It was identified that many children were not able to attend their schools regularly due to illness, illness of other members within the family, economic pressure and environmental problems like eviction, loss of books and rain. Thus, the socio-economic constraint, which is very peculiar for children living on the street, forces them to discontinue from acquiring the basic life skills and confidence to cope with the challenges of daily life.

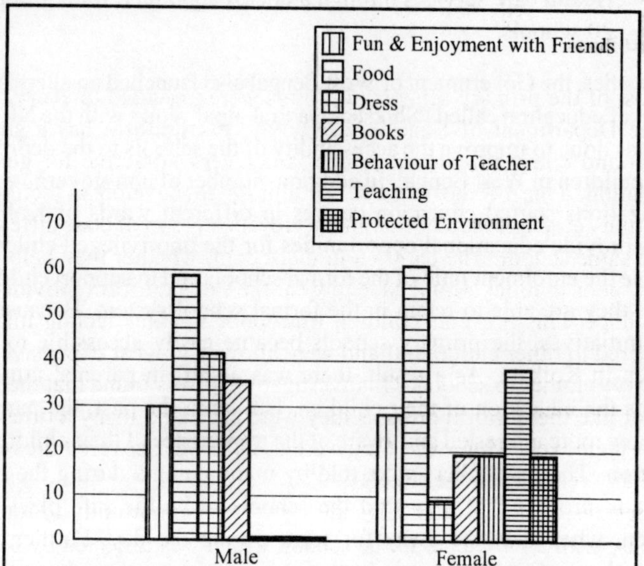

Figure 6.9: Reasons for Children to go to School

The researchers administered questionnaire among the school going children to identify what were the allurements they liked at the schools. The findings were grouped under various headings and are discussed as under:

Food

Of the total number of respondents, 59 per cent boys and 62 per cent girls said that they liked the food that was served to them at the school by the school authorities. It is important to recall the discussion from ***Section 1*** that for the most of the families living on the streets in different areas of Kolkata were not able to cook their food during the day in most of the areas. This forced many children to remain hungry or eat left over from the previous day or consumed unhealthy cheap source of food on the streets. Occasionally, children were forced to pick up food items from the waste bins outside of a restaurant or shop. Thus, the food provided by the school under the mid-day meal scheme was found to be the most important reason for attending the school, and in disguise it helped to improve the educational and nutritional level of the children.

Clothing

In most of the primary schools, uniforms were provided to every child by the Department of Education. Usually, the uniform has a simple design and common colours, which is not very attractive for general population. One of the purpose for this is to develop a feeling of uniformity amongst the students and to prevent any sort of class difference in the same school. The children in the school, whether they belong to rich or poor families would have to wear the same uniform provided by the school. This prevents children from poor families feeling inferior compared to other children, if and were allowed to wear expensive and attractive clothes to schools. On investigation, it was found that the girls did not like the uniform dress as they were short and many a times did not fit them well. Moreover, they were used to wear covered dresses to avoid any remarks on the streets.

Besides, children of both genders liked the opportunity to interact and play with their friends at the school, which was reflected by 37 per cent boys and 29 per cent girls. Also some boys and girls liked the books and teaching materials used at the school for the purpose of education. It was also found that a small percentage of girls felt that the schools were secure and enjoyable place for them to interact with their peers compared to the street environment, where lack of privacy prevails. Also, it was common to find that girls liked their teachers and their way of interaction with them at school.

Abuse within the Educational Setting

Physical Punishment

Globally, there is a movement to stop the practice of corporal punishment as disciplinary measures against the pupil at the school. Taking this forward, the Government of West Bengal and the Department of Education started efforts to improve the awareness of teachers about the positive ways of managing children. The teachers were explained in detail about the adverse effects of beating children at school when they commit mistakes. But, it was shocking to find the practice of corporal punishment within the schools was alarmingly high.

It was identified that the use of corporal punishment by the teachers at school was still a common phenomena, but the incidence was not very high among the formal schools in Kolkata. Among the total children respondents, 27 per cent reported to have faced corporal punishment from teachers. The incidence of corporal punishment was higher (39%) among the boys as compared to the girls. The incidence was found to be much lower than the other national studies conducted where the incidence of corporal punishment was reported to be as high as 50 per cent.

Emotional Abuse

It is also a common to find that the children face emotional abuse within the school environment. The children reported during the data collection that they were humiliated by the teachers for belonging to the families who lived on the streets. And similar incidences were identified by both the sexes who were currently attending the schools and those who dropped out of the school. Some of the common indicators of abusive experience of the children were as under:

- Harassment and insults in front of the other students in the class.
- Labelling them as pavement dwellers.
- Attitude of discrimination.
- Asking about their parents' occupation and their personal food habits in front of other students in the class.

Harassment and Insult in Front of Other Children in the Class

It was identified during the study that the boys faced more humiliation by the school teachers than the girls. There were 65 per cent boys and 30 per cent girls, who reported of being insulted by the teachers in front of other students in the schools. Due to such behaviour of the teachers, they were bullied by their classmates after the school hours. The children narrated that they were not insulted for mistakes in class work or for the poor performance in the examination, but it was probably due to their poor socio-economic condition.

Labelling Children as Pavement Dwellers

The children, who were studied, also felt insulted when their teachers labelled them as street children '*Rastar bachha*' or children of families living on the streets. These children are repeatedly scolded in an abusive language by their teachers. Many teachers hatefully said, "you are worthless"; "you cannot do anything"; and "you will remain poor and continue to stay on the pavement". It was found that all the children attending the schools felt bad due to such behaviour of their teachers.

Discriminating Attitude

The feeling of discrimination by the teachers was also found to be strong among the boys than the girls. There were 52 per cent boys and 32 per cent girls, who stated that they were not loved by their teachers. The teachers only liked the students who do well in the studies and always compare with them in the class. The children felt that due to their poor academic performance and low socio-economic profile, they were not accepted by the teachers and received less appreciation in the class for their conducts. Most of them narrated that the teachers fail to understand their problems of belonging to a family who lives on the streets. The teachers also blamed them for the behaviours of their parents and lack of participation of their parent's in the school meetings. Besides, it was common for these children to be called by funny and odd names and teasing them for their poor performance or habits. On reporting the same to the teachers it was commonly observed that the teacher was not fair and always took sides of students who came from well off families. As narrated earlier that children always suffer from low self-esteem for their family background. All the children stated that they feel embarrassed if the teachers discusse about their parents; profession, food habits or any other personal issues in front of other students of the class.

Relationship of Parents with the Education System

One of the strategies adopted by the education department to ensure continued formal education of the children was by ensuring participation of the parents within the formal school system. Periodic meetings were organized with the parents to exchange feedback between the teachers and the parents. This was very useful to ensure that the necessary support is provided by the teachers at school and similarly, the parents can support the child in a specific area as per the suggestions of the teachers. But, in most of the cases, there was absolutely no participation by the parents in the case of street children. There was a wide gap in the understanding of the problems faced by the children at the school and home as there was absence of dialogue between the teachers and the parents. It was found that the negative approach adopted by the teachers against their children at school, prevented many parents to initiate talk about their children's performance and parents with the teacher. Such close minded approach of the teacher was a common hindering factor to educate the parents how to support the children at home. Thus, the parents did not feel confident and courageous to face the humiliating situation at the school. It was perceived negatively by the teachers as the lack of interest by the parents in the education of their children. With no end to the vicious cycle, it was found that most of the children felt isolated at the school and were sooner or later forced to drop out of the school to prevent from facing various types of abuses at the school.

On further investigation, it was found that some parents were not even aware about the parents-teachers meeting at the school. Probably, this was due to lack of interest by the parents and the children did not want their parents to come to school as the teachers will have lot of complaints and negative feeling towards them, which would further humiliate them. In many cases, where the parents were aware of such meetings, they were not able to participate as they could not take a day off from their work. Moreover, dates available to the parents might not be suitable to attend the meeting because most of them were daily workers. It was also common for parents to feel uncomfortable to confront teachers to know that their children were not performing well at the school and other related problems created by them at the school. It was also surprising to know from the focus group discussion that there were few parents who were not aware whether their children were attending the school or not and if they were, which school and grade were they studying in.

Children's Perception Towards Formal School Curriculum

Since, last few years, the education department is constantly trying to modify the curriculum to make the education more simple and attractive for the students in the formal schools. The curriculum developed by the State Council Educational Research and Training (SCERT) is followed by all the primary schools. The expected outcomes are clearly set in the curriculum according to the academic year. While interacting with children and parents, most of them were of the opinion that the education system was not meant for the children living on the streets. On further investigation, it was found that the children were not able to relate the learning at the school with their daily life situation. To understand this further, the researchers gathered views of the children for their perception of the curriculum of two subjects taught at the school — Mathematics and Bengali. It was not within the scope of the study to compare the data with the expected outcome as stated in the SCERT curriculum. It was collected to get an idea of how useful these subject were perceived by the children living on the streets in their day-to-day life situation.

Mathematics

The discussion was carried out in two groups of 40 children each and equal participation of boys and girls was ensured to understand the differences of perception between different genders. Of the total children 75 per cent reported that they liked mathematics compared to Bengali. The followings were some of the key reasons, why these children liked mathematics as a subject to study at school.

- ★ Mathematics was interesting as they learnet how to count money. It helped them to be more aware while receiving money from their employer at work. They were also able to apply the learning in their day-to-day life on the streets.
- ★ Few children found multiplication and division to be useful when they go for shopping at the grocery shop or any other places.
- ★ The children liked the simple addition and subtraction at school, but they found it hard to remember the multiplication tables.

Opinion of Children Regarding Bengali

Similarly, 60 per cent children of both genders liked Bengali as a subject and they narrated the following reasons for their liking.

- ★ Learning to read and write Bengali enables them to read the name of the shop and identify bus name and number.
- ★ Children liked the rhythms of some action rhymes.
- ★ Used to enjoy write their names and addresses. Some felt that it was good to learn to read and write so that they can write letters to their parents while they are away from home.
- ★ They are able to read few headlines of the newspaper, but still found it difficult to read the whole story narrated in the

newspaper. Children enjoy reading short and simple sentences, but were not able to understand long sentences.

- ★ Children did not enjoy memorizing and re-writing long poems and big paragraphs. They also did not like to read and write questions and answers from the exercise book.
- ★ Interestingly, almost everyone showed eagerness to learn English so that they can interact with non-Bengali population, read colourful hoardings around them, read and save names and numbers in mobile phones, send text messages, etc. According to the children, learning to speak good English was essential as it would help them to explore some better livelihood opportunities in other cities like Mumbai, Delhi and Pune in India and some even felt it would be useful to go and work in Dubai.

It was interesting to understand from the discussion that as the children wish to climb up the ladder of education system, they find it more difficult to relate and apply the learning with their daily life situation. As described earlier, the life of children living on the streets was found to be very insecure and challenging. And it was not possible for the children to relate the teachings at the school with the demanding situations of life on the streets. It was a common expectation of children and parents that the education would help them to access better livelihood opportunities, but it was not practical for almost all of them due to the time involved in the entire process. So, the biggest constraint of the current education system was to relate the outcome of the learning with their day-to-day life and immediate future. It was not possible for the parents and children to prioritize the other advantages of education like mental and physical abilities and personality development. Hence, they came to the conclusion that the education was not meant for the children living on the streets.

While interacting, the parents explained that they cannot afford to pay the fees and manage other expenses related to education for their children to attend the secondary school. From a very narrow perspective, the parents think that if the primary education was not able to add any value to find a better job then what difference it would make if their children achieve higher education. Therefore, they train and engage their children in unskilled workforce from an early childhood so that they become skillful as early as possible. It was evident that there was a huge gap in the expected outcome of the education system and that perceived by the parents, and for this reason, the children were in dilemma and never received proper support to sustain interest in education. All these culminated to lack of conducive environment in the family, resulting into poor performance of children with reference to the expectations of the education curriculum and failing to cope with the system. As explained, the vicious cycle puts the children in an emotional turmoil, humiliation, feeling inferior and poor acceptance with the system of education. As a result, the children are thrown out of the system and are subjected to risky environment, which was open to abuse them.

Street Children in the Workforce

In India, there are lakhs of children are still engaged to work as labourers below the age of 14 years. All this is happening in spite of all the exhortations at the international level. Unfortunately, in India, there is deep rooted history of children working in the production process and so the trends of many generations have made people to think that it is normal for children to work in their childhood. And one of the key factors was the extreme economic deprivation, which forces the children belonging to the poverty stricken families to leave the school and engage themselves in the workforce. The widespread poverty leads to the rapid growth of child labour, which created a far-reaching effects on the economy and the education level of the country. The CRC, ratified by all the countries except Somalia and the United States, guarantees children the right "to be protected from performing any work that is likely to be hazardous or interfere with the child's education, or harmful for child's health or physical, mental, spiritual, moral or social development". The Worst Forms of Child Labour Convention was adopted by the International Labour Organization (ILO) in 1999, and ratified by 150 countries world-wide. Under this, some forms of child labour are flatly prohibited, such as slavery or practices similar to slavery. Other types of work are prohibited if they constitute "work which, by its nature or the circumstances in which it is carried out, is likely to harm the health, safety or morals of children".

As one of the signatories of the international treaties, the Government of India has also amended its existing labour laws and also enacted. The Child Labour (Prohibition and Regulation) Act, 1986. The Government has decided to prohibit employment of children as servants, especially for domestic help or in '*dhabas*' (roadside eateries), restaurants, hotels, motels, teashops, resorts, spas or in other recreational centres. This ban has been imposed under the Child Labour (Prohibition and Regulation) Act, 1986 and was effective from 10th October, 2006.

The Ministry of Labour has recently issued a notification to this effect giving three-month mandatory notice. The Ministry has warned that anyone employing children in these categories would be liable to prosecution and other penal action under the Act. In the Section 4 of the Act, it clearly indicates that appropriate Government agency would conduct time-to-time need-based survey to enumerate number of children working in various establishments that has been declared as prohibited as per the Law. Children working in prohibited establishments would be rescued and provided with safe shelter, food, clothing, boarding, appropriate medical care and educational facilities.

Besides, for the purpose of the rehabilitation of such rescued children, the Act has provision whereby these children would be entitled for free educational facilities, vocational education and training. Some of the free training courses include medical, engineering and computer education as per the aptitude and the need of the child. Also, there are provisions, which will assist such children to identify employment opportunities after the completion of their courses. The Act also recognizes that it is a cognizable offence to employ children or compel children to work as labourers as described under the Criminal Procedure Code (CrPC) 1973 and such act of crime would be punishable with imprisonment for a minimum period of four years, and may be extended up to seven years. But, in spite of these international and national promises, the engagement of children in work force is quite visible. From the interview conducted with the children during the study, it was evident that 82 per cent boys and 100 per cent girls were engaged in such occupations or in such process which were prohibited by the Indian labour laws and/or the Child Labour (Prohibition and Regulation) Act, 1986. Some of the occupations and processes where the children were found to be working during the process of data collection are listed below.

Table 6.9: Occupations and Processes where Children are Involved

Occupations	*Processes*
• Automobile garages and workshops	• Tanning
• Slaughter houses	• Automobile repairing process, welding, lathe work, dent beating
• Domestic work or domestic servants	• Tire repairing process
• Roadside *dhabas*, restaurants, hotels, motels, tea shops, etc.	• Rag-picking and scavenging
	• Skinning, dyeing process of manufacturing of leather and leather products

Besides, there were 12 per cent of the boys, who were engaged in prohibited occupations or processes like cart or van puller, rickshaw-puller, fish and vegetable seller, etc.

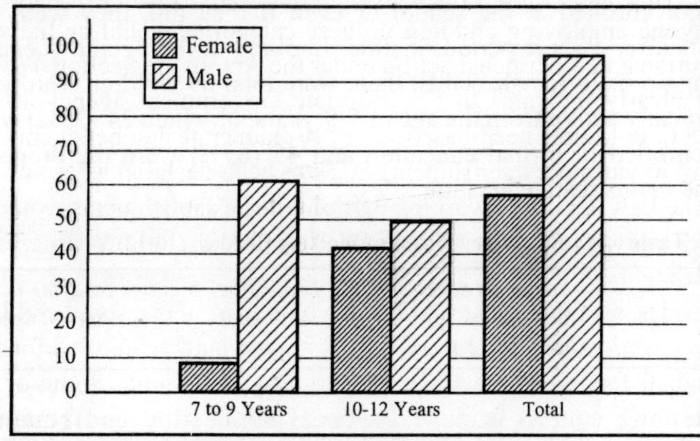

Figure 6.10: Gender *vs.* Initiation of Work

The researcher identified during the field visit for data collection that all the boys and half of the total girls were economically active. Most of them were engaged in some kind of unskilled work or temporary jobs. And it was found that the boys were able to join the workforce earlier than the girls. The usual age for the boys for starting to work was around 8 to 10 years of age and after few years they pass on to the next age group, when they become 'full time' workers. Most of the boys were engaged in different types of work, which includes begging, rag-picking, slaughter houses and cleaning/washing dishes at the road side hotels. Some also worked at the auto parts shop, cycle repairing shop, and garage and construction site. In the case of girls, they usually become economically productive after the age of 10 years. And the girls over the age of 12 years are preferred for work of a domestic help. Thus, it was observed that younger girls were accompanied and trained by their mothers from a young age as domestic worker and later they become independent and earn their own living.

Table 6.10: Educational Status of Working Children (7-9) Years

	Started to Earn between the Age Group 7-9 Years	*Never been to the School*	*Dropout of the School*
Male	57	13 (23%)	44 (77%)
Female	12	11 (92%)	1 (8%)
Total	**69**	**24 (35%)**	**45 (65%)**

From Table 6.10, it is evident that there is a strong co-relation between the age of starting to earn and their participation in school. It is obvious that those children who started to work and earn at an early age never got enrolled at the school or even if they did, they were the dropouts after a short period of time. Looking at the overall scenario covering up male-female status, there were total 69 children who were economically active from the age of 7-9 years, of which 24 (35%) were never enrolled in formal education and 45 (65%) were the dropouts from the mainstream education.

Table 6.11: Educational Status of Working Children (10-12) Years

	Started to Earn between the Age Group 10-12 Years	*Dropout of the School*	*Studying in the Formal School*
Male	57	16 (28%)	41 (72%)
Female	38	25 (66%)	13 (34%)
Total	**95**	**42 (43%)**	**54 (57%)**

When we look at Table 6.11 where children got engaged in the economic activity at a later age, it showed co-relation with the higher ratio of enrolment at school and their education level as compared to the earlier group. It was found that a significant percentage of children who were working did not discontinue their studies at the school.

Thus, it is clear from the above two tables that all the children, who were never enrolled in schools had started economic activities at an early age. And in most of the other children's case, they started to work by the age of 12 years due to the growing expectations within the family and increasing dissatisfaction in the school environment. Though the data does not give the true picture of the work status of the girls as all the girls were engaged in some kind of work, whether they were paid or not. In this study, fifty per cent girls indicated as working who received remuneration for their work but the remaining girls were involved in some kind of activities where they were not paid separately. Their work was considered as their free of cost help to their parents or nearby relatives.

Income of Street Children

It was difficult to estimate the average monthly income of the street children, who were engaged in economic activities, as most of them did not have fixed income. During the process of in-depth one-to-one discussion, it was revealed that children were paid low compared to the amount of work they did and the time they spent after the work. Most of them were engaged in some kind of unskilled work and lacked the capacity to negotiate for better wages in the labour market. Also, many were working in small scale industries or work, which exposed them to hazardous conditions without any protective gears. Though, their effect may not be seen immediately but they may be prone to develop some health ailment at a later stage to such exposure. This clearly indicates the failure of execution of the labour laws in our country.

Children who worked at automobile workshops or garages, slaughter houses, '*dhabas*' (road side eateries), restaurants, hotels and tea shops were usually paid at the end of the day. Besides the daily wages, they had no other benefits of paid leave or medical coverage, in case they required the same. The wages paid to them varied across the city and there was no trend of uniformity in the payment structure compared to the same work done by other children in other area. Everything was dependent on the rapport and the negotiation skill of the children and their family members with the paymasters. During the study, the researchers tried to understand the wage structure of children in comparison to their age, types of work and hours of working.

Table 6.12: Types of Occupation and Income

Occupation in Establishment	*No. of Children*	*Average Income*
Leather manufacturing units	6 (4%)	₹ 50-60 per day
Slaughter house	8 (5%)	₹ 30-35 per day
Garage	4 (3%)	₹ 30-40 per day
Road side food stall	30(20%)	₹ 20-30 per day
Total	**48**	—
Self-employed	—	—
Cycle/rickshaw pulling	7 (5%)	₹ 30-40 per day
Labour at construction site	12 (8%)	₹ 25-30 per day
Vegetable vendor	15(10%)	₹ 20-35 per day
Rag-picking	46(31%)	₹ 10-100 per day
Domestic help	36(24%)	₹ 200-400 per month
Total	**116**	—

From Table 6.12 it can be said that out of the total 150 economically active children, 116 (77%) were self-employed whereas 48 (32%) were working in some kind of establishments in and around the city. It was also found that the children enjoyed the power to earn money, though there was lot of pain involved at the work place. As they belong to poor socio-economic group, no one wants to trust them and give them a chance to work in the beginning. And it is not uncommon for these innocent children to get tortured and rudely behaved by other people at work, including the employer. But, they continue to work so that their income can supplement the monitory needs of the family. It was also common to find that the children were involved in more than one job at a time due to the pressure from the insecurity of the job market and their pressing needs. It is always a big challenge for the children to get into the mainstream of the job market, but still they continue to struggle to survive and earn their living to sustain their lives on the streets of a metropolis.

Children Working in Some Establishment

Children Working at the Tea-stalls, Restaurants and Hotels

The researchers identified that 20 per cent of the total children, especially the boys were involved in the above occupations during the field visit. And these boys were required to work for a minimum period of 14 hours each day, during which they cleaned and mopped the floors, cleaned tables, emptying the garbage bins, taking orders from the customers, supplying and serving food and helping in the kitchen. And for such slogging hard work, they would receive ₹ 20-30 per day as remuneration. Usually, they work all the days of the week and are not expected to take long breaks or leave. They are expected to work as per the order of the employer and are not expected to complain. In return, the employer may provide them with two square meals a day and a place to sleep at night. Besides this, there are no other benefits as they are hired on a temporary and illegal basis.

During the interview session, the children revealed to the researchers that they were forced to work long hours by their employer, for which they are paid a tiny some of money. Also, they do not get any overtime for any extra hours of work done for the employer. At the same time, if they happen to reach late at work or take a day off, their remuneration is accordingly deducted. Also, it is common for them to lose the job if they remain absent for a couple of days, in case they or their family members fall sick. Hence, it is common for them to change jobs frequently.

Most of the working children reported that it was common for them to receive harsh treatment by the employer or senior co-workers. Of the total children working at the tea-stalls and *dhabas*, 65 per cent reported that they were victims of severe forms of physical abuse. Besides, they were commonly exposed to burns, cuts and other physical injury during their work in the kitchen or near the stove. They also commonly suffered from body-ache, stomach-ache and other forms of physical problems due to consumption of stale, unhealthy and spicy food provided to them and lack of sufficient rest.

> Raju, a 14 year old boy worked at a road side hotel near Shobha Bazaar metro station. He started to work since he was of 6 years of age and so far he has changed more than 8 work places. He is presently working in a place for three months. Prior to this job, he was involved in a similar job at another restaurant. He was forced to leave the previous job due to work pressure and the cruel treatment by the employer and his co-workers. He found this current job through one of his friends, who also works in the same place. Raju works six days a week and prefers to take one day off to spend time with his friends. But, he mentioned that his family members and the employer want him to work all days of the entire week. Every morning, his day starts at 5 o'clock and ends at mid night. During the day, he is given a couple of hours of rest when there is no work. With all the hardships, he makes about ₹ 180 every week, which comes to about ₹ 30 a day.

Children Working at the Slaughter House

The slaughter houses are located in the eastern parts of Kolkata. For common people, slaughtering of animal is a loathsome activity and they do not prefer to know how and what is being done inside the slaughter houses. It was found that of the total children, there were (5%) who worked at the slaughter house, which is prohibited as per the labour law of the country. The working condition inside the slaughter house in Kolkata is worse than working in a sewerage drain pipes. As one gets inside these houses, there are carcasses of cows and buffalos hanging from the stuffed yards. The dregs from the slaughter houses are thrown in the open drains and get dumped without any chemical treatment as per the guidelines of the pollution control board. In such pathetic environment, the children get exposed to unhygienic and brutal activities inside the slaughter houses. These children are made to move the animals inside the slaughter houses, help them in the process of slaughtering, remove the internal organs, clean and removed skin and dispose the waste. For such a filthy and horrifying job, they get paid up to ₹ 30-35 per day. They have no fixed hours of work, and they usually work for more than 7-8 hours per day.

Some children were also found to be involved in the process of cleaning and drying of the intestine and skin of cows, sheeps, and goats. The income of these children varies depending on their involvement and amount of time spent in the process of cleaning and drying. It was surprising to know that the dry layers of intestine of cows and sheeps are used as the raw materials for the manufacturing of absorbable surgical instruments. There are many families, who are involved in the process of extracting the raw material in the eastern part of the city. Such raw material produced in the households is collected by the middleman and is supplied to the surgical supply manufacturing industries. While interviewing a boy, the researchers were told that he works at one of the slaughter houses in eastern part of Kolkata and he felt proud that they were supplying the raw material to well known companies like Johnson & Johnson for making of absorbable surgical sutures.

Children Working at the Tanneries

In India, West Bengal stands at the top for its exports finished leather goods in the international market. More than seventy per cent of the leather goods produced in West Bengal gets exported due to high demand in the global market. And, India is proud to have the Asia's largest manufacturing complex developed in Kolkata. The well known areas for leather manufacturing are Tiljala, Topsia and Tangra in the eastern part of the city. The Government is in the process of relocating these factories from the main city to the sub-urban areas of Kolkata to reduce the levels of pollution due to these industries. Though, the Government has banned the use of children in the leather manufacturing process, still there were some children identified during the data collection who worked in the leather processing industry. To protect the industries from any litigation, they use the back door entry to engage children with a poultry amount. Usually, the leather factories hire people on contract through the labour contractors and these children get employed by the greedy contractors, who pay them ₹ 15-20 per day for their exposure to hard and hazardous work. They are engaged at the tanneries to carrying carcasses, process the skin removed from the dead animal with different chemicals and laying the chemically treated skins for drying. Many a times, these children work as a help to their parents, who are employed through labour contractors on temporary basis.

Children Working in the Garages

Of the total participants, there were four children found to be working in garages. They were involved in different repairing processes, which include welding, tire reconditioning, restoration of car battery, cleaning and other activities involving lifting of heavy parts. They also worked with unguarded machinery like welding and grinder, which exposed them to the risk of injuries. Occasionally, children injure themselves while carrying heavy loads and from falling of objects or machinery. They were also exposed to hazardous chemicals of wet cells and fumes and for such tasks, the children were paid ₹ 35-40 per day and were required to work for more than nine hours a day with only a short break in between.

Children as Domestic Help

Since 2006, the Government of India has imposed a ban on the use of children for domestic help. But for the younger girls living on the streets, it is a lucrative job. And so, many mothers train their daughters to get skilled with domestic work, which includes cleaning, washing and cooking. For the purpose of the study, only those girls who worked as part time help were included as they had access to their friends and families. But, there was no way to get in touch with the girls who were working as domestic help round the clock. However, it was reported that there was a growing demand for the full time domestic help and most of the girls and their family members aspire to get such jobs. The families, who live on the streets, always strive to get their daughters in a safe home of a good family, where she can work and stay. This would eliminate the pain and struggle of living on the streets, where the child may also encounter various forms of abuse, including the risk of getting sexually abused.

Self-employment Activities

It was observed during the study that the children, who were self-employed, were involved in number of activities to generate some income to supplement their family income. They were able to identify various mechanisms to survive and sustain themselves in the competitive market and amongst the challenges of living on the streets. The study identified about 16 per cent of the children to be involved in more than one activity in a day to earn their living. Besides, they were forced to change their activities frequently, due to changing market needs and competition.

Children as Rag-Pickers

One of the common self-employment seen amongst the children living on the streets is rag-picking. Of the total, there were 46 (31%) children engaged in the process of picking up recyclable material from garbage and similar scavenging activities. Of these 46 children, there were 14 girls and 32 boys and their income varied from ₹ 10-70 per day, depending upon what they find from the garbage. Many children start doing this at an early age and they tend to earn ₹ 10-15 per day, but with time, they pick-up the work very well and spend more than 10 hours a day and their income is around ₹ 60-70 per day.

It was found that this work is done in a well coordinated manner by the children and their families. The children and their families get divided into small groups and they are given specific areas of operation, where they roam on the street and scan the garbage bins to collect recyclable items. During the day, they travel few kilometers in search of recyclable items. They search on the streets, in the garbage heaps by the side of the road, factory garbage, around railway and bus station and near hotels. These children collect items like soft drinks cans, aluminum foils, plastic bottles and polythene carry bags, metal pieces, glass bottles, paper and any other recyclable items. At the end of the day, the collected items are sorted out into neat piles by their respective categories in an open space or by the side of the road. Each recyclable item fetches a different rate depending upon its capacity to be refused and the demand in the market. The items collected by the children and their family get sold and a share of money is given to the children based on their contribution. Some children also hire carts (vans), so that they can move around faster and pick-up more and heavy material while they roam on the streets in different parts of the city. Usually, their target is to reach in the bins of hotels, restaurants and dumping grounds of Kolkata Municipal Corporation. In such cases, their earning is usually higher than the other children, who are involved in scavenging by walking around with a large plastic bag to collect items. Their earning varies from ₹ 70-100 per day.

Dismantling automobile batteries, which is made up of recyclable lead, is a work done by specialized group of such children. Children break the battery to remove the dry cell from which they extract carbon rods, plastics and zinc covers, which get sold in the market. While they struggle to survive from the income generated by selling the recyclable waste material, these children are exposed to various unhygienic and filthy environments. They are exposed to injuries, while searching for items from the pile of garbage without using any protective gear. Many a times, the heap of garbage is put on fire, which releases hazardous fumes from the burning of plastic, rubber and other waste. Such exposure also makes the children to suffer from upper respiratory tract infection. Also, they easily contract disease due to their exposure to filthy waste for the entire day, without any source of basic amenities to keep themselves clean.

Vegetable Selling

The other common source of earning amongst children, who were self-employed was to sell vegetables near Sealdah railway station. This station is considered as the gate way to Kolkata as a large population flows in and out of the city through this station. Besides, it is also an important junction for both rail and road route. It is through Sealdah that the city connects with other important areas of the state as well as the neighbouring states. Sealdah is hub for distribution and sale of fresh vegetables, fruits, fish and other livestock products, which are then transported to different parts within and outside Kolkata. It was found that many children living with their families on the streets close to Sealdah station were involved in loading and unloading of these products. While working as loaders, they manage to get some vegetables and fruits from the large load, which they sell to other small scale vegetable vendor to make some money. Many were reported or beaten up for stealing vegetables from the packages, while they worked as loaders. However, their parents did not perceive it as something wrong and supported their children for such act of stealing. In case of some children, the entire family was involved in the loading and unloading work at the Sealdah Station, making it a primary source of income. It was common for children to be exposed to vulnerable situation. There were many occasions when they were treated harshly and were exposed to injury or accidents due to the risky nature of the job. For many children, back pain, bodyache and minor injuries were something which goes without being registered till it turns out to be a chronic debilitating condition.

Besides, they were also involved in several other activities for their secondary source of income. They were found to be involved in selling lottery tickets, newspapers, clean train compartments, and assist in smuggling of electronic goods, brown sugar and country liquor in plastic pouch.

Unfortunately, the country has several laws to protect the children from working, but in reality, there is sheer lack of system and personnel to enforce them. It has been clearly notified by the Government that involving children in several activities and processes is illegal and strictly prohibited. But due to the miserable condition of the families living on the streets, the children are pushed by their parents to work in such hazardous and difficult occupation from a very tender age. For the parents to support the family, it becomes essential for their children to be working to supplement the income of the household. Their struggle is helping survive the family in the deplorable living conditions of the streets. In such situation, it is not possible for the family members to think whether the occupation is causing any negative impact on the development of their children.

On the other hand, there are individual owners of business or small scale units, who prefer to employ children as a cheap labour. They keep them as illegal workers to avoid paying higher wages and benefits to regular worker in their establishment. This helps the greedy businessmen to avoid the legal obligation of providing and welfare to the employees. Most common places, where children get engaged are garage, roadside eateries and restaurants. They make the children to work at the whims and fancies of the employer and do not hesitate to bend or break the regulations, which give protection to the children. The children are made to do slogging work for more than 8 hours a day without proper pay or basic facilities. And due to their vulnerable nature, they cannot negotiate with their employer otherwise the employer may replace them with other children. In the labour market, there is no dearth of cheap labour and so, the children tolerate all the pain of hard work in unhealthy condition to keep up with the job. Many children are exploited by exposing them to hazardous conditions of which they are not aware and could have detrimental effects on their physical and mental growth. So, the children are constantly searching for a better job to jump one step higher. And with time, they develop many other survival mechanisms to protect themselves from the negative effects of poor working conditions. Consequently, many a times they also get lured by the anti-social gang, who involve them in various deviant actions to make a better living. Though these activities are also not free from hazards and exploitations, but they prefer to pick-up such work as they are not to work at the caprice of their employer.

Physical Abuse

While recalling their experience of last six months, 68 per cent of the boys reported to have faced physical abuse by their employer, co-worker or other person at the work place. Some of the common forms of abuse were to get beaten up, slapped, kicked or pushed away.

Table 6.13: Types of Grievous Injuries Experienced

Types of Hurt Experience	*Boys Working in Establishments*	*Self-employed Boys*
Physical abuse causing swelling and hematoma	18 (50%)	12 (38%)
Physical abuse leading to bleeding and laceration	8 (22%)	4 (13%)
Physical abuse causing burns and scalds	6 (17%)	0
Physically abused with or without injury	36	32
Total	**48**	**52**

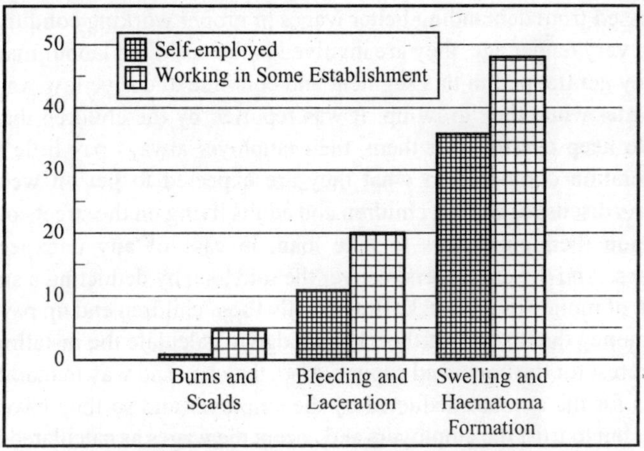

Figure 6.11: An Experience of Boys at Work Place

While going through the boys experiences of last 6 months, 68 per cent of the boys reported to have faced physical abuse by either the employer, co-workers or other persons at the work place. Of the total 48 children working in some kind of establishment, the incidents of physical abuse was found among 75 per cent of children. It was comparatively low in the case of self-employed children, i.e. only 62 per cent. The same can be seen in the above bar diagram.

An Experience of Girls at Workplace

The girls working as a part time domestic help were less affected by the physical abuse compared to the boys and other girls working as full time domestic help. Out of 36 girls, 15 (42%) reported to have faced physical abuse at their employers' residence. In none of the cases the intensity of abuse was severe. It was observed that girls who worked as part time domestic help were much more empowered and oriented to their safety measures. Usually, such part time workers stayed up to 2 hours at their employees place. In a city like Kolkata there is a growing demand for domestic help and so if they find any threat of physical abuse, they easily change to a different location of job at a short notice.

Economic Abuse

Apart from getting physically abused, the children who are in workforce are often victim of economic abuse by their employers. It starts with hiring of children at a cheaper rate compared to the adults and they are suppressed from demanding better wages or proper working conditions. From a very tender age, they are involved in the unskilled labour market and they get trapped in this segment and continue to derive low wages, even latter when they grow up. It was reported by the children that in order to keep control over them, their employer always pay little less remuneration compared to what they are expected to get on weekly basis. As discussed earlier, children and adults living on the streets often rely upon their employers to take loan, in case of any unexpected expenses. And the employers recover the said loan by deducting a small portion of money every week. But, usually these children end up paying more money due to lack of their knowledge to calculate the installment and interest for the borrowed capital. Also, they have no way to maintain records for the amount deducted by the employer and so they have no choice, but to trust the employers and accept the wages as calculated and paid by the employer. Besides, the employer also takes advantage of the vulnerable situation of the children by making them work extra and long hours in return of the obligation of lending the money during the time of emergency.

Street Children in the Immediate Community

The children often get exposed to various forms of abuse within their immediate community due to the poor socio-economic, lack of solidarity and absence of value system among the people living on the streets. While interacting with the children, it was found that children do not have faith and respect towards the adults of their surrounding community. They believe that they cannot trust those adults as they lack self-control and can easily take advantage of an opportunity to abuse them for their selfish interest. Also, the children expressed the feeling of fear from the other people living in the area during one to one interaction. On further investigation, it was found that the girls living on the streets were more fearful for getting sexually exploited by the people living around their shelter on the streets. Whereas, in the case of the boys, they were afraid of getting exploited for money by the community members in which they reside. It was common amongst both the gender that they were quite cautious about any stranger around them and they were believed to have a reasonable sense of judgement to identify the intention of any approaching person.

It was found that out of total 100 girls, 74 per cent responded that they do not have any faith in the adult members of their immediate community. Of these 74 girls, there were 8 (11%), who disclosed that they were sexually abused by the known adults living in the nearby area. In addition, there were 43 (58%) girls, who were aware of such abuse occurring by the known people. Also, there were 23 per cent girls, who were aware that there are some adult persons in the community, who try to show their private parts to the girls.

In the case of boys, there were 63 per cent of them who were aware of incidence of sexual abuse occurring to someone whom they know from their peer group. The most common form of abusers were the vendors (21%), leader among the street children (24%) and other influential people (12%) in the community. The children also reported that they feel the threat of abuse from the other youngster and taxi-drivers in the community. And, if the children do not agree to their demands then they become furious and try to molest them, when they are alone. One of the boys during the interview revealed that they were allured to perform oral sex initially and later he was forced for anal sex, which was a very painful experience. Similarly, during the focus group discussion, some of the children narrated the following incidences of abuse perpetrated against the children.

- Children are often offered free movie tickets and tasty snacks to become friendly with them. Once the perpetrators gain the little faith of the children, they lure the children to accompany them to watch a movie in the nearby cinema hall or video parlour. This helps to establish rapport with the children after which they are taken to cinema halls to see pornographic films. Here, the children are forced to involve in the sexual activity with the perpetrator. These incidences commonly occur among both the genders Similar attempts are also made by elderly men, who try to allure children by fondling their private parts and then force them to entertain with sexual activity.

- To start with, thc children are lured with cinema tickets, tasty food and cosmetics but later, the perpetrators lure them with money by throwing five rupee coins on their shelter. Many timcs, the child gets trapped and follows the perpetrator. And the perpetrator engages with the girl in sexual activity promising her for marriage. They engage in such relationships for few months and then withdraw once they lose interest. Many girls understand this and so they try not to accept the money at the first instance.

During an interview, Reens, a 13 year old girl said, "I felt very disheartened; when I saw the persons I loved the most has betrayed me. He was interested for only physical relationship with me. . . . He has not only exploited me but was playing similar games with my other friends also. . . . He had promised to marry and take me away from the pathetic life on the streets . . . promised me of a good house . . . good food . . . but now I can realize that he was a liar . . . after three months of intensive relationship, he handed me over to three of his friends . . . who abused me and tortured me brutally . . . now, the same person is doing the same thing with one of my friends. . . .

After repeated incidence of abuse like in the case of Reena, many girls are pushed in the flesh trade. These girls lose the emotional attachment in life and become sex worker due to its vast demand. It fetches them easy money in a short period of time. Gradually, they learn the tricks of the business, where the customer throws coins on the shelter and they pick-up and follow them. Then, such perpetrators take the children to some lonely place and engage in sexual activity by promising to give good food and extra money. Many a times, these children get into the racket of pimps, who are involved in the arrangements of girls from the streets to entertain their clients. From the streets, these girls move as per the directions of the pimps and are taken to hotel and vacant flat for sexual engagement. In such places, they are given to get ready, allured with good cloths, cosmetics to wear and food to eat. Subsequently, they are forced to sexually entertain multiple clients against a meager amount of money.

Besides, the sexual assaults by the known adult members of the nearby community, the children also reported of incidence of abuse by an elderly person from the community. The children from the south zone described that they have seen many older persons of the community abusing young girls and boys in vacant places near parks, beside cinema halls or inside a taxi.

> A man of around 60 years of age was well known in the community for his behaviour and love for children. He was known for helping parents to take care of their young children while they are out for work. Parents were also relaxed as there was someone from the community who was taking care of their younger children at home. He used to bring candies and gifts and played with the children for most of the evenings. One day, while playing with the children saw a 3 year old girl lying unconscious in one of the lonely places behind the park. Her dress was drenched in blood and she had marks of injuries all over the body. Children informed people in the community and the child was immediately taken to the hospital. Later on, it was found that she had severe injuries near the genital area as someone had raped the child. After a day, when the child regained consciousness and narrated her horrible experience with the same old man of 60 years of age, people came to know that he raped the girl, whom they trusted to be a fatherly person and left the children under his supervision when they went out for work. They also came to know that he had attempted to abuse many other children in a similar fashion.

> Ratan, a 13 year old boy, worked as a rag-picker and was also engaged with some local smugglers. He provides help to the gang to traffic brown sugar through the international border with Bangladesh. Occasionally, he travels to Bangladesh *via* Bongaon boarder and transfers the goods to another Bangladeshi boy, whom he meets there. He stays in Dhaka for a few days before he returns back to Kolkata. He makes good money for doing this work but he is also scared of the security forces at the border. Once, he was caught by the BSF (Border Security Force) and was detained for a day, but was released as he had nothing in his bag while returning back to Kolkata. He was aware of the risk factor involved in this type of work but was enjoying the thrill to overcome those challenges. Also, it was helping him to earn handsome money.

> Sheikh Salman, a boy of 11 was locked up in the police custody for two days. He was caught by some local residents while he was running away with a stolen fan from a nearby primary school. He

was beaten up by the people on the street as he was caught red handed and later public handed him over to the local police station. Police detained him in custody and after a prolonged negotiation with the primary school authorities and on the request of the local influential members and parents, the police released him. During the group discussion, the participants introduced him as 'criminal'. It was observed that during the entire session, the child remained silent and never participated. Later, the researchers conducted an in-depth interview with the Salman, during which he revealed the following:

> "I was hired by one of the local persons. . . . I will not mention the name . . . he gave me an advance of ₹ 50 to do the job of stealing a fan from the primary school. I was accompanied by two other local youth, who were around 19 years. They broke the window and helped me to get inside the classroom, after which I opened the wooden window of the school so that they can come inside. I had helped them to bring the fan down from the ceiling. Immediately, after that they ran away and asked me to carry fan to a nearby place. When I came outside the building with the fan, I was caught by one of the local residents. He called other people and they beat me very badly. I was bleeding from my mouth. They handed me over to the police, where I was again beaten. But I could not disclose the names of the other accompanies. In our group, we do not disclose each other names. The person, who had hired me, helped me to get out of the police lock up. He was given ₹ 500 to my family members for not disclosing his name. I worked for him before and was able to complete the given task successfully. And I will continue to work with them".

Though it was very difficult to enumerate the exact number of street children getting trafficked each year, but it can be assumed based on the above case studies that it must be very common. During the data collection, the researchers came to know about two girls from the North Zone, who were trafficked by a woman from their own community. The girls were lured by the woman to get a good job as a domestic help at an old lady's home. The parents also agreed as the woman promised of good salary and other facilities like stay and food. One day, she left the area with the two girls promising that they will return back in few hours after meeting the old lady, who was in need of domestic help. The woman assured to the parents that if the old lady agreed to hire the girls then the parents can visit and negotiate the remuneration and other benefits of the job. But, after she left, the woman never returned back nor did the girls. The members of the community lodged complain with the local police station but they were not able to trace her. On investigation, it was found that the woman was also a pavement dweller as she was thrown out of her home after getting a divorce. It was believed that she belonged to a good family and worked as a domestic help in the nearby vicinity. But in reality, all these were stories she told to the community members to create a goodwill and rapport with them. In fact, the woman behaved in a manner to gain trust of people and later betrayed them by trafficking their girls by luring them with false promises of employment.

Excluding abduction and forced trafficking, the younger girls were also lured by their peer groups. Once a girl becomes a victim, they try to entice other girls of the community to become like them. And most of the times, they are successful to allure them. During the study, there were 4 incidences were reported from 5 zones, where girls were taken by their friends with the promises to get them a better job. Once they trust them, these girls usually fall in the racket of child trafficking.

Similar problems were also seen in the case of boys, but the number of incidence were less as compared to the girls. They were usually trafficked or abducted to train them to get into antisocial activities like trading and transporting of drugs, country liquor, imported electronic goods and other smuggled goods from dockyard and/or from railway yards. The boys were also lured to get involved in other antisocial activities like prostitution, pick pocketing, shoplifting and burglary. And after the initial period, these children are lured to do life risking jobs with the expectation to earn large amount of easy money.

Peer Group Abuse and Different Deviant Behaviour

It was observed that children adopt various deviant behaviour to cope and adjust with the street environment, where there is poor supervision and lack of societal control. Some of the practices adopted by these children are to get involved in a gang culture, use of intoxicating substances, deviant sexual practices, watching of pornographic films, gambling and living in a world of fantasies

Gang Culture

The boys living on the streets believe in gang culture to protect themselves from any external threats. Such gangs operate in a confined area, where they usually reside and they lack any constructive guidance to utilize the energy of young members in constructive activities. They are often influenced by the local political leader for their mutual interest. Of the total 100 boys, there were 87 who reported of their affiliation with one or more such gangs or groups. During the discussion, it was found that the some members of the gang were already involved in some form of deviant activities and they are best used by the political parties for their interest. As these gangs operate under the umbrella of political parties, they receive protection against their act of violation of law and order in the society. It becomes very attractive for the children to gain such power by joining the gang and they get exposed to activities that violate the law.

To ensure that they remain well accepted in the gang., they get in the habit of substance abuse and gambling, which are the common recreational activities among the gang members. The new children joining the gangs are instigated to get involved in these activities. And, in most cases, they force themselves to inculcate this behaviour to get acceptance by their peer group. The members of the gang usually get involved in various types of competitive activities to prove their capabilities and ranking amongst the members of the gang. It is a sign of power and prestige in the gang to develop tolerance for different types of substance abuse, have multiple sex partners, be the winner in gambling and other rebellious activities. It helps them to get promoted within the hierarchy of the gang.

The boys are usually members of more than one group, and they tend to affiliate with the more powerful and influential group as one of the protection strategies. These groups and its members are not always from the same communities. And, it is common to find that the new children joining these groups get abused by other senior children, who force them to watch adult movies and make them consume intoxicating substances. The habit of gambling is also very common in the gang and often the young and new members get cheated by the senior and influential members.

The senior members of the gang often encourage the young and new members to engage in law violating activities to vent out their frustration from the past abusive experiences and deprived of life on the street. It was found from the discussion that the children mostly developed rebellious behaviour against the law enforcement authorities, who were one of the perpetrators of abuse. Besides, they also have a lot of bitterness from the ill treatment received from the economically better class of people living in the nearby area. And the other means to compensate for their limitations in life, the children tend to derive satisfaction from their masculine power of their capacity to procure expensive materialistic things. They do this to show their power and attract beautiful girl friends, who can accept them as a 'real man'. By doing so, they try to estimate their acceptance amongst their peer and young girls in the community.

It was also revealed from the discussion that the children in the gang develop different alternative activities to satisfy their psychosocial needs. Among such behaviour, homosexuality and sexual relationship with girls at an early age with limited knowledge about the reproductive and sexual health. It was identified that of the total 100 boys, there were 3 who were married at the age of 13-14 years and were already managing a separate family on the streets with their own children.

While there are advantages of being a member of a gang, there are many disadvantages. It was reported that a large number of children get abused by the senior members of their gang. Often, they steal or snatch their hard earned money and on resisting, they get physically assaulted. Of the total 87 children, who were involved in the gang culture, 37 (43%) reported that they were physically abused by the senior members when they first joined the gang. But there were also 34 (39%) children who reported of abuse by their senior members of their gang, even after being in the gang for some time. Thirty nine children also reported that the senior members use abusive language to prove them inferior in the gang. They reported that senior children snatch their money or personal belongings. Besides, sexual abuse by the gang members was also common behaviour of the gang. Twenty six children reported of being forced to get involved in a sexual relationship with others in the group during the first few days of joining the gang. But there were 34 (39%) children, who reported of regular sexual relationship with their peers.

Substance Abuse Among Children

As described earlier, the life of the children living on the streets is quite stressful. And in order to relieve some stress, the researchers found that the children were using various addictives. There were 85 per cent of the boys and 48 per cent of the girls, who use addictive substances like snuff, tobacco, alcohol, brown sugar, *gutka* (a preparation of tobacco and betel nuts), and *hashish*. Similar trends were seen across the five zones of Kolkata city, except North and Central Zone, where the children were found to have access to intoxicating substances like brown sugar, dendrite, glue, nitragipum (N-10) tablets and petrol.

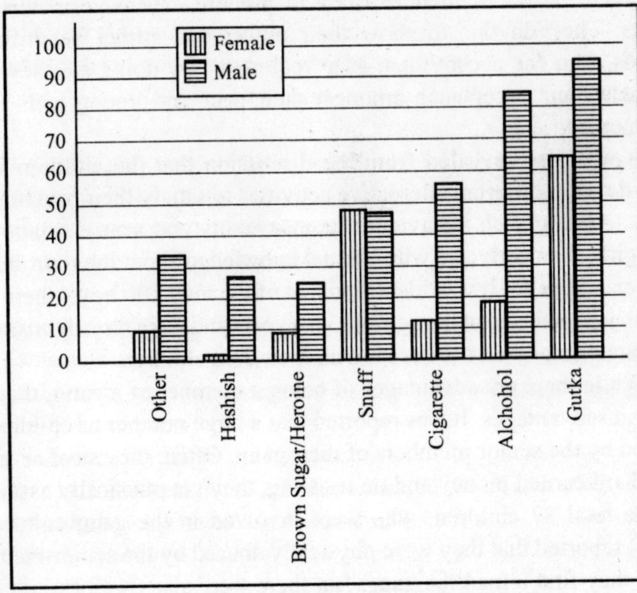

Figure 6.12: Use of Substance among Children

Based on the data collected, it was found that the consumption of *gutka* was the most common form of substance abuse among the children living on the streets. Almost 95 per cent boys and 64 per cent of the girls were found to be eating *gutka* on a regular basis and they reported it was difficult for them to feel normal without consuming it.

Table 6.14: Substance Abuse among Children

Gender	*Gutka*	*Alcohol*	*Cigarette*	*Snuff*	*Brown Sugar/ Heroine*	*Hashish*	*Others*
Male	95	85	57	47	25	27	34
Female	64	19	13	48	9	2	10
Total	**159**	**104**	**70**	**95**	**34**	**29**	**44**

The second most commonly abused substance among the children was alcohol. The rate of alcohol abuse was 85 per cent among the boys and 19 per cent in the case of the girls. Most of the children reported to use alcohol regularly to get relief from the body ache and fatigue at the end of the whole day's hard labour. There were 3 girls who reported the use of alcohol regularly during the winter season to keep them warm from the cold weather at night. Some of the girls were in the opinion that the intoxication of alcohol helped them to tolerate the pain of spending the whole night under a tree of small shade during unfavourable environmental conditions. Besides, there were 3 girls who revealed that they were lured to use alcohol and other substances before they were forced to sexually entertain some of the clients.

The third most commonly substance abused by the children was tobacco and snuff. It was found to be a common practice of many children to sniff the powder of tobacco as well as keep the powder under the tongue to get the kick out of the addictive tobacco. In addition to sniffing, there were 57 per cent boys and 13 per cent girls who reported the use of cigarette and *bidi* (local made cigarette). Another common form of addiction among children is to use *Patta* (brown sugar/heroine), which is legally prohibited in India to be used by any individual, including adults. It was found that 25 per cent children procured and used *patta*, whereas other 50 per cent were aware of their friends being addicted to brown sugar. Though it was not common for the girls to use brown sugar for addiction but there were 9 per cent, who admitted to have experienced it. Similarly, *marijuana* (Cannabis) and *hashish* were used by 20 per cent of boys and 2 per cent of girls. Those children, who were not able to have access to costly addictives, inhaled different forms of solvents like petrol, glue, and dendrite as substitutes. There were 44 per cent children who reported the use of such alternative addictions on regular basis.

> Around 7 o'clock in the evening, Rana, a boy of 12 years age, was playing cards with three of his friends, the researchers came to know that he used alcohol as well as brown sugar (*patta*) regularly. Rana narrated he could not work without the use of alcohol. He works as a rag picker and earns around ₹ 70 per day. But, he is forced to spend almost all the money on his addictions. He uses a pouch packet of alcohol every morning and goes out for work. He has a group of friends with whom he shares *patta*. In a day he takes almost 4 to 5 packets of alcohol and 5 to 7 packets of *patta*. He finds it difficult to manage money for his addiction and is forced to borrow money from others.
>
> Rana's father was also a rag-picker and an alcohol addict, who died in a road accident. His addiction started from his home, soon

after he started to work as a rag-picker at a very tender age. Every evening, he suffered from pain due to excessive physical stress of work during the day time and he learned from his father that consumption of alcohol helps to relieve the pain. Since, childhood, he has witnessed regular conflicts between his parents and he was used to sleeping without food for many nights. He knew that his mother used to go away with some clients to earn money. Rana and his elder sister used to take alcohol from his father to get relief from hunger and physical pain. After the birth of Rana's younger sister, his mother left the house leaving Rana and two younger sisters behind. She got married to another person and now she works as prostitute. Rana and his elder sister started to work with their father in the scavenging work.

After the death of Rana's father, he and his sisters are now staying at their grandmother's place. The grandmother works as a maid and takes care of the cost of their living. Rana can not remember when he started the use of regular alcohol and *patta*, but he cannot manage his day and life without these substances. He wants to supplement the income of his family but cannot manage to save money. He borrowed some money from the alcohol shop owner and from other friends, who used him to smuggle brown sugar and other substances from one vendor to another. He makes little money from it and repays his loan. Most of the nights Rana spends with his friends and desperately tries to find some work so that he can earn money to buy alcohol and *patta*.

Gambling Practices among Children

It is very common to find that the children living on the streets were involved in gambling. There were many ways of doing it and some of them were to buy lottery tickets, play cards, use of gambling machine like 'Super Lotto' or video games. But of those, the most common means of gambling was to play cards on the streets. It was found to be the most enjoyable way of earning easy money by the children, who actively participated in the card games, which gave results in a short span of time. Many children took a chance by playing with their day's hard earned money to gamble and try to make a large sum of money by fluke. The data revealed that out of 200 children, there were 62 (31%), who gambled regularly. Of the total children who gambled, 1/3rd of them were boys and 1/4th was girls.

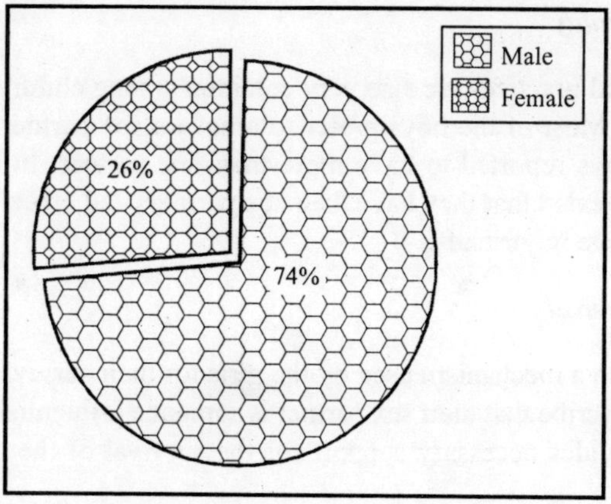

Figure 6.13: Gambling Practices

Different Forms of Sexual Activities

It was surprising to know that most of the children living on the streets became sexually active at a very early age, when compared to other children who were not living on the streets. Homosexuality, heterosexuality and group sex were common amongst these children. It was found that most of the boys aspired to have sex partner from their young age and many a times, they are able to identify more than one sex partner. Besides, physical relationship, it was common for these children to watch pornographic movies. And they had an easy access to such movies through the video parlour, which are available in all the zones of the city. During the focus group discussion, all children were not found to be open to disclose their experience and practice. So, it was allowed to them to report of any sexual behaviour they were aware of about their friends. Some of the findings from the discussions and interviews are described under various categories.

Homosexuality

Of the total boys, 70 per cent reported that their friends were sexually active and they enjoyed having sex with same sex (MSM). Most of them reported that their friends engage in such act for fun during the leisure time. Practices of homosexuality, however, were not common among girls. Only 10 per cent of the girls reported that their friends were involved in homosexual practices.

Heterosexuality

Heterosexual practices are also very common among children living on the streets. Most of the boys prefer to a have a sex partner and of the total, 20 boys reported to have more than one partner. In the case of girls, 27 revealed that they have their sex partners and other 16 reported that they have boyfriends.

Sex for Survival

Sex was also a mechanism used by the girls for their survival. They felt proud to describe that their sex partner is someone influential in the area and he provides necessary support for the survival of the girls on the streets.

> Santoshi, a 14 year girl narrated "on a rainy night, a person offered me to come inside and take shelter. I accepted the offer and the man gave me good food, drinks and place to sleep. In return, I allowed him to have sex with me".

> Malati, a 13 year old girl was known for having good relationship with the local official authority. She offered herself for physical relationship to the local influential persons and return she got the BPL card. Now, she is able to get regular ration from the local Public Distribution System dealer and plastic sheets during the rainy season.

Pregnancy and Unsafe Abortions

Unfortunately, the young children, who were sexually active, were found to be having very limited knowledge about safe sex and contraception. And due to the immediate cost of the contraception, many boys did not bother to use them. As a result the girls were subjected to the risk of pregnancy. Due to poverty and limitations for access, the girls adopted traditional methods of prevention and termination of unwanted pregnancies. But, all these resulted into unsafe abortion by putting the life of the mother at risk. During the study, the children narrated two incidences of death in their area due to unsafe termination of pregnancy procedure adopted by the girls. Similarly, there were 13 girls who revealed that their friends had experienced the problem of unwanted pregnancy and they were forced to take the help of the traditional methods of abortion.

In the North Zone, the girls reported of one of their friends, who had an unwanted pregnancy. She identified about it at a late stage and was forced to deliver the baby. Later, it was found out that she was not able to keep the child and sold her baby to some unknown person. Similarly, the children also reported that the problem of unwanted pregnancy of street girls was also common in the Central Zone area. They reported that there is a charitable institution which supports the street children to safely deliver the unwanted babies. And they help the girls with required medicines and food during the time of pregnancy and delivery. Later, if the girls decide to give away the baby, the institution takes the responsibility of the child.

Thus, it was observed that children adapt to various forms of high risk behaviour to satisfy their psycho-social needs as well as to survive in the street environment. Moreover, these behaviours are promoted within their societies due to lack of parental supervision, ability of parents to support their children's basic needs and wide acceptance of deviant practices within their society.

Interaction of Children with Legal Authorities

As one of the signatories of the CRC, the Government of India promises to take appropriate legislative, administrative, social and educational measures to protect children from exploitation and abuse. However, it seems that a change is taking place in the socio-legal system of the country after the ratification of CRC. The JJ Act (Care and Protection of Children) was enacted in the year 2000 and further amendment in 2006 to plug few loopholes. A separate Ministry for Women and Child Development was formed, which drafted a scheme on Integrated Child Protection. Further, a draft Bill of the new Offences Against Children Act, 2006 was drawn up by the Women and Child Development Department, under the Ministry of Human Resource Development.

The JJ Act, 2000 has given a new dimension to the whole Juvenile Justice System of the country. Most of these acts now lay more emphasis on the treatment, care, protection and developmental needs of the children by adopting a child friendly approach in the adjudication and disposition of the matters for the best interest of the children. Focus has also been given on the voice of children towards identification and solution of their own problems. But, it does not encourage children to access police system to lodge complains in case of violation of their rights. The Act also states to constitute a Child Welfare Committee for every district or a group of districts. It encourages children in need of care and protection to produce themselves before the Child Welfare Committee in case their basic rights get violated. Despite the enactment of all these legislations a wide gap is visible between the law enforcement bodies and primary beneficiaries, i.e. children. The JJ Act encourages children and other primary beneficiaries to access the system but it does not emphasize to modify the system to make it easily accessible for the children.

As described in the literature review that as one of the signatories of "The Standard Minimum Rules for the Administration of Juvenile Justice" and Child Rights Instrument, the Government and its law and order machinery must adhere to the international standard of dealing with juvenile offenders. For such compliance with the international treaties, the Government of India has established separate juvenile justice system and amended its rules to deal with juvenile offenders. As per the recommendations, Juvenile Justice Board has been established for every district or for a group of districts. These boards are entrusted to deal exclusively with all proceedings related to child in conflict with law. The Government also recognizes that the juvenile justice system shall accentuate on the well-being of the juveniles. The system must ensure that any reaction to juvenile offenders should always be in proportion to the circumstances of both the offenders and the offence. It also clarifies that appropriate judgement should be allowed at all stages of proceedings and at different levels of juvenile justice administration, keeping in view the special need of the juveniles as well as the variety of measures available. Appropriate scope for discretion should be allowed during investigation, prosecution, adjudication and the follow-up dispositions. Police is one of the important players in the entire justice system of the country. As an important law and order machinery, they must play a significant role in prevention of crime, investigation of cases and also extend requisite assistance in the prosecution of offenders.

The JJ Act, 2000 recognizes the adoption of a "child friendly approach" during dealing, adjudicating and disposition of cases to protect the best interest of the children. But in reality, no guideline or procedure has been designed to make the system 'friendly' for the children to take necessary support when they need in the time of crisis. So far, people recognize police as their first contact point of the law and order machinery. And geographically the police stations are reachable and accessible to common people due to its location in strategic and well connected places. They act as a liaison point between the community and the justice system. And as per the new Police Act, 2006, it recommends a separate child and women desk in each police station to provide easy access to the system for the vulnerable people. In this section of the research, efforts are made to understand and analyze the interaction of people living on the streets with the law enforcement agencies. The researchers have tried to understand and record the perception and experiences of children dealing with these law enforcement bodies and their adherence to the juvenile justice system in dealing with the children living on the streets.

Perception of Children Towards Police

To understand the level of interaction of the children with the justice system, they were asked to draw pictures of police eliciting some of the characteristics they are familiar with. After the drawing exercise, the researchers facilitated group discussions, followed with in-depth interview with few children to understand their perception. The findings from these exercises are described as under.

Table 6.15: Perception of Children Towards Police

Perception of Children	*Male*	*Female*	*Total No.*	*Percentage*
Eviction without any notice	82	78	160	80%
Take away belongings	56	49	105	53%
Physically assault the children	78	23	101	51%
Arrests and detains children without any valid reason	58	34	92	46%
Always suspect street children as criminal and gives harsh punishment for petty offence	76	16	92	46%
Gives trouble to street children for petty cases	34	22	56	28%
Take bribes to release especially during occasion of festival	67	20	87	44%
Does not listen to the children and discriminates against them	66	57	123	62%
Forces children to work for the police station and do not give remuneration to them for their work	17	5	22	11%
Police can trace missing people	22	7	29	15%
Ensures safety to only elite people	38	27	65	33%
Few police personnel are good and do not beat them	15	18	33	17%

It was interesting to find that the children had a very negative perception towards the police and law enforcement systems. About 80 per cent of the children stated that the police are known to conduct surprise raids at night to evict the families living on the streets without any prior intimation. More than half of the children reported that during the eviction drive the police would throw or take away their personnel belongings, which includes cash, cooking utensils, clothes and bedding. Many also reported that they were physically assaulted by the police during such eviction drive.

Children reported that the poor families living on the streets were discriminated by the law and order machinery as they were vulnerable and could not use any influence to defend them. More than 58 per cent of the boys reported that they were detained by the police and put in the lock up for no reason whatsoever. They also complained that police officials always suspect the families living on the streets for being criminal and occasionally arrest them for some petty criminal cases. The children were also subjected to harsh treatment for any minor offence and their families were compelled to pay bribes to release them from the police lock up. Few children also reported that the police officials make them to do work at the police station and never pay them for their hard work.

In spite of these negative feeling amongst the children, 65 per cent also had some positive experiences with law and order machinery. More than 14 per cent of the children believed that the police have very strong administrative network throughout the country and they can easily trace missing people. They perceived that the police is the only agency who can ensure safety and protection of the city. However, most of the children complained that police listen to only elite and influential people and do not care for the poorer section of the society. About 16 per cent of the children cited the example of a few good police officials, who had extended support to them and never assaulted them.

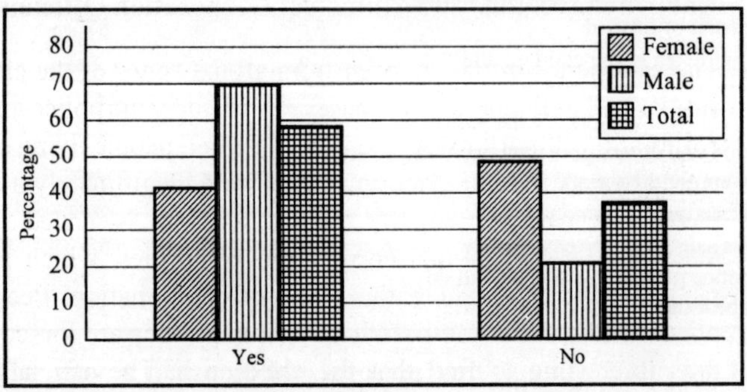

Figure 6.14: Children Visited Police Station

It was identified from the collected data that of the total respondents, 61 per cent children had visited police station at least once or more in their life time. The ratio of the boys was comparatively higher than the girls for visiting the police station. And, the negative perception of the children showed strong co-relationship with the children who visited the police station at some point of time. While describing the reasons of visit, it was found that none of the boys went on their own. They were taken to the police station, either when they were detained or were arrested for petty crimes. Also, many boys for the streets are rounded up by the police when a serious crime takes place in the locality to identify, if there was anyone from the streets involved in the case. It was rare for the boys to seek out help at the police station to safeguard their rights.

But in the case of girls they often visited the police station to negotiate with the police officials to return their belongings, which they might have taken during the eviction drive. As the police was softer with the females, the women and girls living on the streets would represent the families to negotiate with the police officials. Similarly, they also went to the police station to request for the release of their children, who were detained or arrested or to lodge a complaint against any rival groups on the streets. It was also observed that more number of girls has accessed the police station to seek legal support against any abuse that they may have experienced. However, in most of the cases, their visits to the police station were accompanied by other adult members of the family and influential members of the community.

Through the focus group discussions and in-depth interview with the children, the researchers were able to cite different forms of abusive experience of the children. The inputs from the children are described as under.

Abuse by the Police and Municipal Corporation Officials (Hallagiri)

The experience of the children from all the zones of the city was quite similar with reference to the abuses subjected by the police and municipal corporation authorities. As mentioned earlier, people living on the streets were always afraid of eviction as they were illegitimately occupying the pavements. And occasionally, the eviction drive is carried out jointly by the police and municipal corporation authorities, which mostly takes place around midnight without any prior intimation. People call this phenomenon as *Hallagiri*. When it happens, they are forced to evacuate the place without their personal belongings. The officials commonly demand for money, take away some precious belonging and throw the rest of the things off the streets. The authorities use abusive language to drive them away from the area and subject to physical assault, if anyone gets caught by them. Children also reported that the police was known to snatch away their hard earn money during the eviction drive.

Besides, the police officials suspect that the people living on the streets are criminals or they are closely linked with people who are involved in serious crime. Hence, the police conduct surprise raids in the settlement, when any crime takes place in the area as a part of their investigation. They were also known for harassing the boys living on the streets and many a times, they are picked up by the police for further investigation. Of the total boys, there were 37 who were detained by the police and placed in the lockup at some point of their life. Of these 37 boys, there were 24, who were charged for some petty crime and their parents had to pay a heavy bribe before they could be released from the lock up. There were 5 boys, who also reported that police had forced them to work in the police station and denied to pay any wages for the work done by them.

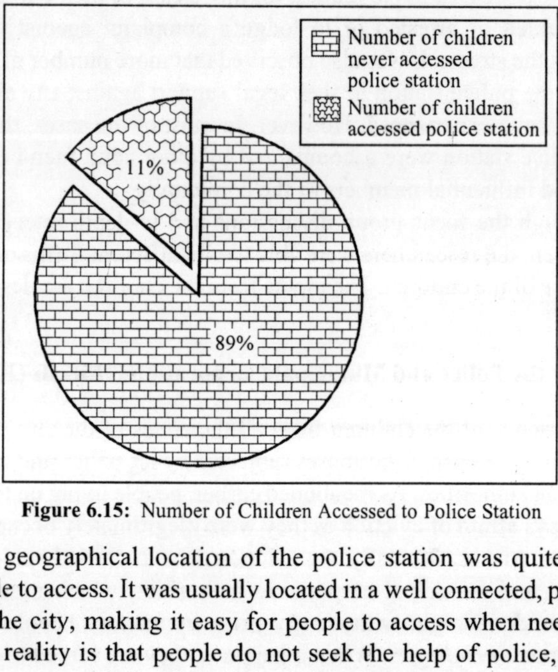

Figure 6.15: Number of Children Accessed to Police Station

The geographical location of the police station was quite suitable for people to access. It was usually located in a well connected, prominent area of the city, making it easy for people to access when needed. But still, the reality is that people do not seek the help of police, unless it becomes very critical. Thus, it was found that there were only few children who actually accessed police station to lodge complaints against any abuse perpetrated against them. Of the total 200 children, there were only 22 (11%), whoever went to the police station to lodge complaints for any abuse against them. Of these children, there were 9 boys and 13 girls, which indicate that the boys resorted to other means of protection rather than seeking help of the police. In the case of girls, the help of police was sought especially when the abuse was gross in nature. But still the number of girls accessing the services of the police is much less compared to the incidence of abuse taking place against them. And, for the cases of abuse in which the police was the perpetrator, it was not possible for either gender to access the same police system to seek justice for the crime of abuse against them.

Table 6.16: Reasons for Lodging Complaints at Police Station

Reasons	*No. of Children*
To report incidence of a child missing	3
To lodge complaint against sexual abuse	5
To report economic abuse against an employer	5
To report the incidence of physical violence against a few youth	9
Total	**22**

Besides, the children also had the feeling that the police have a strong network, which can identify missing children or individuals. Of the total respondents, there were 3 children who accompanied their parents to lodge a missing diary for their missing brother or sister, at the nearest police station. The children reported that the police personnel helped them a lot and referred them to few non-governmental organizations which also helped them to trace their missing brother/ sister. They felt that due to their poverty and illiteracy they faced obstacles in accessing the services available for the recovery of missing children. As the children were the witness of the process of lodging a complaint at the police station, they described some of the following problems they faced to lodge complaints:

- When the police request for a recent photograph of the missing child but they were not able to provide the same at the time of lodging a complaint.
- The police gave names and addresses of the NGOs work to trace the missing children. But they had to go from one organization to the other to search for the records to find if their brother or sister is found and kept there. The children felt that there was lack of coordination between the police and the NGOs in keeping the data of the missing and unfound children.

- Of the total 3 missing cases, 1 missing child was found from a NGO run institutional care facility. The organization requested for residential proof and relationship certificate from their parents, before they could hand the child back to them. But, these families living on the streets had no such records and had to go through a lot of trouble before they could get the child back.
- In the other 2 cases, the police were not able to trace the missing children as the family members were not able to provide a photograph of the missing child. The family was referred to the Missing Person Squad and other children's homes, where there was some possibility of finding the missing child.

During the discussion with the children and parents, they reported that the people living on the streets face lots of problems to access the facilities provided by the Government as most of them do not have any official identity such as residential certificate, voter identification or ration card. They also informed that most of them do not have photographs or any such documents, which can help them to trace the missing person or the child. They also expressed that due to their temporary pattern of settlement and frequent displacement, they cannot preserve important government documents. And, for multiple reasons, they get harassed by the government authorities and remain deprived of their basic rights and opportunities.

Problems Faced to Lodge Complaints against Sexual Abuse

Of the total children, there were only 5 girls, who sought the assistance of the police to file a complaint against the perpetrator of abuse. These girls informed police to file a complaint that they were subject to much harassment by the police, relatives of the perpetrators and the prosecutors. On further investigation, it was found that the 5 girls who took initiative to register a case against the perpetrator did not receive satisfactory response from the system. And it was found that the following was not done in accordance with the Juvenile Justice System of the country, with reference to the respective cases:

- In all the cases, the children found that a literate person was required from the community who can do the needful paperwork for filing a case at the police station. In most cases, the trial continued for more than a year.

- Due to manipulation of the case, none of the perpetrators were convicted and sentenced for the crime by the court.
- Children did not get any legal and financial assistance for the preparation and presentation of the case.
- Children were required to appear before the judicial court and were compelled to testify against the abuse perpetrated against them.
- Of the 5 cases, 2 underwent the medical test after the required period of validity from the time of abuse. The children and the family members were not oriented about the objective and the pre-requisites of the test. Thus, in none of the cases the medical test reports could be used as clear evidence against the perpetrator.
- In all the cases, the children were kept with their parents on the streets, and so they were not protected from the threats of the perpetrator, friends and relatives.
- Of the 5 cases, 3 children reported that they were taken to the judicial court in the same vehicle along with the perpetrator.

During an in-depth interview, all the children reported that because of their illiteracy they had to face lots of difficulties to understand the required official procedure at the police station. There were 2 children, who reported that if the language of communication was in Bengali, they could have understood what they had written. It was observed that in one of the cases, children were taken to take safe places after the occurrence of abuse. Children were not produced before the Child Welfare Committee (CWC) and no effort was made to provide emotional and psychological support to these victims.

> Suman, a 13 year old girl reported that she was a victim of sexual abuse and visited the police station, with her parents, on a couple of occasions to lodge her complaint. Her parents admitted her at the hospital and she was unconscious for about two days. She was found lying on the street, after the incidence of abuse under the influence of some intoxicating substances. At night, the people living around her found her unconscious near one corner of a lonely pavement in North Kolkata. For two days, when she was unconscious, nobody knew who the perpetrators were, but, on the third day, when she came to consciousness, she was interrogated by the police. The girl said, "I was not feeling comfortable to reply in front of other patients in the hospital". She could only remember that S.K. Rajjak,

offered her a glass of cold drink before the incident. S.K. Rajjak is one of the taxi drivers, who parks his taxi in nearby garage of their locality. Suman had undergone a series of test in the hospital and after four days of her stay, she was discharged from the hospital. She had severe injuries in her anal areas and faced many difficulties to manage her life after the incidence on the pavement. After returning to the pavement, she came to know that police arrested S.K. Rajjak and would produce him in the court. In the morning, the police officials took Suman and her mother to the police station as they had to appear before the Judicial Court. They were taken to the court with S.K. Rajjak in the same police van. During the trial period, Suman had to face very awkward questions of the prosecutor hired by S.K. Rajjak. Suman said "that all want to prove that I had sexual relationship with many male members of the community and they have abused me. I am intentionally taking the name of S.K. Rajjak to get some monitory benefit from him". Suman also said she had to visit the court for couple of months, and for all these days, her mother had to take days off from her work. They had to undergo lot of problems, while dealing with the court. The prosecutor continued to ask silly questions and Suman said that she was very much confused as she was not been able to recall the entire incident. One day, the prosecutor revealed the report of Suman's medical test, which said that she had intercourse with multiple partners. Suman said "I could not understand what they said during the trial, most of them were using English words". During one of the trials, the prosecutor asked Suman about her personal relationship with one of the boys staying in the same locality. Suman had to admit that once she was involved with him in a physical relationship, but that was in the past. Next day, that boy was arrested from the locality. Suman had to face lots of criticism and pressure from her immediate community and the influential persons from her locality, as well as friends of S.K. Rajjak. After all these incidences, Suman's family decided to leave the place and went back to their native village without informing anybody. After a couple of months they came back to Kolkata and decided to settle down in another pavement of Eastern Zone of Kolkata. Suman was almost crying and continued, "I cannot wipe off these unpleasant events from my memories".

Complaint Against Economic Abuse

The researchers were able to identify 5 respondents, who took help of the police to resolve their problem of economic exploitation. But in all the cases, the children approached the police station with their parents. Due to illiteracy, the children made verbal complaints against the employers to the police and the police did not bother to document the same and so the cases were never registered in the police diary. The police tried to settle the case outside the police station even though it was not the role of the police to do so. Thus, the children living on the streets have no faith in police officials of the law enforcement agency and they believe that the police did nothing to resolve their problem of economic abuse. They felt that in most of the cases, the police take the side of economically better off people and thus, they cannot fight for their rights to be protected from getting abused.

Reporting the Incidence of Physical Violence by Youths

Of the total 200 children, 9 went to the police station to report a case of violence against few members of their rival group. The incidence of rivalry between two groups is quite common among the children on the street. There are many groups and each one has distinct characteristics and are highly influenced by the material aspirations due to the media. Many a times, they get in conflict with the other group to show more power and influence over the children in their locality. It is quite common for them to imitate the characters of film actors and perform stunts like the movies in front of the other members. Occasionally, there is a fight between the competitive individuals, which may get extended to the entire group.

The other reasons for the conflict between the gangs were for the craving of power between the groups. There is always a gulf between the senior leadership and other members of the group. The group leader is the one who dominates and intervenes in all the affairs of the group members. But, within the group, there are other strong members, who try to exert their power upon others and many a times it leads to conflict between them. As mentioned earlier, most of these groups are affiliated with some political party members. The local party members try to dominate the community through these youth groups. Thus, if any individual tries to get rid of the dominance of the group, the local party leaders intervene through the local youth. On the other hand, the rival group/s also takes advantage of the situation and influences the victimized individual to lodge complaints against the youth group in the local police station. In all the cases the police take the role of a negotiator and try to settle things between the two parties.

Reasons for not Accessing the Legal Assistance Against the Abuse and Exploitation

The majority of the children believed that the police do not listen to them and they cannot independently lodge complaints at the police station. In all the cases, where children lodge complaints at the police station, they were always accompanied by adults. It was believed by the children that they must be accompanied by adults and there has to be someone who is literate to do the necessary paperwork for lodging complaints.

Thus, the children told that they were restrained to take any legal assistance against the perpetrators, if they were not supported by the family members. And in most of the cases, the family members refuse to support their children when the perpetrator is a member of the family, or influential member of the community or senior government official.

Moreover, children had experienced that law and order machinery is guided by the adults and they do not let the children to participate in the entire process. There is no means for children to get any legal and supportive services so that they can take independent action against the perpetrator. Hence, they believe that taking legal assistance without the support of the family will push them into more vulnerable situation and they will face further difficulties to cope with the situation. As a result, the children living on the streets have learned to accept the abusive experiences as a part of their life and they try to adopt other survival mechanisms to continue their insecure life on the streets.

Experience of Children who were Identified as 'Children in Conflict with Law'

> Rajiya, a 13 year old girl was abused by her step-father, when she was 10 years of age. Her step-father had taken her to a nearby house and given her an intoxicating substance. She was partially unconscious and was shocked to see that her father was sexually assaulting her. She was badly injured around her private parts and tried to disclose the matter to her mother. But her mother took her to hospital for treatment and asked her not to disclose the case to others. Still, she lives with her mother and step-father, but she can no more tolerate her step-father. She wants to report the case to the police, but her mother does not support her. She knew that she cannot take any step alone. Thus, she had to keep quite.

Of the 100 children interviewed, 37 per cent complained that the police abused them in form of detention, beating, extortion or verbal abuse. And of these, there were 37 boys, who complained of arbitrary detention on one or more occasions. Of these 37 children, in 25 cases, the guardians were not informed about the arrest or the reason for the same. In rest of the cases, the police arrested the children in front of their parents, but did not inform about the reason for the arrest. From those children who were arrested, there were only 5, in which cases the police was able to justify the arrests. The police also arrested a few adults for the 2 cases out of the previously mentioned 5. The children reported that in most of the cases, there are adults involved in the crime, but the police fail to arrest them for various reasons. In the cases where the children were arrested, they were kept at the police station for more than five hours. Except for one child, all other children reported that they were kept in the police lock up for the whole night. And out of the 37 children, 30 reported that they were placed in the same lock up along with the other adult criminals. Also, of the 37 children arrested, 22 reported that the police took bribes in form of money to release them from the police lock up. It was agreed by all the children that the police do not pay any attention to the words of the street children and force them to admit or extract information about the crime.

> Sukdev, a child of 12 years of age was arrested by the Narkeldanga police as a suspected offender for the case of burglary. He spent the whole night in the police station but not in the lock up. The child mentioned that because of the provision of the law that children cannot be placed in the lock up, the police kept him outside the lock up, but tied with a chain in the police station.

All the children reported that the police commonly use verbal abuse and physical torture in form of beating with fists and slapping at the time of interrogation. The children reported that police believed that the street children are always involved in some criminal activities or the other and are aware of the actual offender, when a crime takes place in an area. Thus, the police apply physical force to elicit the information from various suspects. It was found that 2 children were produced before the civil court and jointly charged as adult offender. After the production, both the children were referred to "*Aryadha*", which is an observation home for boys in conflict with the law.

Conclusion

There are countless children living on the streets, who continue to suffer violence resulting in physical injury, psychological trauma, within and outside the family setting. It was very unfortunate to find that in many cases, the parents or close relatives of the child were the one who exploited the child. Added to this, the social and economic instabilities within the family spoils the healthy environment required for the growth and development of a child. Due to the stress of managing the basic needs of the life, the parents fail to provide required affection, care, psychological and emotional support, supervision and control to their children, which is an integral part of the psycho-social growth and development of a child. But, unfortunately due to the prevalence of domestic violence, addiction and substance abuse by parents, problematic parental behaviour and insecure environment leads to the development poor self-image in children. Later, when they grow up, they tend to engage themselves in substance abuse and develop trends of destructive behaviour. These children get pushed at a budding age into vulnerable situations due to combination of different socio-legal and environmental factors. And, as commonly seen, many children also were forced to enter into the workforce at a very tender age, which is a clear evidence of denial of their basic rights. Children were also exposed to physical risk and violence within the work environment.

As described in the earlier chapters, the temporary settlements on the pavements are looked as illegal population or settlement of unwanted people, though they are living over there for many years. The illegitimacy of their residence is the main stumbling block for the families living on the streets to access the required support from the law enforcement agency. The fear of eviction looms largely over these people and they view police as a force which is meant to trouble and evict people like them on the street. On the other hand, police have negative feeling for the children living on the streets and they are viewed by them as drifters and criminals. Thus, the illegitimate status, fear of eviction and poor preparation by the police officials towards the people living on the streets result into a defiant attitude towards the existing legal system of the country.

While it is true that street children are sometimes involved in petty crimes, drug-trafficking, prostitution and other criminal activities, it is wrong for the police to assume that all the children living on the streets are involved in criminal activities or associated with criminals. Due to such negative attitude of the police officials, the rights of the children get grossly violated and many a times, the perpetrators are the officials of the law enforcement agencies themselves.

SECTION 6.3

Abuse and the Perpetrators — Perception of Parents

Like any other parents, families living on the streets do love and care for their children. The researchers interacted with many parents living with their children on the streets. It was common amongst many parents to start a happy married life with equal sensitivity amongst both the parents for their children. The role within the family was clearly defined, where the mother was expected to bear the responsibility of child rearing and household jobs and the father was expected to earn the livelihood. But, over a period of time, the stress of poverty caused lot of destruction and shifting of the roles and responsibilities. The parents succumbed to the struggle of survival and were no longer in a position to offer the ideal parental role to their beloved children. It was common to observe that most of the families were victims of unplanned family growth, disease, substance abuse, death of one or both parents and separation of parents. These situations were mainly responsible for the neglect of the child in an unstable family environment. In addition, there were external factors like the threat of eviction, illegitimate status and other environmental coercion which made the family situation much more vulnerable for children to get abused.

Road Accident

It was identified that the commonest concern among parents was for accidents on the road. It can be observed in Figure 6.16 that of the total respondents, 67 per cent of the parents raised their concern about the same. The pavement dwellers tend to settle beside busy roads or market places, where they have easy access to livelihood options. These roads are congested and overloaded with traffic. Moreover, the erratic nature of driving and speeding of vehicles causes frequent accidents. It was found that the parents were afraid for their children becoming victims of road accidents. Also, they lacked any support system to take care of their children, if they had any minor injuries. Thus, parents were found to be anxious for the safety of their children who remain unsupervised while they are away for work.

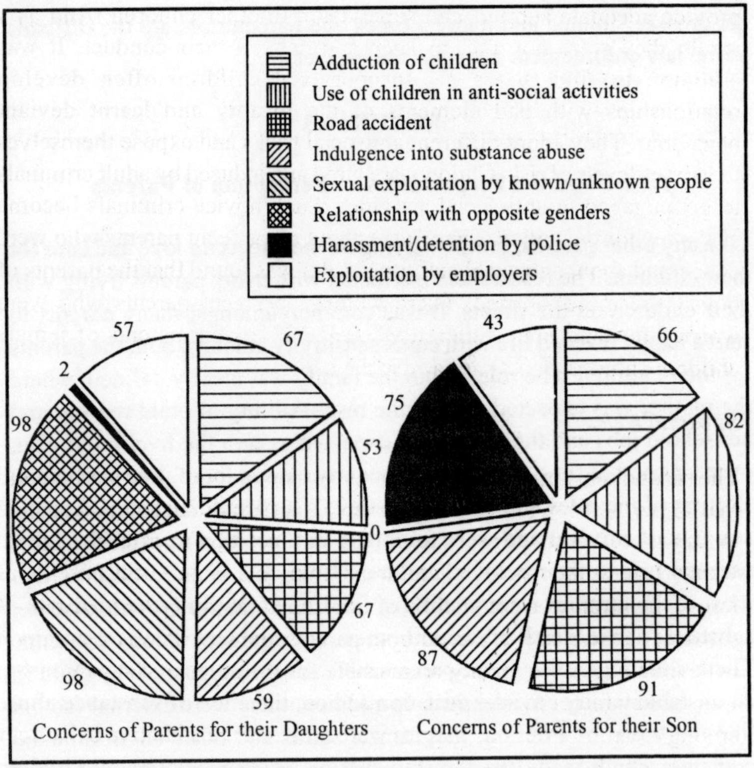

Figure 6.16: Concerns of Parents for their Children

Abduction of Children

Abduction by strangers understandably receives the most attention and generate the most fear among the parents of street community. Abduction of young children and girls are the most prevalent in street community. And the obvious reason for abducting children is to traffic them for prostitution, domestic workers, induce them into begging and use them in illegal activities. Thus, parents are always on an alert and they try to keep an eye on the strangers and take necessary action to prevent abduction at night. The above diagram shows that the fear is more prevalent among the parents of female children (78%) and 66 per cent among parents of male children.

Anti-social Activities

Many parents admitted to the researchers that they were not able to provide adequate support and supervision to other children. And as a result, they were not able to keep a watch on their conduct. It was common to find that such unsupervised children often develop relationships with bad elements of the locality and learnt deviant behaviour. They adopt different antisocial tricks and expose themselves to various levels of risk. Children are lured and induced by adult criminals to get engaged in anti-social activities. Such novice criminals become easy prey for the police. There were about 68 per cent parents who were concerned about antisocial activities and it was found that the parents of boys were more worried. There were 82 per cent parents who were worried for their male children whereas 53 per cent parents of female children showed anxiety for antisocial activities.

Substance Use

The second most priority was given to substance abuse. The study found that 73 per cent parents were concerned for their children getting addicted to substance abuses. From Figure 6.16, it can be observed that, there were 87 per cent parents of male children and 59 per cent parents of female children who felt that their children were exposed to the risk of substance abuse due to the poor street environment. It was a common believe amongst most of the parents that the wrong type of companionship was the key factor for the initiation and continuation of substance abuse among their children. The parents were aware of the addictive behaviour of their children and they found that majority of adolescent children used cigarettes, alcohol, *marijuana*, heroin (*patta*), dendrite or illicit drugs. And, they acquire the knowledge about different addictive substances from other children in the community.

Sexual Exploitation

It was found that parents of most of the girl children were concerned about sexual exploitation and molestation of females on the streets. Similar to the children's response, the parents also admitted that lack of privacy for females on the street environment and due to exposed environment, the girl children are easy victims of sexual exploitation. The common perpetrators of sexual molestation are by unknown drunk people at night. Figure 6.16 shows that there were 98 per cent mothers who reported that they received threats from known and unknown people for abusing their daughter from their very childhood. Also, it was felt that such people can easily abduct the girls living on the streets for the same purpose. On the other hand, the parents were not very concerned about the abuse by incest, i.e. sexual abuse by family members or close relatives of children. In case of parents of male children, they were not at all worried about sexual molestation. They believed that male children do not face the threat of sexual exploitation.

Exploitation by Employers

Due to the pressing needs to survive in the street environment, the parents are forced to engage their children in the work force from a very tender age. It is almost impossible for most of the parents to meet the needs unless their children work and contribute to the family income. It was experienced by most of the parents that children are exploited by the employers both physically and economically as they bear poor negotiation power. Such concern for exploitations was found to be much stronger among the parents of the female children (57%) whereas it was about 43 per cent among the parents of male children.

Relationship with Male Members

It was found that most of the parents (98%) were concerned about their girls for developing relationship with male members living on the streets. Parents were skeptical that such relationship can lead to premarital sex and unwanted pregnancies, which was not acceptable by the society. The parents were aware of the fact that there are many local youths who try to lure their adolescent girls to develop relationships with them.

Harassment by Police

It was reported by the parents that they face harassment by the police officials during the eviction. Such eviction drives are conducted during the night without prior notice and they subject the pavement dwellers to unwanted harassment. The parents were of the opinion that the police have a negative attitude towards the street living families and suspect them to be criminals. They occasionally conduct surprise raids in the settlements whenever any crime takes place in the area. It is also common for the police to harass the children and many a times these children are detained for investigation at the police station without proper procedures. There were 75 per cent parents of male children who were afraid of such harassment and detention. Similarly, the parents of the girl children were also afraid but their percentage was quite low. There were only 2 per cent of the mothers living near Sealdah Railway Station who perceived such fear for their daughters and the harm caused by the police.

Perception of Parents Towards Perpetrators of Child Abuse

Parents

Parents did not perceive parents as abusers. They agreed that due to poverty and insecurities they cannot take proper care of their children and fulfil their material needs. So, it may appear to be an unhappy family environment, but none of the parents have an intention to abuse their children. The parents also admitted that they occasionally scold their children as a disciplinary measure, and this is done to control and shape the behaviour of their children.

Family Members

The Figure 6.17 shows that there were only 2 per cent of the parents of girl children, who felt that their family members can also abuse their children. And, this could happen when one of the parents is a step parent. It was common to find that the step parents force the children to

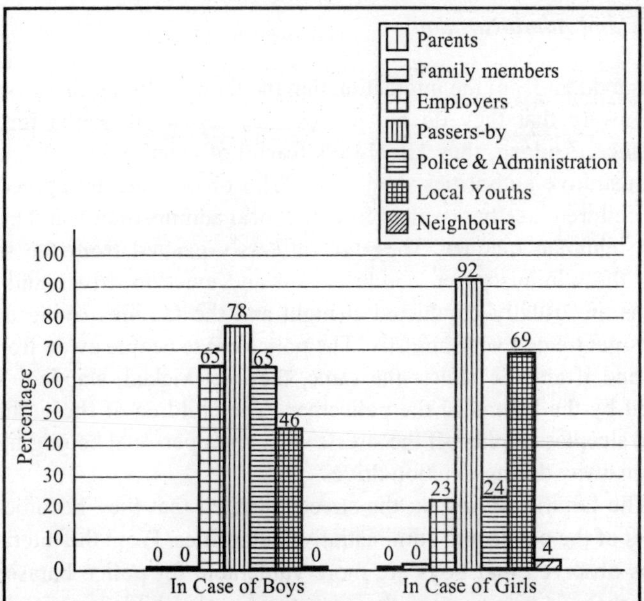

Figure 6.17: Perception of Parents Towards Perpetrators of Child Abuse

do all the household work, torture them and serve less food. On the other hand, the parents of normal families would always try to protect their children from any form of external evil. Parents do feel that exposure to family violence is common among street families because of their poverty, substance dependence among male members and other daily struggle of the street life. They felt that it is difficult to hide their emotional outburst from their children because of lack of privacy.

Passers-by

Like children, 92 per cent of the parents of girl children and 78 per cent of parents of male children perceived unknown people or passer-by as abusers. They felt that affluent people enjoy watching miseries of the poverty stricken people. They hate people who live on the streets and use abusive languages, while addressing them. Moreover, there are many people who seek the opportunity to sexually molest female members as well as adolescents' girls living on the streets. Those parents also reported that abduction of children from street families is also a common phenomenon. Thus, they try to protect themselves and their children from any unknown passer-by.

Police and Administration

It was evident from the interaction that the families living on the streets were aware that they do not possess any legitimate status for their residence. And, so, they are always fearful of eviction by the law and administrative authorities. Majority (90%) of the patents' agreed that their children face harassment from the local administration and behave in an inhuman manner. They are ruthlessly evicted from the streets when the administration conducts raid and eviction drives and such actions are usually conducted at night and the families living on the streets get treated very unjustly. The police chase people away from the area and if anyone resists the same, they get kicked, slapped, hit or jabbed by the batons of the policemen. The children of these families spend sleepless nights off the streets when their personal belongings are thrown away during eviction drives.

The families living on the streets narrated that they become easy targets of the police and administrative authorities. From the interaction it was observed that boys are more vulnerable for police harassment. More than 64 per cent of the parents of male children voiced their concern for police harassment. The parents of female children were less concerned for the same problem. Parents narrated that whenever any criminal activities or incidence of burglaries take place in the nearby areas, the police conduct routine round-ups of street families upon suspicion of involvement in the crime. It is common during such time for the male members and adolescent boys to be detained in the police lock-up overnight. There were also frequent reports of severe police brutality against the children and adults both at the time of arrest and particularly during interrogation at the police station.

The families living near the Sealdah Railway Station reported that the Railway Police Force (RPF) officials occasionally physically and sexually harass the children and women. The parents reported that the RPF officials force their children to lift goods from the train during the unloading process and they do not remunerate them. Similarly, the women headed families are considered most vulnerable and they are forced to please the RPF officials by having physical relationship with them. Hence, the parents living near the railway stations are very cautious for the physical and sexual violence of RPF officials against their children. And the perception of the parents regarding the law enforcement authorities as the perpetrators of abuse was also shared by the children.

Local Youth

The parents also reported that their fear from the local youth. They perceived that the youth of the area are involved in varying degrees of antisocial activities, and the parents of adolescents girls narrated that they try to keep an eye on their daughters and do not allow them to interact with the local youth. They are apprehensive that these local youth can lure their daughters and involve them in a relationship, which may lead to premarital sex. Such emotional decisions can ruin the future of their daughters. All the parents aspire for a better and secured future for their daughters. They believe that marriage with a well established person is the only solution to get their daughters away from the life on the streets.

Parents of 46 per cent of the boys were also apprehensive of the local youth. They think that the local youth could use their sons for criminal purposes and later the police will harass their sons and the whole family for being involved with such groups. They also perceive that these youth entice children to indulge into substance abuse. The parents also reported that they have less control and supervision over their sons as they spend most of the time with their peer groups. Thus, they cannot do much to protect their sons from abuse though they are always worried for the same.

Conclusion

Parents who live on the streets with children also believe that every child has the right to grow up in a safe and supportive family environment. And the parents do have a decisive role in protecting their children from potential harm. Because of poverty they are forced to keep children on the roadside without any support system and also engage them in some work from a tender age to support their family. Thus, parents feel that they cannot provide the required support and protection to their children, but can try to adopt different mechanisms to protect their children from potential harm from the perpetrators.

SECTION 6.4

Self-protection Mechanism

We have realized that families living on the streets are exposed to various risks and exploitations. Illegitimacy of stay prohibits these families to access essential amenities of life and to enjoy the basic Constitutional rights. Thus, it was observed that people have to readjust and modify themselves to survive in the society.

Heterogeneity of social and cultural groups, lack of cohesiveness, semi isolation and predominance of primary relationships are the main characteristics of the social groups live on the streets. Families living in these semi-isolated groups do not have any structured social control system and are highly influenced by external culture.

These families and individuals develop and modify their coping mechanisms and adopt different strategies to safeguard themselves from external risks. It was observed that children living on the streets learn to adjust themselves and reframe their own perceptions.

In this section, we tried to understand the perception of children and their family members about feeling of safety and insecurities. Attempts were made to understand different self-defense strategies that the children and street families developed as a social group to protect their children from abuse and exploitations.

Opinion of Children Regarding their Feeling of Safety

Safety is a feeling of well-being which can evolve through a family and the community where the children stay. Here, insecurity means the feeling of anxiety or fear that comes from physical, social and emotional insecurities. The causal factors of these feelings are based on perceptions of children, families and communities about potential harm that they will bear as a consequence of being on the streets. The insecurities reflect from the outlook of other city dwellers towards the street communities, attitude of unknown passers-by, support system they have, helping attitude of the administration and welfare authorities as well as the socio-economic profiles of these children and cultural belief systems of the street families. Data was collected from children to understand the factors that help them to feel safe within the environment irrespective of their vulnerable situations. Qualitative as well as quantitative data were also collected from the children and their family members to understand different forms of protection mechanisms that children and their families adopt to survive on the streets.

Feeling of Safety within the Environment

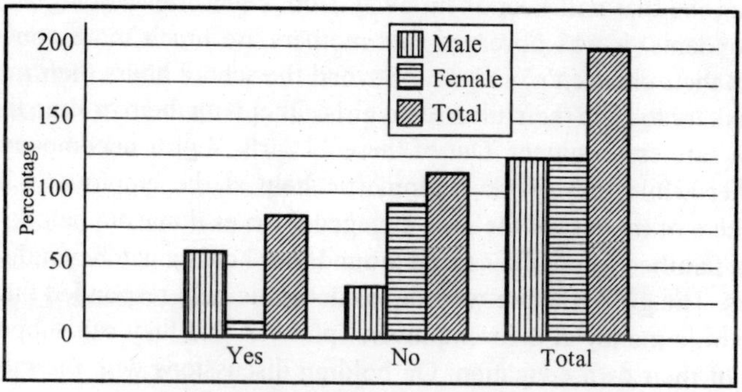

Figure 6.18: Feeling of Safety within the Environment

Table 6.17: Feeling of Safety

Gender	*Yes*	*Percentage*	*No.*	*Percentage*	*Total*
Male	65	65	35	35	100
Female	11	11	89	89	100
Total	**85**	**42.5**	**115**	**57.5**	**200**

From Table 6.17, it is identified that the feeling of insecurities are significantly higher among girls than the boys. Among the girls, 89 per cent reported that they do not feel safe within the environment. While only 11 per cent of girls said that they feel safe.

The following factors were common among these girls:

- They are not worried as they stay with parents.
- They all attend formal schools as well as NGO run education centres.
- They have positive perception about school and attend schools regularly.
- All the children are from nuclear families and the size of the family are relatively smaller (4-5 members).
- Mothers are literate which means they can help their children to read and write.
- Mothers work as domestic workers and have stable monthly income that is (₹ 600-1100) per month and bear the maximum cost of their family.

During the interview with the parents it was reflected that their parents do not allow children to spend much time on the streets. They try to keep their children either in education centers or involved with some jobs that will keep them away from street life. Among all these respondents, it was observed that mothers are much more concerned about their children's' security. Beyond the school hours their mothers always try to keep their adolescent girls either with them or keep them in some safe environment. Out of these 11 girls, 7 girls accompany their mother while they work as domestic help at the employer's house. Mothers of the rest of the girls engaged them as domestic help in some good families where they spend around four hours a day beyond school hours. The girls who are working as domestic help responded that they save little money at their employers' place so that they can support the cost of their own education. On holding discussions with the mothers, the response from them was that they do not want to make their children like other girls who live on the streets. They dream for a secured future for their children and they do not want their children to suffer as they have suffered on the streets. Another respondent mentioned that the girls are not their property so they are responsible to protect them until they rich a mature age, when they can get married into a good family. One of the mothers recalled that she was from a very poor family and her father forced her to get married at an early age and could not continue her education at her village school. Yet still, she believes that they should get their daughters married at an early age so that they can get rid of the street life as early as possible.

Among the boys, 65 out of 100 responded that they feel safe within the environment. While depicting reasons, it was observed that the feelings of securities among boys are depending on the following factors:

Table 6.18: Reason for Feeling Safe

Reasons	*Frequency of Response*	*Percentage*
Association with a powerful group	32	49
Power of negotiation with outsiders	32	49
Regularity of income	28	43
Muscle power	8	12
Knowledge about the environment	5	7.6

Out of the 65 boys 32 (49.2%) responded that they feel safe as they are affiliated to some powerful gangs. These children do not feel insecure as their groups pose strong negotiation power and influence on local community. Thus, they can be protected from external risk and exploitations. Among boys, 12 per cent responded that male members should not feel insecure because they have muscle power where as 7.6 per cent said that they have good knowledge about their area and people. Thus, they know how to protect themselves from abusers; they know safer places to hide and seek assistance of others if they are threatened. The remaining respondents felt safe in the environment as they get the opportunity to earn money on a regular basis.

Thus, it was visualized that girls are more dependent on their family members for their personal securities. The feeling of insecurities among the girls comes from the attitude of family members towards their girls. On the other hand, boys are not dependent upon their family members for their personal securities. They seek assistance from their peers and group members for their personal protection.

Feeling of Safety and Exposure to Education

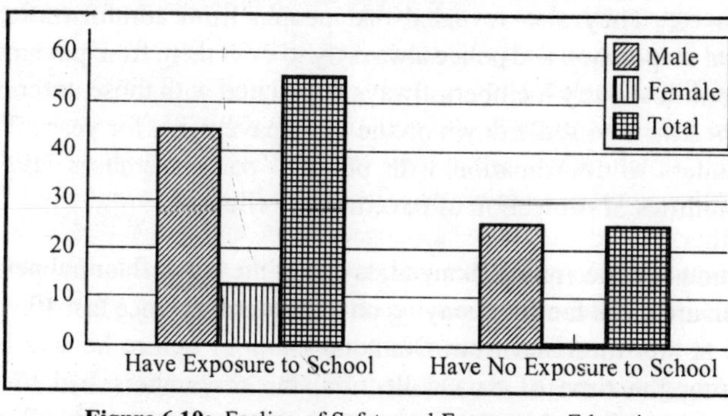

Figure 6.19: Feeling of Safety and Exposure to Education

It is observed from the data analyzed (Figure 6.19) that children's participation in education has a positive correlation with the feeling of security. If we analyze the educational background of street children who feel safe in the environment, it can be identified that a significant number of children (72%) have exposure to education. Among boys, 44 (67%) children had attended schools while among girls it is 100 per cent. From the discussion it came out that the children who can read and write feel more confident because it ensures protection from economic exploitations.

Thus, it can be inferred that schooling, has a positive association with the feeling of safety of the children living on the streets.

Protection Mechanisms

As preventive mechanism, children and their parents generally adopt the following means to protect themselves.

Protection Mechanism of the Street Communities

Families Always Settle in Clusters

Families living on the streets always settle in clusters. They try to keep cohesion among the families by living in same cluster. From the cluster of families, one person who has leadership skills emerges as leader. They turn into a key influential member of that area. In all the areas, it was observed that these leaders are affiliated to some political party who support them to deal with external problems. All these areas are affiliated to one or other political party leader who help these street families to get emergency support like admission to government hospital, free/subsidized treatment facilities, negotiate with police and administration during eviction, etc. They also revealed that people from administration of municipal corporation and police always try to evict them from pavements, but the political party members always negotiated with those authorities and helped them to settle down on the same pavements for years. Thus, local leaders in coordination with political party members take the responsibilities of protection of pavement dwellers.

> Bishnu aged 38 (name changed) is one of the key influential persons of an area. His family is staying on the pavement since last 40 years. His family migrated from Diamond Harbour before he was born. During the time of data collection, the researchers had to take permission from him to interact with other pavement dwellers. It

was identified that pavement dwellers were not allowed to give information to any outsiders without the permission of Bishnu. The researchers had to explain the purpose of the interaction to Bishnu who in turn gave the permission after a thorough discussion with their local political party leaders. The cluster is affiliated by a sub-committee leader of a political party. They maintain very good relationship with all the members living on those pavements through Bishnu. The political party members conduct medical checkup camps on a regular basis and also provide trampoline to the street families during rainy seasons. Bishnu maintains the liaison among political party leaders, local administration and street families. In all the zones, similar type of social support system had emerged among the street families to protect their own interest.

Mechanism Adopted by the Family Members to Protect Children

- In all the zones, parents said that they perceive schools as a place where they can keep children for a few hours. In most of the areas it was found that families prefer to send their girls in more than one school to keep them away from unsafe environment. For the younger children, families use schools as a crèche and like to send them to schools when they are out for work. Thus, it was observed attendance of younger children in school is better than adolescent boys and girls.
- At night some mothers keep girls tied to their bodies with pieces of cloth so that no one can take them away.
- Sexual exploitations among adolescent girls are very common in all the zones. Thus, parents always try to adopt some mechanism to protect their girls from sexual assaults and exploitations. It was reflected from the data that children as well as girls experience maximum threat of sexual exploitation during night. In all the areas they alleged that unknown drunk people/commuters try to assault adolescent girls. They enter into their plastic sheds and try to touch their private parts. The experiences were common across the zones. Thus, to protect girls all the female members sleep inside the plastic sheets. And male members sleep outside so that they can protect girls. In a few areas the families who have adolescent girls sleep together in group. Mothers/older female members sleep at both ends of the row and keep their girls in the middle. In central Kolkata, female members have divided their responsibilities

and take turn to keep watch in shifts. A few members keep themselves awake for few hours at night and in turn other members also do so. Thus, they try to sleep early (by 8.30 p.m.) as they can not sleep comfortably at night.

- Majority of families are nuclear families having no support service within the city to look after to their young children. Thus, when parents go out for work they are compelled to keep the younger children tied with rope to prevent them from getting into any harm.
- Engaging adolescent girls as domestic help is also a mechanism as it helps to keep girls stay away from street life. Thus, they always look for good families where they can engage their children as domestic help. To ensure regular food and security, parents are also interested to engage their adolescent girls in fulltime domestic jobs with good families.

Mechanism Adopted by Children

- Boys living on the street prefer to stay with friends in groups to protect themselves from outsiders. These groups take on certain behavioural pattern and culture. These groups generally play in groups and get them associated with local political party leaders and compete with others to gain power. In most of the cases they define power as their intimacy with influential party leaders and negotiation skills with law and administrative authorities and outsiders. These groups are led by young adults who have strong hold over the community. Group members tend to satisfy their various needs within the group which they cannot satisfy otherwise within the family environment. Each group operates within a distinct mode of operation and gratifies mutual interest and provides protection to its members.
- Boys living on streets always believe in gang culture for their own protection. They also try to get themselves attached to some strong powerful groups. Though exploitation within the groups is common, but they in turn ensure protection to their group members. These groups are also supported by some powerful persons in the community. In most of the cases those influential persons are connected to some political party. They always use that connection to influence or negotiate with others. Thus, because of these influence and power boys feel themselves more secure than girls.

- During the discussion girls revealed that they always take the help of mothers, elder sisters, sister in laws and other female members of their communities. They always openly discuss with them regarding any type of abuse they face. Their mothers and elder female members also always train them about different self-protection mechanisms. During the time of discussion they revealed the following methods they adopt to keep themselves safe:
    - ★ They do not talk to unknown people.
    - ★ Do not take any gift/food from any unknown people.
    - ★ Do not roam or stay alone in any place.
    - ★ Talk with male members from distance.
    - ★ Use covered clothes.
    - ★ Do not allow any male members (even known people/ relative) to hug or to touch them.

Support Taken from NGOs

In a few areas NGOs provide night shelter facilities to children. Parents and girls also prefer to avail the night shelter as it provides a safe place to their children to sleep at night. In these shelters children enjoy at night along with bathing, nutrition, recreation, personal lockers (to keep their belongings) facilities. But these types of facilities are not accessible in any of the areas except in central Kolkata.

Conclusion

Street living families try to settle in small groups and adopt various methods of defensive behaviour to protect them from personal harm. Though lack of cohesiveness and individualism are predominating characteristics of these families, but they try to organize in groups to pursuit their common interest. Families try to derive common strategies from the conditions of their localities and extend mutual support to protect their interest. Children also adopt various tricks to defend themselves from abuse and exploitations. Girls are mainly dependent upon their family members for their protection where as boys try to organize themselves in groups for their own good. Besides, children learn to adopt different strategies to safeguard their interest and fulfil their own needs. Night shelter facilities are not accessible throughout the city, but children and their family members long for this support to protect their children during the night.

SECTION 6.5

Child Rights — Perception of Children and their Parents

During the study, efforts were made to understand how children living on the streets perceive their rights as an individual. For this purpose, various techniques like one-to-one interview, drawing exercises and group discussions were used with the children. Through these exercises, the children came up with a list of immediate needs that affect their daily life. They also expressed their desires for the future through these exercises. The children were facilitated to state their right based on their experience of daily life, insights and desires for the future to lead a quality and meaningful life. It was a common plea of most of the children living on the streets that they do not want to be ignored by people and they would like to be a part of the society. The following is the list of basic rights as perceived by the children.

Table 6.19: Perception of Children Towards their Rights

Rated Priority	*Rights of Children*	*Frequency Boys (%)*	*Frequency Girls (%)*	*Average*
1	Regular food/Right to good food	85	82	83.5
2	Safe shelter/safe place to sleep	32	62	47.0
3	Clean environment to live	27	58	42.5
4	Privacy of their family life	42	46	44.0
5	House to stay	42	58	50.0
6	To be safe	10	87	48.5
7	Not to be tortured	78	47	62.5
8	Proper clothing	77	84	80.5
9	To be cared and loved by parents	19	78	5.0
10	To be cared and respected by others	15	67	48.5
11	To have freedom	71	54	41.0
12	To purchase thing of their choice	79	51	62.5
13	To get proper rest	65	52	58.5
14	To get job market oriented education	16	27	21.5
15	Not to be forced by others to get married	0	55	27.5
16	To have proper medieval attention	34	54	44.0
17	To get support and decent behaviour from law and order officials	36	74	55.0

The researchers also interacted with the parents of street children to find out what they felt about their children's rights. It was found that the parents had a desire to provide the needed support to ensure proper development of their children. However, the parents were also aware of their socio-economic condition and limitations in achieving their aspirations. The researchers also conducted some exercises to identify rights of the children as perceived by their parents. It was found that there was a strong recognition that parents and governments are mainly responsible to ensure that the children receive necessary support. The following is what the parents perceive as the rights of their children.

Parent's Perception of Child Rights

- Right to have regular food
- Right to have a safe place to sleep and/or safe shelter
- Right to get educated
- Right to have decent life
- Right to have clothes to wear
- Right to be cared and loved by their parents
- Right to have proper medical attention
- Right of decent behaviour from law and order officials

Regular Food

More than 83 per cent children and their parents felt that children should have the right to have regular and proper food. Parents of 87 per cent boys and 79 per cent girls believe that '*right to food*' as one of the prime rights of children, but unfortunately due to poor socio-economic condition they were not able to endure four square meals a day for them. It was identified that the parents had a bias for male children in terms of the needs and their priority for the distribution of food within the family. They believed that male children required more nutritional food than females as they perform heavy physical work to earn a living as compared to the female children.

Safe Shelter

The study found that there were 47 per cent of the children and 75.5 per cent of the parents who believed that the children should have the right to safe shelter. And, it was not surprising when parents of 95 per cent girl children and 59 per cent boys considered safe shelter as one of the important factors which can prevent children from getting abused. For obvious reason, parents of girl children believed that the requirement of safe shelter is more significant for girls than among boys.

Education

The data revealed that more than 21 per cent children and 54 per cent of the parents thought that education is an important aspect of life and every child should have the right for proper education. The perception was stronger among parents of boys (65%) than that of the girls (43%). While interacting with parents, most of them were of the opinion that '*education system is not meant for the street children*'. On further investigation, it was found that the children living on the streets were not able to relate learning of the school with their daily life situation. Thus, children as well as their parents voiced for an education system that can help children to learn required skills to earn money, so that they can lead a decent life.

Clothes to Wear

It was found that more than 73 per cent of the parents and 80 per cent of the children believed that children living on the streets should have the right to have proper clothing. It is essential to protect them from climatic changes and also it is helpful to prevent children from getting abused. Parents of 89 per cent girls felt that proper clothing is an important requirement for girls living on the streets to help them ensure their privacy.

Love and Care by Parents

It is well known that for the proper development of a child, it is essential that the child receives proper care and adequate love from the parents. In this study, it was found that 78 per cent of the girls were of the opinion that no children should be denied from parental love and affection. On the contrary, there were only 19 per cent boys who identified love and care as one of the rights of the children. But, the parents of both boys and girls were of the opinion that the children should have the right to receive love and care from their parents. Also, it was surprising to observe that 64 per cent parents of girl children had a feeling that girls require more care than boys as they are much more vulnerable on the streets.

Proper Medical Attention

Parents as well as the children believed that '*proper medical attention*' should be made available to all the children and it should be one of the most important child rights. Over 64 per cent of the parents and 44 per cent children felt that all the members including the children should have the right to proper medical assistance, when needed. People living in sheer poverty cannot ensure proper treatment to their family members due to sky high cost of medicine and treatment. Also, there is an opportunity cost involved when a member of the family falls sick and other members need to take care of the sick family member. It was a common experience of many families that they cannot rely upon the government hospitals as they are always full and is almost impossible to find a vacancy for admission in case of emergency. Moreover, they have to depend upon the local political party leaders and counsellors for recommendation to the hospital to waive the charges and provide free treatment. This obligation can also be a source of exploitation and abuse at a later stage.

Decent Life

There was a common feeling among 77 per cent parents that the children should not be discriminated against because of their socio-economic status. It was perceived that the children should be treated equally in the society. And, it was essential for the street living children to have a healthy environment for growth and development. The study found that the perception was almost equal among parents of both the gender, i.e. 77 per cent among boys and 78 per cent among female. The inputs from the children indicated that they want to receive equal treatment like other children in the society. More than 41 per cent children felt that they should not be denied from equal treatment due to their socio-economic conditions.

Right to Freedom

The study revealed that more than 62 per cent children were of the opinion that all the children should have the right to freedom. It means that no one should force them to work and they should have the right to use their hard earned money in the way they like. The children also felt that they should have the right to move around freely. The data analyzed indicated that 79 per cent boys valued freedom as their rights whereas 55 per cent girls perceived other aspect as their rights.

Privacy for their Own Family Life

In this study, more than half of the children perceived that they should have a private family life and that should be one of the important child rights. The feeling of privacy was found equal amongst both the genders. It was found that the children had a strong desire to keep the daily life struggles, family life tensions, poverty and family violence as private as possible. They felt embarrassed to expose the difficulties of their life to outsiders. They feel that the right to privacy of street living families gets denied as their life is exposed to the strangers.

Decent Behaviour from Law and Order Officials

During this study, it was found that the parents as well as the children firmly believed that they should have the right to fair and unbiased treatment from law and order officials. Parents of 73 per cent boys felt that their children should not be harassed by the police and the parents of 43 per cent girls believed that the law and order agencies must ensure that their children are protected. Similarly, 44 per cent children also believed that they should have the right to get adequate support and protection from law and order officials.

Right not to be Bullied by Others

The children narrated to the researchers that because of their filthy clothes, appearance and poverty, they are bullied by others at the schools, play grounds and work places. Their access to the play grounds is denied and they face humiliating comments. They, therefore, felt strongly that all the children should be treated equally in the society. The data analysis did not reflect any gender disparities where almost 65 per cent of both boys and girls perceived "right not to be bullied by others" as an important aspect of child rights.

Right not to be Forced into Marriage

Girls believed that almost all the girls in the society are forced by their parents and relatives to get married to the strangers. Once children are married, parents and family members generally deny taking any responsibilities of their lives. Thus, over 55 per cent of the girls stated that they should be protected from forced marriages.

Conclusion

Overall, it was observed that children's opinion were not very different from adults. From the discussions with children it was felt that they were skilful and analytical enough to identify and analyze their rights based on the struggles of their daily life and perceived needs. Children were much more involved and vocal in analyzing their rights and denials as that of their parents. Throughout the discussions, children and parents pleaded for the right to equality in the society and demanded for basic human dignity to lead a decent life. They felt that extreme poverty of the family is the core issue that results in denial of basic human rights and restricts access to basic services required for a respectable life. They believed that it is the responsibility of the society that includes parents, government and other members to provide required support to promote their rights. It is important to note that children viewed the above mention rights not only as "*child rights*", but also as "*basic human rights*". Though in the earlier sections, children identified various perpetrators as abusers and it was their need to get oriented enough so that they do not exploit others. They also appealed for strict action to be taken against the perpetrators who commit repeated abuse within the society.

SECTION 6.6

Perception of Police Towards Street Children and Child Protection

Roles and Responsibilities of Police

One of the key objectives of this study was to identify areas to make the environment child friendly so that children remain protected from all kinds of abuses. This cannot be envisaged without the involvement of the police. Hence, the researchers felt the need to understand and analyze the roles and responsibilities of police under the newly amended Police Act. The researchers interacted with various ranks of police officials during various training programmes conducted by the researchers to impart training on Child Rights and Juvenile Justice Act in Kolkata. In this section, efforts have been made to understand the perception of police towards the street-living children and their role in protecting their basic rights.

The new Police Act was drafted after the amendment of Juvenile Justice (Care and Protection Act) 2000. The roles and responsibilities of police officials of different ranks were modified to incorporate the expectations of Juvenile Justice Act, 2000, besides many other changes which were required to improve the functioning of the police department. Realizing the need to replace the 146 year old Police Act, 1861, the Ministry of Home Affairs, Government of India, ordered the formation of a committee of experts, under the Chairmanship of Dr. Soli Sorabjee, former Attorney General, Government of India. In September 2005 the committee came up with a draft of the new Police Act, which could meet the growing need for efficient policing and fulfil the democratic aspirations of the public. While working on the draft, the committee incorporated the changes that were required in the roles and responsibilities of police officials. It was expected that the changes in the Police Act would give a new vision to the police department and would help to change some of the rudimentary assumptions of the past. In the new Police Act, it has clarified the relationship of the police establishment and the political executives, civil administration and general public. In the chapter IV of the new Police Act, the details of the duties, responsibilities and powers of police are clearly described.

In chapter IV a significant change has been made where power and authority are replaced with roles, functions, duties, social responsibilities and emergency duties.

It describes in details the general duties of the police like promoting and preserving public order, investigating crimes, identifying problems and situations that are likely to result in commission of crimes, reducing opportunities for commission of crimes through preventive patrolling and other prescribes police measures, creating and maintaining a feeling of security in the community, etc. In addition, it states the duties of the police towards the weaker section, poor people and general public. Section 44 of this chapter states that it shall be the duty of every police officer to guide and assist members of public, particularly the poor and indigent, disabled or physically weak and children who are either lost or find themselves helpless on streets or other public places.

The Police Act has defined the following roles and responsibilities of police personnel:

- Upholding the law and order and public peace under all circumstances.
- To protect life, liberty, property and human rights of the public.
- To provide as first responders all possible help required to people in disaster and thereby, if necessary, to provide active assistance to other agencies for relief and rehabilitation.
- To regulate traffic on roads and highways.
- To counsel and resolve conflicts in the community, to protect internal security and therefore prevent crimes or investigate crimes, if any.

Social responsibilities of police include:

- Behaving with the public with due courtesy, particularly, while dealing with women and children.

- Guiding and assisting members of the public, particularly children, women, poor people and physically or mentally challenged individuals, who are either lost or helpless on the streets or other public places for help or protection by self or person or by any organized group.
- Caring of vulnerable sections of society and upholding human rights.
- Arranging for legally permissible shelter to every person in custody and also give information on legal aid schemes enforced by the State.
- Preventing harassment of women and children in public places and public transport.
- Providing required assistance to victims of crime and of road accidents and give prompt medical aid, irrespective of formalities.

The new act lays greater emphasis on empowerment of the police constabulary and outlines the training required for them to adopt to the newer way of working with a community friendly attitude. It has also redefined its administrative procedure and had made the police force more accountable for their conduct and deeds. Under the new act, every police station should have a reception-*cum*-visitors' room, separate toilets for men and women. Separate lock-ups for men and women and a separate Women and Child Protection Desk, which will be staffed by a woman police official. It requires a prominent display of all the information required to be made public under the Right to Information Act. This act includes the Supreme Court guidelines, which orders for a public display of the list of persons arrested and held in lock-ups.

The hierarchy of Kolkata police and their roles and responsibilities are described in brief as under:

Commissioner of Police (CP)

The CP is the in-charge of the overall metropolitan district; he/she enjoys the power of a Class 1 Magistrate; he is also responsible for special reports like of a dacoity, drugging, forgery, etc. In the absence of CP, the additional CP carries out the duties.

The **Joint Commissioner of Police (JCP)** is in-charge of a particular division. The responsibility of the **Deputy Commissioner of Police (DCP)** is to ensure inspection within designated division; to supervise special report cases and in areas of communal riot. The **Assistant**

Commissioner of Police (ACP) within the designated sub-divisions holds discussions with Investigation Officer on cases to be tried by the Session Court. **Inspector of Police** act as the Officer in-Charge (OC) of a particular police station. His/her responsibility is to maintain the Police Station record keeping, delegate work among the **Sub-Inspectors** and **Assistant Sub-Inspectors**. The OC to the Sub-Divisional ACP and has to keep the ACP updated with daily reports. Sub-Inspectors are called **Sergeants** or **Duty Officers** in absence of OC. In Kolkata, there is **female Sub-Inspectors** who has been given additional responsibility to work as **Child Welfare Officers (CWO)**. Some of the key responsibilities of SIs are as under:

- Filing charge sheets in court, as the first investigating officer.
- General Diary (GD) entry.
- Manage all non-cognizable offence, enquires, investigations, and producing cases in the court.
- Manage Sergeant-out-reach programmes and maintaining traffic and law and order.

An ASI (Assistant Sub-Inspector) is in the charge of a police station in absence of the OC. They are not authorized to file charge sheets, but can only investigate on behalf of a SI. ASI will handle all cognizable offences in their jurisdiction. The responsibility of *Constables* are as follows:

- To escort and guard cases.
- Accompany on investigation, call witnesses and effect arrests.
- Maintaining note books.
- Conducting out-reach services.
- To collect definite information, under special orders of OC.

The responsibilities of *Head Constable* are:

- Keeping footpaths clear of obstructions.
- Checking movements of registered old offenders in his area on regular basis.
- Collecting names of nearby hospitals, public institutions, etc. and becoming acquainted with these places.

Functions of the State Police Board:

- To frame policies and guidelines to ensure that the police services are carried out efficiently and effectively. And the same should be made accessible to the public.

- To systematically review and evaluate organizational performance of the police officials using the indicators like public satisfaction, victim satisfaction, etc.
- Of the total 9 members of the Board, there will be 5 members from the fields of academia, law, media and NGO, who shall act as '*Independent Members*' and would facilitate to design and review the system periodically.

On the whole, the new Police Act is a welcome change to make the police force more efficient, service oriented and community friendly. Besides upholding the law and order system, the act also lays emphasis on prevention, emergency support and rehabilitative duties of police personnel to protect life, liberty, property and human rights in the society. To make the functioning efficient, accountable and public friendly, the legislation has focused on making the system free from extraneous influences. It has also emphasized on capacity building needs to bring about a positive change in the attitude of the police personnel. Excluding these positive initiatives, it is wearisome to observe that the Police Act did not make any effort to converge with the Juvenile Justice (Care and Protection) Act, 2000 though it was amended long after the amendment of JJ Act. As a signatory of Convention on the rights of child and the Standard Minimum Rules for the Administration of Juvenile Justice, Government of India amended its JJ Act in 2000 and tried to adhere to the international standards for dealing with children and juvenile offenders. As one of the implementers of Juvenile Justice Administration, JJ Act, 2000, has laid down the specific resolutions and responsibilities of police personnel to uphold and safeguard the rights of children. The Act provides more significance on treatment, care, protection and developmental needs of children by adopting a child friendly approach in the adjudication and disposition of matters for the best interest of the children. Focus has also been given on the voice of children towards identification and solution of their own problems. It has also mandated that a Juvenile Police Unit is to be set up, to deal with child related issues. However, besides the forming of women and child desk in the police station, the new Police Act has not designed any operational protocol to deal with child related cases. Moreover, the new police act did not make any effort to coordinate with other Juvenile Justice Administration to promote child protection. Thus, the new police act again reflects the government's attitude and negligence in upholding child protection issues. It can be assumed that, without any further amendment in the Police Act, police personnel will continue to neglect child related cases because of lack of priority, inadequate resources and lack of capacities to deal with children. Therefore, the role of police personnel in safeguarding child rights will continue to be an uncertain issue in near future.

Perception of Police Towards Street Children and Child Protection

It was reflected from the earlier chapter that a wide gap exists between the law enforcement authorities and the street living families. Overwhelmingly, negative experiences were recorded by the researchers from the children living on the streets against the law enforcement authorities. The families living on the streets did not perceive police as trusted machinery for the protection of their rights. Added to this, the illegitimacy of stay restrains street living families to access the required support of the law enforcement machinery. It was also found that the children living on the streets had developed a strong feeling that they were widely discriminated by the law enforcement authorities due to their poverty and illiteracy. They reported that they cannot participate in the legislative procedures as they cannot understand the procedure and language of communication. As a result, their rights are widely violated and the families living on the streets could not take any steps to safeguard their best interest. There has been a widely held perception among police officials that child protection work is something that sits out beyond the fringe of "*Real Police Work*". Moreover, JJ System does not offer children any measures to take legal steps to safeguard their own interest.

Most of the people including street living people are not aware of the whole gamut of JJ System and none of the authorities other than police are physically accessible to them. Though in Constitution, Indian legislation recognizes the arbitrary detention is prohibited but the illegal detention of street children was observed as a very common phenomenon. Though, because of their socio-environmental reason many children were involved in criminal activities but they have the right to know the ground of arrest and also to get other legal support to protect their own interest. Overall, the current system fails to take into account the individual needs of children, ensure participation and confidence of street living families in the system. Thereby, the system does not offer the opportunity to uphold inherent dignity and equal and inalienable rights of street living children.

- During the interaction with the police officials it was observed that they were over burdened with different acts and its amendments. No official training programmes are organized for these officials to update their knowledge about the recent amendments. It was found that most of the officials were aware of the title of the new JJ Act, but were not inducted on the special features of the same and their individual role in its implementation. It was also surprising to find there were some police officials who were not aware of the latest definition of a child as amended by the Government of India. Thus, most of the measures they take while interacting with children do not match with the standards set in Juvenile Justice (Care and Protection) Act, 2000.
- It was a general perception of the police officials that they were not trained enough to deal with the children. Most of them felt that police cannot earn the trust of children and thus cannot establish proper communication channels with them. Therefore, they were not able to ensure children's participation in the process of interrogation and investigation of the legal matters.
- It was reported by the police officials that they do not have sufficient staff and resources to carry out their desired role with emphasis on the treatment, care, protection and development needs of the children. The police were found to be more concerned about the punitive aspect of crime rather than the protective aspect. Most of the police officials had their own perception about the child friendly approach which was largely predisposed by their own socialization process. Moreover, there were no standard operational guidelines to deal with child in need of care and protection and children in conflict with law.
- Another group of police officials reported that the police stations are not equipped to handle problems of the children. They do not have necessary facilities to take care of them and so the only thing they can do to refer them. But in most of the situations, police officials were not aware of various referral centers and their services available for the needy children. With reference to the production in Child Welfare Committee (CWC) and Juvenile Justice Board (JJB), police were found to be aware of it but they did not have sufficient monetary and human resources to transfer the children to safe places or CWC or JJB.

- Police do acknowledge that street children are one of the most vulnerable sections of the society, but they are forced to carry out frequent eviction drives in order to keep streets clean and free from obstructions. It was also found that the general perception of police about most of the street children was that they are involved in criminal activities. Thus, they take action against these children to keep peace and safety within the community. Police also acknowledged that the street children face lots of difficult situation and abuse, but police cannot intervene unless someone lodges complaint at the police station. It was also seen that the police did not feel the prevention activities were under the purview of police system. According to police, children are not entitled to lodge complaints in the police station unless they are accompanied by an adult person. They strongly felt that they should not encourage children to directly lodge any complaint to police station. As per their opinion, children should be accompanied with adult/s who should support the children to lodge the complaint. According to the police, children take whimsical decision, and thus on the basis of their complaints police cannot take any legal action against the perpetrator.
- Moreover, police have other priorities to deal with and so they cannot provide adequate attention to child related cases.
- Most of the time they categorize cases and conduct investigations according to their own perception. The JJ system does not offer children any measures to take legal steps to safeguard their own interest.
- A few police officials had been identified as *Child Welfare Officer* who is responsible to deal with child related issues.
- It was found that police had no idea as to how to involve a child in the identification of a problem. Sometimes they are apathetic and do not involve themselves in actual investigation beyond what they can see. They act according to their prior experience. Thus, they do not understand the uniqueness of cases and keep applying same technique or approach with every child. As a result, they end up in superficial solutions by providing sentences to the young offender living on the streets, but do not take any long-term action to actually get the child out of the trap or vicious cycle of the situation.

Conclusion

It was felt that an adequate convergence between the JJ Act and the Police Act is needed to create a safe environment for the children within the community. It is essential that the Government does not fail to execute its commitment of promoting child rights and this can be done by clearly stating the roles and responsibilities of police personnel in line with child rights and JJ Act. The role of police personnel in child protection will continue to be a tentative issue unless the roles and responsibilities of the police in the implementation of child related laws are clarified in the Police Act. Special emphasis is required to be given to equip police officials to deal with child protection issues through capacity-building initiatives, adequate resource allocation and appropriate coordination with the other functionaries of Juvenile Justice Administration. Moreover, a standard operating procedure within the police discipline code needs to be developed to create a child friendly approach in the adjudication and disposition of the matters for the best interest of the children.

SECTION 6.7

Opinion of Children Towards Law Enforcement System

To capture the opinion of children regarding the child friendly police system various qualitative research methods were used. Focus group discussions were conducted with the children to understand children's perception about child friendly police system. It is significant to mention that children were not given any orientation on child rights or existing laws to facilitate the FGDs. The ethics of confidentiality were maintained while narrating the case studies. Venn diagram exercises were conducted with the children before the discussion to facilitate them to plot the existing protective instruments available in their surroundings. Children were also facilitated to depict their ideas in the form of colourful circles. Children identified various institutions as machineries available for their protection and ranked them with size as per their scope to access those.

- Local party leaders.
- Youth groups.
- Police stations.
- Police help desk.

- Police mobile van.
- GRP office.
- Courts.
- Formal schools.
- NGOs.
- Child line.
- Kisholaya and Sukanya (CWC).

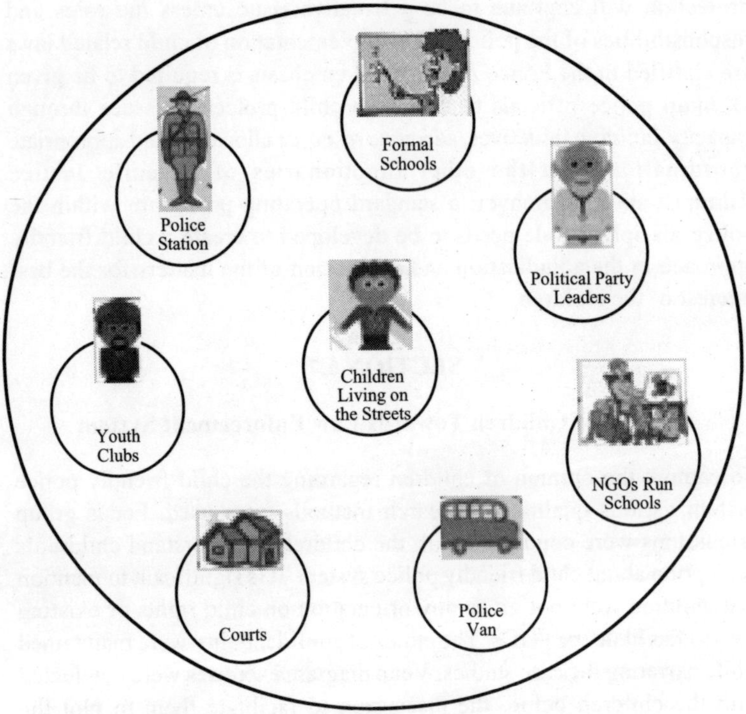

Figure 6.20: Venn Diagram

It is worth mentioning that only 4 children identified CWC as one of their protective instrument. These children had previous experience of interaction with the CWC authorities. But they had less faith on the system as their protective instruments because of the physical distance from their community and lack of clarity on the responsibilities of the CWC in child protection.

Ten children were aware of child line but did not know the help line number. These children were reached out by some Non-Governmental

Organizations and taken part in an awareness programme conducted on child line. They have faith on the system but narrated that PCO personnel do not allow them to make calls from their booths. They also narrated that public telephone booths remain close at night so it is not effectively accessible for children at night. Following are the expectations of children from the law and order machineries and their protective machineries.

Access to Police Station

- Children should have access to police stations.
- Police should honour children as an individual, listen to them and recognize their problems.
- Children should have the permission to lodge complaint at the police station independently with or without the support of any adult member.
- Police should officially acknowledge complaints lodged by children and paraphrase what they have written at their register as most of the children living on the street are illiterate.
- Each police station and police help desk should have a complaint box. Children who are not willing to come in direct contact with the police or afraid to disclose his/her identity can drop his/her complaint.
- Each police station should have a recording system where children will register their case with voice recording system. Police should also write the case in their register and use both during the time of investigation.
- A few children suggested that complaint forms should be attached to that complaint box with instruction to facilitate children to describe their problem. The instructions in the forms should be simple and both in written (Bengali and Hindi languages) and pictorial form so that children as well as illiterate people can also understand.
- Each and every police station, police help desk, mobile police van, schools should attach a board at a visible place where punishment for child abuse will be described.

Children in Conflict with Law

- Jail for the children should be clean and well ventilated.
- Good food should be provided to children in the lock-up.
- Police should not behave too harshly and listen to children so that they get the chance to tell the truth.

- Police should not keep children in same locker with murderer.
- Police should not assault children without any valid reason.
- Police should also trust the child offender and give them enough protection so that they can disclose the name of the actual offender.
- Police should not always suspect street living children as criminals.
- Police keep all the personal belongings of the children under their custody before sending them to jail. Police should return children all the belongings after the trial or the punishment is over.

Investigation

- Police should investigate the case in consultation with the concern child and punish the offender.
- Police should be transparent in investigation and should not take bribe from the offender to settle the case.
- Punishment for police personnel should be there for taking bribe.
- Confidentiality of the child should be maintained as they are not safe on the streets.
- Police should investigate the case in a different way so that the perpetrator cannot identify the child who has lodged the complaint.

Trial System

- Children and their family members should have access to free legal system. Children narrated that people living on the streets should have access to lawyer who will fight cases for the children living in deprived situation. A few children narrated that most of the time, perpetrators are influential persons and children or their family members cannot fight to protect their rights because of their ignorance about legal system.
- Children should not be forced to give testimony in front of adult offenders.
- Judge should listen to the initial recorded complaint of children and then read police documents.
- Children feel threatened and ashamed during the process of interrogation (especially in child rape cases) and in most of the

cases children and their family members do not understand the questions they have been asked.

- Trial process prolong for long time. Therefore, victim child and their family members lose their day long income to participate in the process of trial. So, the families prefer to settle cases outside the judicial system to avoid their economic loss and further complicacy. Thus, children suggested avoiding the process.

Punishment

- Strong punishment should be given to the perpetrator for the offence of child abuse.
- Any officials found to have violated children's rights should be dismissed from the official capacity and should be punished.

Opinion of Parents Towards Law Enforcement Systems

Parents narrated that because of their sheer poverty people who alive on the streets do not get a fair chance from law enforcement authorities because of their illegitimate status in the city. Also, they have inadequate means to access legal services to protect their self-interest in case of violation of their rights. Police should give an ID to all the residents living on the streets to prove their citizenship and legal status.

Access to Police Station — Parents reported that they seek the assistance of police personnel to trace missing or abducted children, lodge complaints against abuse and to negotiate violence within their community. From their experience of dealing with police they highlighted the following expectations from the law enforcement authorities. Parents pleaded that the police should not evacuate street living families without any prior intimation.

Tracing Missing or Abducted Children — List of all rescued individuals with their photographs should be displayed in each police station. Parents reported that they face lots of troubles to trace their missing children. They are to run from one police station to another or in different.

Lodging of Complaints — Parents suggested that families living on the streets should get fair chance from the law and order machineries to lodge complaints in the police station. They emphasized the suggestion of having voice recording system as a tool to lodge FIR. They stated that for any illiterate person lodging written complaints is very difficult.

Thus, police should give equal priority to voice recording system as written complaint as an official process.

The Time of Trial should be Expedited — Parents suggested that the time of trial should be expedited as it hampers the income of the family as well as it harasses children who are the victim of the abuse.

Simplified Trial Process — During trial, lawyers should use simple words so that they can understand and respond to the queries. They also suggested that the lawyers should not embarrass children with offensive questions.

Safe Custody During Trial — Parents suggested a safe custody for their children during the trial process as they face lots of threats from the accused person while they are on the streets.

Free Legal Aid — Parents recommended access to free legal aid lawyers who can help the children and their families to understand legal procedures and can fight for their rights.

Equal and Fair System for the Street Living Families — Parents depicted that police should not be biased during settling the case. Employers exploit children economically and physically. Police should take up those cases and help them to negotiate without any prejudice.

Besides, parents raised the Following issues to avoid harassment:

- ★ Police should not detain children without any valid reason.
- ★ Police should not perceive all the street living children as criminal and give due respect to the street living families.
- ★ Police should explain the reason to the parents before arresting the child.
- ★ Police should not take bribe to release children from custody.
- ★ Moreover, parents appealed that police should listen to children and their family members and treat them with respect.
- ★ Police should not physically assault children without any concrete evidence of crime.
- ★ Parents admitted that many a time children commit offence but they are lured by adults. Thus, police should also arrest the adult offenders who has lured the child to commit the offence.

Conclusion

All the children and their parents narrated that system of law and order machineries should be simple and transparent so that children as well as illiterate people can keep faith on the system, access them to protect their own rights. Children's expectations from the law and order machineries were compiled according to different stages of intervention.

7

SOCIAL WORK PRACTICE WITH STREET CHILDREN *vis-à-vis* CHILD ABUSE

The practice of social work has gone through major changes because of various factors like demographic and political changes, social and policy level transformations, and the then, again, the recent economic crisis in the world. Hence, in order to be "**up to speed**" as a professional, various social work theories and approaches have been evolved to deal with seasonal cycles of social as well as individual problems. Here, we will discuss briefly about the evolution of social work, its definitions, broad objectives and various pertinent approaches of social work practice. In the context of the present study, the researchers used various social work theories to understand the different contributory factors of child abuse and its effect on the children living on the streets with their families. An attempt has been made here to have brief descriptions of the conceptual paradigm of social work and the pertinent way it can address the problems of child abuse along with some specific role of social worker at different levels.

Evolution of Social Work Approaches and Its Practices

Western World

The modern occupation of social work emerged from religious, church sponsored charitable enterprise in an age when private voluntary charity and statutory poor law represented in their shared conception of the 'deserving' and the 'undeserving' poor a profound ideological and institutional division. The division centered on the issue of class relations and the proper degree of state intervention in society. The question of poverty focused and symbolized issues about class relations in Victorian society in such a vivid and powerful way that the subject has continued to exercise a high degree of fascination and partisanship for scholars.

The Church of England under political and social attack and threatened with the possibility of disestablishment experienced a profound religious revival which issued in an attempt to come to grips with the new urban-industrial society. The moral welfare and settlement movements were important elements of the response to urban poverty. Equally the Charity Organization Society attempted to cope with the breakdown of traditional communal relations between classes and end the consequent abuse of the disorganized charitable system through systematic and scientific casework methods. Also, it aimed to pre-empt the necessity for the expansion of state charity beyond its limited role under the poor law.

Those who were employed to operate the poor law were minor functionaries working to a bureaucratic routine and recruited mainly from elements of the working class itself. The ethos of the poor law and the attitudes of its servants militated against the adoption of professionalism as an ideology and occupational practice. Such influence as professionalism had in the poor law — and it was always limited — was carried there by middle-class men and women such as doctors and nurses, and much later by social workers. At the level of political process, professionals and intellectuals played a growing part in pressing for the reform of the service.

It was chiefly from among middle-class women seeking to create occupational opportunities that the impetus came for the adoption of professionalism as a form of occupational development and control in social work, nursing and teaching. These women shared the ideology of professionalism with the men of their own class, such as doctors and lawyers. They adapted it and combined it with the caring ideology of familialism which conventionally defined the role of woman in society. Professionalism in social work was strengthened by the influence of psychiatric theory with its scientific roots which issued in the creation of a new social work occupation, psychiatric social work, in the late 1920s.

There was a separation in the early twentieth century of social administration from social work in dealing with the problem of poverty. The **neo-liberal** [Neoliberalism is a political philosophy whose advocates support economic liberalizations, free trade and open markets, privatization, deregulation, and enhancing the role of the private sector in modern society] and **Fabian Socialist Approach** [The Fabian strategy is a military strategy where pitched battles and frontal assaults are avoided in favour of wearing down an opponent through a war of attrition and indirection. While avoiding decisive battles, the side employing this strategy harasses its enemy through skirmishes to cause attrition, disrupt supply and affect morale. Employment of this strategy implies that the side adopting this strategy believes time is on its side, but it may also be adopted when no feasible alternative strategy can be devised] was through state action on the basis of the insurance principle and the management of unemployment *via* employment exchanges. Social work was regarded by the proponents of such policies as patronizing and irrelevant. Yet, the disruption of war — particularly to family life — and the weakening of the deterrent principle of the poor law and the moderation of its practices by the penetration of middle-class professionals, especially women, led to a convergence during the inter-war years between the practices of voluntary agencies and state agencies.

The repeal of the poor law in 1948 and the takeover of its responsibilities by the National Health Service and the local authorities created the opportunity for the employment of social workers by the local authorities, particularly in the new occupation of child care. The disappearance of the poor law removed the long-standing division which had blocked the integration of social work into the state welfare system.

The struggle for professional unification among the several social work occupations had begun between the wars, but in the post-war period the movement towards an integrated managerial structure of state welfare services was deeply influenced by the professional interests of social workers. Managerial integration could reduce functional divisions among the social work occupations and lead to professional unification. There was a thrust towards a single professional association controlling the process of recruitment, entry and educational qualification.

Autonomous professionalism was never a serious possibility for social workers, partly because of the drive towards state managerialism, but also because of limited market opportunities. What in fact emerged was a hybrid form of organization for social services which was reflected in the Seebohm report [*The Seebohm report of 1968 is what changed the delivery of welfare services into social services. It resulted in the combination of children, elderly and mental welfare departments into one social service. This was a bid to cut costs and save on resources.*] and incorporated in the reform of local government in 1974. This form we have called bureau-professionalism. In practice Scotland achieved such a unified structure for social work; in England the probation service bulked both at incorporation within the administrative structure of the social services and at the proposed unified professional association of social workers.

Indian Scenario

Historically, social work in India is as old as the Indian society. In brief, the evolution and historical backdrop of social work in India could be glanced through the following periods:

1. Ancient and Medieval Period

In ancient and medieval India, there was a widespread tradition of giving alms and donations to the needy people. The responsibility towards community welfare was shared by the Government and the individual members of the community. Welfare work was regarded as an integral part of religion. Besides the joint family system and caste organizations also used to provide help and assistance to the needy and disabled persons. During the Ashoka's reign there were many charitable institutions for the purpose of helping the poor and disabled. Ashoka did many works of public utility. He opened separate hospitals for men and animals. He got built national highways, rest houses and wells for the welfare of common people. Similarly, during the Gupta period there were village republics in the form of village panchayats. In addition to village administration, village panchayats were also responsible for the protection of and welfare of weakers and minors. The Gupta Kings did many works for the good and welfare of the people, made arrangements for irrigation and opened hospitals providing free medical facilities to the people. There were many charitable institutions maintained by the state. During Vardhana empire the state used to operate many activities relating to social welfare. It is said that Harsha after every five years donated all his wealth to the monks, orphans and poors.

During the period of Parmars, many works of public utility were undertaken. King Bhoja built many temples in his kingdom and freely donated money for such purpose. In the same way during the Rajput era, village administration was looked after by village institutions. The village assemblies contributed to the safety and security of the people. Arrangements regarding education, hospitals and sanitation were made by gram panchayats.

During Muslim period, India witnessed the spread of Islam. But welfare activities remained as an integral part of religion. Many welfare activities were undertaken during the reign of Sher Shah. He introduced effective reforms in the system of communication and built roads and Sarais at frequent places. Besides many charitable institutions were established. Charity was given to the needy people. Sher Shah personally took interest in the problems of cultivators and helped weak, disabled and destitute persons. Thereafter, welfare measures were again organized during the rule of Akbar. Akbar stopped the evil practice of *sati* and child marriage and encouraged widow remarriages. The practice of enslaving the war prisoners was also stopped.

2. Social Work during the British Period

During the British period, social work evolved in the form of social reform movements. In the beginning of 19th century, the condition of India became deplorable. Native rulers and Nawabs established their small kingdoms that always used to fight with each other. After the battle of Plassee, East India Company established its hold on the major portions of India. For commercial gain, the company established peace in its occupied areas and could not pay attention towards the well-being of vanquished people. Indian society became orthodox and custom bound. People had immense honour towards *Shastras* and *Karma Kandas*. Every kind of custom received sanction under the cover of religion. The custom of *sati*, dedication of women to temples, untouchability and casteism and other obnoxious customs widely prevalent. Consequently, many reform movements came to limelight.

Reform Movements

Brahmo Samaj

The movement was started against the evil customs and practices of Indian society. It is often called the Protestant movement of Hindu religion. It raised public opinion against the practice of sati and prohibition of widow remarriage.

Arya Samaj

In the middle of the nineteen century, Swami Dayananda Saraswati gave again self-reliance and Kshatriya grace to Hindus. He removed the different faiths and religions and propagated Vedic religion. He opposed to idol worship and caste distinction at birth.

Ram Krishna Mission

Ram Krishna Paramhansa preached his precepts through examples in his household talk. He preached spiritual and practicable matter like a saint. According to Ram Krishna, the mystery of religion and its essence is experience of God. When there is experience of God, all discussions of *Shastras*, *Karma Kanda*, and precepts are extinguished.

3. Social Work after Independence

After Independence, a new orientation has evolved in the field of social work. The sources of welfare activities are inherent in the Constitution. It is only on the ideals of the Constitution that the Government has adopted a social welfare programme. Schemes are being implemented for the development of welfare programmes and social services. Many acts relating to marriage and family have been passed. We can discuss these measures under the following headings:

(a) *Social Legislations*

In order to encourage social reforms, many Acts have been enacted by the Parliament. The Special Marriage Act, 1954 has been passed for the interest of those persons who solemnize marriage not as a religious sacrament, but in civil court. That is why this Act is also known as the Civil Marriage Act. The Act has prescribed minimum age for marriage.

In 1955, another Act known as Hindu Marriage Act was passed. Except the member of Muslim Community, this Act applies to all other people. The Act prescribes a definite age for valid marriage — monogamy, guardianship of mother and provision to be for divorce. Thereafter, the Dowry Prohibition Act, 1961 was passed. According to this Act, if a person gives and takes dowry, then he is liable to be punished. Similarly, for the purpose of enforcing Article 15 of the Constitution, the Central Government passed the Untouchability Offences Act, 1955. The Act was amended in 1976. The Act prescribes punishment for the practice of untouchability in any form of manner.

(b) *Social Welfare*

After Independence, there has been immense development and intensification of social welfare activities (Singh,1982). These activities promote the welfare of the people by securing and protecting a social order in which justice and equality shall be available to every citizen. Social welfare services have sought to serve the development and rehabilitation needs of the weaker sections of society especially the physically and socially handicapped, and women and children from the vulnerable sections of the community in rural and tribal and urban slums.

(c) *Establishment of Central Social Welfare Board*

The Central Social Welfare Board (CSWB) was set in 1953 to promote and accelerate voluntary action, throughout the country. Among its main activities are: survey of the needs of social welfare organizations, evaluation of their programmes and co-ordination of assistance and render assistance to voluntary welfare agencies.

(d) *Social Education*

During recent years, special emphasis has been given to social education and women's education. The changing socio-economic scenario in the country demands development of human resources. The programme of social education has been geared to meet these new demands of the society as well as of individuals. Similarly, numbers of steps have been taken to stimulate the education of girls and women.

> Social work is a recent branch of knowledge which deals with the scientific solution and treatment of the psycho-social problems (Fink, 1955). Its main aim is to increase human happiness in general. Therefore, it is oriented toward the attainment of two ends, first, the creation of those conditions which help to make a more satisfying way of life possible, and second, the development within the individual and the community as well of capacities which help to live that life more adequately and creatively.

Characteristics of Social Work

- ★ *Professional Service* — In its present form, social work is a professional service which assists individuals, groups and communities. On the one hand it attempts to help the individuals in the social milieu and on the other hand it removes the barriers which obstruct people from achieving the best which they are capable.
- ★ *Based on Scientific Knowledge* — Social work is based on scientific knowledge and technical skill. It has its own methodology which distinguishes it from other types of welfare activities.

- *Humanitarian Philosophy* — Social work derives its inspiration from the humanitarian philosophy. It seeks happiness and prosperity for the individuals, groups and community.
- *Solution of Psycho-social Problems* — Social work aims to solve the psycho-social obstacles which prevent the effective functioning of groups, community and society.

Philosophy of Social Work

- Each individual, by the very fact of his existence is of worth.
- To respect individual, group and community differences at the same time as seeking to harmonize them with common welfare.
- To recognize the worth of the individual human being, regardless of the circumstances — status, race, religion, politics or behaviour; and to foster the growth of human dignity and self-respect.
- Human suffering is undesirable and should be prevented or at least alleviated whenever possible.
- All human behaviour are the result of interaction between the biological organism and its environment.
- Social work rejects the doctrines of *laissez-faire* and survival of the fittest.
- There are important differences between individuals and they must be recognized and allowed for.
- The rich and/or powerful is not necessarily fit while the poor and/or weak are not necessarily unfit.
- A major responsibility for the welfare of its members rests with the community.
- Public assistance should be based on the concept of need.
- Each individual has responsibility towards self, family and community.

Values and Ethics of Social Work

- Commitment to the primary importance of the individual in the society.
- Respect for confidentiality of relationship with clients.
- Commitment to social change to meet socially recognized needs.
- Willingness to transmit knowledge and skills to others.
- Respect and appreciation for individual and group differences.

- ★ Willingness to keep personal feelings and needs, separate from professional relationship.
- ★ Commitment to developing clients' ability to help themselves.
- ★ Willingness to persist in efforts on behalf of the clients' despite frustration.
- ★ Commitment to social justice and economic, physical and mental well-being of all in society.
- ★ Commitment to a high standard of personal and professional conduct.

Role of a Social Worker

Enabler — enabling is the process through which the social worker make a meaningful effort to make adjustment between the available resources and the clients' need of the hour or the future.

Advocate — Social workers should sensitize, inform and make the client aware. Social workers communicate on behalf of the clients and help to reach out for the organize people, and sensitize the government on behalf of the community.

Broker — The social worker will make an effort to render maximum services with minimum cost.

Activist — Those who are actively involved in the war for change and stabilization in the society.

Skills of a Social Worker

- *Skills in Human Relations* — Social worker should be competent in building rapport and forming relationship. Social work graduates are identified because of their special skills in building relationships.
- *Interviewing* — Training is given in the way of interviewing and assimilating the findings after the interview.
- *Observation* — Getting a perception by seeing and thinking. To understand the facts and make an idea about the situational problem.
- *Listening* — In the client-worker relationship the worker needs to be patient listener and should give space to the person who is speaking. Good listener tries to find depth of the words which he is listening and then understanding.
- *Communication* — Good skills in articulation are a necessary prerequisite in any profession, more so in social work where the professionals mainly deal with human beings.

- *Analyzing* — Qualitative and quantitative analysis of data, social events, social situations and human behaviour is very necessary.

In Summary, the main features of social work as pointed out (P. Seed, 1989) are:

- It is a helping activity.
- It is a social activity established for the benefit of community and not for profit motives.
- It is a liaison activity which the disadvantaged individuals or groups may tap community resources.

So, far as India is concerned, social work has not yet acquired a professional status and is considered an activity to help economically dependent persons. The aim of social work, as generally understood, is to remove social injustice, to relieve distress, to prevent suffering and to assist the weaker members of society to rehabilitate themselves and their families and in short, fight the five giants evils of (1) physical want, (2) distress, (3) ignorance, (4) squalor, and (5) idleness. Social work is a dynamic activity undertaken by public or private efforts in the implementation of social policy, with a view to raise the standard of living and to bring about social, economic, political and cultural well-being of the individual, family and the group within a society irrespective of social development.

Conventional Social Work Approaches in Relation to Child Protection

The concept of a state sanctioned child welfare system dates back to **Plato's Republic (380 BC)**. Plato theorized that the interests of the child could be served by snatching children from the care of their parents and placing them under State custody. The current provincial or State Government's child protection legislations also empower the government department or agency to provide services and to intervene in families where child abuse or other problems are suspected. The agency that manages these services has various names in different provinces and states, e.g., department of children's services, children's aid and department of child and family services. There is some consistency in the nature of laws, though the application of the laws varies across the country.

Broadly, the present child welfare services designed to provide an array of prevention and intervention services to children and families, particularly children who have been or are at risk of abuse or neglect; children with special medical or mental health needs; delinquent children; and children who do not have adult caregivers. This '**system**' has been dubbed by an amalgamation of programmes with efforts to prevent out-of-home placements, reunify families, and provide long-term care and solutions to families in need. Regardless of how it is characterized, the child welfare system is designed to support families and to protect children from harm.

All the child protection related legislations enacted before 1989, were predominantly designed to provide services both to the neglected and delinquent children through institutional and community-based services. From the inception of child protection services the role of social workers were mainly to use the empirically derived interventions to help child victims and their families to achieve their optimum level of psycho-social functioning, including: psychological, emotional, behavioural, educational, developmental and relational functioning. Predominantly, different theoretical and practical approaches focusing on individuals were used to help the child victims and his/her family to restore their normal functioning. Social workers in this field assess children's needs and offer assistance to improve their situation. In assessing needs different social theories like Psycho-dynamic, Analytic, Behavioural and Cognitive theories are used to analyze specific psychological problems to be worked on and accordingly, rehabilitation programmes are designed. Allied agencies and services are coordinated to assist the child or family. These services include assistance to single parents in finding day care, arrange adoptions, or help find foster homes for neglected, abandoned, or abused children. The social workers also provide specialized services in dealing with specially abled children, addiction, adoption, homelessness, domestic violence, or foster care. In dealing with these problems social workers mainly practice case work and group work methods with children, his/her family and with children's groups.

Thus, in conventional child protection services, child centric services are provided to help the alienated children to come out with their own problems and to readjust in the mainstreamed society. As mentioned before, in these individual oriented approaches social work theories are used to manage contingencies which affect the relationship between the children and the social consequences. However, it overlooks the social, economic and structural aspects that have attributed problems within the children and his or her family.

Emerging Social Work Approaches in Child Protection

In 1948, the United Nations had addressed child abuse as human rights issue, adding a section specifically on children in the Universal Declaration of Human Rights. The Convention on the Rights of the Child adopted in 1989 further provided a universal set of child protection standards to be adhered to by all countries to protect children and child offenders from being abused. For the first time in the history, children were recognized not as a passive recipient of benefits but as the subject or holder of their rights. Children were acknowledged as individuals and as members of a family and a community, with rights and responsibilities appropriate to his or her age and stage of development. Focus was given on participation of children towards identification and solution of their own problems. It has also empowered children to raise their voice in case of violation of their basic rights. It also encourages children to express their opinion freely and to have that opinion taken into account in any matters or procedure affecting them (Sears, 2001). This treaty has a profound impact on the child related laws and child protection services throughout the world. Moreover, child participation is a very new concept introduced in child protection and its approaches are still emerging. Thus, the role of social workers in the area of child participation and protection is evolving as a field of practice. Different Governmental and Non-Governmental agencies are coming up with their own child protection policies and designing behavioural protocols for their organizations to adhere to the child protection standards. However, involvement and recognition of children in decision-making is still tentative and subjective.

Against this backdrop, the researchers feel that a combination of radical approach and individual centric approaches are required to ensure child protection standards. Still, child abuse is dealt as a private matter instead considering this as a social or public issue. Macro-societal structures, cultural codes, social position, influences of social policies, have direct relationship of children both within and between families, groups, organizations and society. It also determines the social position of children. Thus, the structural analysis of child abuse, analysis of social controls and functions of children within different settings have predominant role in child protection services (West, 2007).

Most importantly, in understanding child abuse and child participation, adults' sharing and control of power, decision-making and information sharing with children are important areas of understanding. Thus, in the present context of child protection, the social worker has an important role in redrawing the world of adult through empowerment and organizational advocacy, so that the children are given an opportunity to be heard (Finkelhor, 2004). Thus, the radical social work approaches are required to enable children to use sources of power according to their stages of development to achieve satisfaction of human needs that they are entitled to. It entails adults' listing and making space for children so that children are encouraged to develop and refine their competencies and put democratic values into practice.

In the context of India, the implementation of child protection programmes suffer from poor implementation, lack of professional approach, less political commitment and limited resources. Moreover, the problem of child abuse among the children of families living on the streets is a social problem. The social, economic and structural aspects of these families are the main attributors of the problem of child abuse. Thus, the concern of child protection programmes can not only be dealt with the children, his/her families, small groups or sub-groups within which these families operate (Hollway, 2008). Therefore, a structural change through policy level modifications is required to ensure basic securities and amenities for families living on the streets to ensure a safe environment for their children. On the other hand, child centric support will be required to restore the normal functioning of alienated children. Thus, integrated approaches of social work are required to reduce vulnerabilities of children, provide justice, and ensure participation to reintegrate child victims into the mainstreamed society.

At an ideological level, we believe that structural factors have close correlation with child abuse, neglect and deviant behaviours of children. Thus, the social worker can play an important role in assessing the social transactions of children using the theory of system approach to human behaviour. System approach to human behaviour makes two general substantive assumptions (Giaretto, 1981):

1. The state or condition of a system, at any one point in time is a function of the interaction between it and the environment in which it operates.
2. Change and conflict are always evident in a system. Individuals both influence their environment and are influenced by them. Process of mutual influence generates change and development (Mrazek, 1983).

Based on this theory, we can analyze family structures and the environment within which street families operate. Socio-economic profile of street families, transactions of street children within their families, peer groups and within larger community, education system and legal system can also be assessed to understand their influence on behaviour of children. To understand various dimensions of child abuse and neglect, overlapping and mutually reinforcing dimensions of injustice, power relationships, discriminative factors can also be analyzed. The social worker can use his/her professional skills in assessing the environmental factors of child abuse and its effects on children. In doing this, we have used our critical thinking skills within the context of professional standards and use our knowledge, analytical abilities and values to assess individual, interpersonal, and inter-organizational needs within primary institutions, groups, organizations, and communities of street living families (Rafferty, 1991).

In the case of a partial disclosure, where the child's word is accepted as *prima facie* evidence of abuse, a social worker, together with the police, will initiate and pursue the investigation of what has happened, the family circumstances and relationships surrounding the child, and questions of appropriate immediate protection. This is likely to include the setting up of a *disclosure interview*, which is most appropriately conducted conjointly by a trained social worker and police officer. It may also be at this time that the first and crucial contact will be made with the child's care-givers or mother. The social worker may accompany the child to the medical examination. At the subsequent case conference an assessment of the safety of children in the family, as well as a plan for protection and therapy, will rely to a considerable extent on information gained by the social worker, under the same well-established procedure accepted for physical child abuse (Jones, 2001). The task of child protection which falls on the social worker, particularly when accompanied by statutory requirements, is a very complex one, raising the question of the feasibility of combining a legal and therapeutic role. If the child's safety is deemed to require statutory support, the family and social worker enter into a required relationship, the existence of which is not in the power of either party, but rather in the hands of the court, or of the child abuse legislation. Although viewing the social worker's position in this light may seem to render her or him powerless, it can become a liberating context. It enables the social worker to be freed from becoming the target for potential attack or rejection by the family, and allows the social worker to join with the family in working towards a common goal, namely, the dissolution of their required relationship. The social worker's task becomes redefined as seeking to enable the family to convince society that the children's needs are now being adequately met within the family and no longer require outside surveillance. The social worker thus temporarily becomes part of the therapeutic system.

It is clear from all that has been said that social workers who are key workers in this field require support, supervision and recognition from within their own hierarchy of the heavy burden which child sexual abuse cases impose (Glaser and Frosh, 1988).

Against this background, more specifically, the role of social worker can be categorized under two broad heads:

Micro-level

Community-based Services to Assist Children to Deal with their 'Life Stressors' and Maladjustment — Because of the exposures of metro-cities, children living on the streets develop high level of aspirations that lead to frustrations and internal conflicts because of their limited capacities and access to resources. These problems arise among children because of their maladjustment between their own environment and their needs, capacities, rights and aspirations. Social workers can use this knowledge of social psychology to capture the understanding children about their own needs, rights and perceptions about their own environment. As a method of practice social workers can use different qualitative tools to ensure active participation of the street living families and their children in the assessment of their 'life stressors' that includes their perception about their own family settings, environment, educational system, work environment and legal and administrative system. Thus, social workers can play a important role in designing community based services to assist children to deal with their life and frustrations.

Facilitating Children to Identify Perpetrators within their Community — Social workers can facilitate children to capture children's perception about different types of abuse they experience within different settings and how they perceive different perpetrators. Social workers can also facilitate children to coordinate with different allied system like NGOs and police stations. Thus, they can use their skills of participatory tools to identify and manage the problems of children within community settings through an active coordination with supportive and legal system.

Facilitating Families to Move from Un-authorized Areas — The survival mechanisms of families and the children can be assessed using the broad conceptual framework of Social Darwinism. Through this study, the researchers tried to analyze different underlying and largely irresistible forces acting within the communities of street families that drives them through an evolutionary process. These social evolution processes create natural conflicts within their own groups. Consequently, the 'best adapted' families or individuals survive these conflicts and design their own psycho-social coping mechanism to make them fit within their environment. Globalization has helped raise the standard of living for many people world-wide. Conversely, it has driven many deeper into poverty. The democratization of technological option is a primary characteristic of globalization which has created tension among the people who have limited skills and resources. Moreover, it has created unemployment and shrinkage of economic opportunities for the poor, living in the deprived and rural areas of India. These factors have further pushed these poor families from the socially and culturally homogenous community to a complicated and heterogeneous community with less social support. The families settled on streets suffer from illegitimate status, constant threat of eviction and lack of all the basic social and legal support system. The 'best adapted' families who could win the struggle move from unauthorized to authorized settlements and access basic amenities of life. The families who stay back on the streets suffer from internal as well as external conflicts resulted in psycho-social problems within the family and attribute to neglect and exploitations towards their own children. On the other hand children also adopt different coping mechanisms and survival tricks to adapt themselves within the much complicated system. Children became prone to adopt deviant survival avenues to make them fit within the environment. Social workers can play an active role in assessing positive factors of the evolutionary process and help other families to move from unauthorized areas to authorized slums through reinforcing the positive factors active within their community.

Identification and Reinforcement of Self-protection Mechanism of Street Community — Building on the idea of self-organizing and self-sustaining autopoetic system found preliminary in biology and cybernetics, the social worker can strive to capture the self-organizing and self-sustaining structures evolves within the street living families and among their children. Families try to settle in clusters, develop their own social support systems and affiliate themselves with the powerful political party members to sustain themselves within the unauthorized areas of the cities. On the other hand children affiliate themselves with the powerful gangs which are also supported by political party members.

The role of social worker should be to amplify the positive determinants of self-organizing structures to switch them in a desired direction.

Management of Abused and Traumatized Children — Social workers can use the empirically derived interventions to help child victims and their families to achieve their optimum level of psychosocial functioning including — psychological, emotional, behavioural, educational, developmental, and relational. Social workers can use different theoretical and practical approaches based on psycho dynamic, analytic, behavioural and cognitive theories to restore the normal functioning of alienated children and his/her family.

Facilitate Children to Access Legal Support — Social workers can also play an important role to facilitate children to access legal aid and other legal support systems. They can use their professional skills to ensure children's active involvement during lodging complaints in police stations, investigations, trials, and adjudication to protect their best interest.

Macro-level

- ★ It is well recognized that families living on the streets have multiple needs. Thus, a combination of health, education, livelihood and protection schemes can be used uplifting the quality of life for families living on the streets. In this sphere, a social worker can play an active role within the democratic as well as bureaucratic systems to facilitate integrated policy designing process for the families living on the streets through using specialized knowledge and skills of social work.
- ★ While assessing the factors of child abuse, the researcher felt that social workers need to emphasize on a changed environment focused on transaction of social environment. Thus, social workers can use their professional ability to analyze the impact of international and national level social policies, social welfare legislations as well as implementation of the policies for the children of families living on the streets. In doing this, the social worker can assess policies and schemes of Government of India, Juvenile Justice Systems and can assess the interaction of children and their family with law and order machineries. Thus, the social worker can play an active role in designing need-based policies to promote structural change at macro-level. They can also play an important role in ensuring active partnership of street living families based on '*mutuality and*

reciprocity' in designing need based policies to address their felt needs.

- ★ The role of social worker can also be envisaged for the customization of education and legal systems to fulfil the capacity building and protection needs of the children of the street living families. Thus, they can also work with the education system to design needs driven education curriculum and system for the children with different needs.
- ★ Overall, the researchers tried to respect the voice of children through their active participation in their own situational analysis, abuse identification and in designing child friendly police systems and processes. Hence, the social workers can be envisaged with the juvenile justice system to customize the protection system for the children.
- ★ Designing and institutionalizing child protection policies within different governmental and non-governmental system can be another important role of social workers. They must play an active role in designing recruitment procedure for the staff who will be directly dealing with children, defining behavioural protocols for the staff and designing the monitoring plan for the proper adherence of child protection policies.
- ★ Punishment of offenders involved in child abuse is also an area of concern. The present Juvenile Justice Act does not ensure the punishment of adult offenders. Thus, social workers can play a pivotal role in designing effective coordination between Juvenile Justice System and Criminal Courts to ensure proper punishment of offenders. They can also facilitate the administration to design effective database to record details pedophilic cases through an effective coordination between Police and Juvenile System so that these people can be retained to directly work with children.

The role of social workers has broadened over the last few decades throughout the world. Still, in India, social work has not yet acquired a professional status. However, with changing socio-economic situation, globalization and with the enhancement of activities of international charities in India, scope and field of social work is also expanding. Simultaneously, the roles of social workers are also broadening with the increasing demand for such services in the country. A number of social work institutes have come up in India over the last few decades to meet the demand of professional social workers. However, the number of trained professionals is less than the demand. Therefore, people from different fields and expertise are also joining the sector and performing the expected role of the professional social worker. Understanding and practice of social work has been gone through a process of infusion. The researchers feel that all the professionals expected to perform the role of social workers should be educated with the philosophy and broad conceptual framework of social work to enrich the developmental sectors of the country. As the role of social work in the area of child participation is still an emerging issue, more social work theories and practices need to be devised to build up the skills of social workers to ensure children's participation in the area of child protection.

8

MAJOR FINDINGS AND SUGGESTIONS

The faster growth in urbanization and industrialization process in India would accelerate the process of migration from rural to urban areas. Consequently, that would result in faster growth of families living on the streets in urban cities. It is unfortunate that in this phase of upward growth of urban population, the government has not yet come up with a comprehensive strategy to absorb the steady inflation of poor families in urban pockets. Thus, it is implied that vulnerability of children living on the streets would continue to be a significant issue in the near future unless an integrated strategy is adopted.

The Government of India vowed to ensure rights to all children without discrimination and recognizes the right to minimum standards of living and a favourable environment for the physical, mental, spiritual, moral and social development. Though the primary responsibility of the children lies with the parents to provide adequate support for holistic development but still the State has the responsibility to oversee and ensure that such duties by the parents are fulfilled. But, unfortunately, our society is unable to reciprocate uniform level of care and protection to its every young citizen. It was observed during the study that children who are living in poverty are excluded from their basic rights to survival, protection, care and opportunities to develop, and participate in the affairs of mainstream society. Furthermore, the situation of children living on streets gets worse by illegitimacy of stay, miserable environmental conditions and lack of protection mechanism. Children are exposed to abuse and exploitations within their families, peer groups and within their immediate community. A wide gap is perceptible between the law enforcement authorities and street living families because of unauthorized status of settlements, lack of coordination among the agencies and lack of understanding of the poor families about their own rights. Therefore, children adopt different survival tricks to deal with their '***life stressors***' and expose themselves to further vulnerabilities.

To get a very clear scenario of the phenomenon, 200 children of both genders; of the age group 12-16 years, who lived on the streets, were purposively selected from 5 administrative zones of Kolkata. The socio-economic and legal status of these children was analyzed to understand various risk factors of children living on the streets with families. Among the whole gamut of Juvenile Justice System, interface between police and street living families were analyzed to identify the gaps in the Juvenile Justice Administration. Further, the newly amended Police Act was also reviewed to understand the newly framed role of police with special reference to Juvenile Justice (Care and Protection Act), 2000. Moreover, the outlook of children and their parents was also assessed to voice their opinion for a child friendly police system and its procedure.

The Major Findings of the Study

- The families belonging to the same caste refer to stay together in a cluster.
- Of the total 200 children living on the street, 40 per cent migrated from various parts of the West Bengal; 37.5 per cent migrated from Bihar and remaining 22.5 per cent came from Jharkhand, the neighbouring State of West Bengal.
- The most common push factor among the migrant families was the lack of livelihood options in their native villages.
- Out of the total 200 children living on the street, 30 per cent and 48 per cent had migrated more than 20 and 10 years before respectively. Similarly, another 23 per cent families were found to have migrated within last five years to search for employment in Kolkata.
- Because of illegitimacy of stay, families cannot provide minimum shelter to their children and are forced to stay in open spaces without any permanent or temporary shelter and denied of basic amenities of life.
- Male members of the families are commonly engaged in low wage sectors like labours, rickshaw pullers, artisans, loaders, hawkers and rag pickers, whereas the females generally worked as domestic helps, vegetable sellers, unskilled labourers, rag pickers and beggars. It was identified that 57 per cent male and 88 per cent female earning members of the family received pay below the minimum wages fixed by the government.

- More than 45 per cent children attended one type of schooling system as parents felt it to be safe to send their younger children to school instead of letting them to roam and play on the streets.
- It was found that children were much sensitive towards the emotional abuse as over 98 per cent children recalled the occurrence of the same in the recent past. Girls had identified sexual abuse as the most devastating forms of abuse in the streets because of the unsafe and exposed environment. Whereas, there were more than 85 per cent of the boys, who had reported of harassment by the legal and administrative authorities as their key problems.
- Children perceived unknown people passing on the streets as the most common abusers, while they lived on the streets. Besides, they also perceived threat from the government authorities like police, municipal corporation officials, and traffic controllers. Children also identified local youth, political party members, employers and in few cases the parents themselves as the perpetrators of child abuse.
- Families cannot meet daily requirements due to their irregular earnings and hence, they are forced to borrow money from money-lenders or from employers to meet their daily needs as well as for dealing with emergencies. The idea revealed that about 90 per cent of the families had to take loans for each hospitalization episode and this pushed them into a vicious and ominous cycle of poverty and disease.
- Families were found to be without the basic entitlements. There were more than 88 per cent families who did not possess voter identification card. Among the respondent, only 5 per cent of the families had the BPL (Below Poverty Line) cards. Thus, over 95 per cent of the families were denied of facilities meant for the people living below the poverty line.
- It was found that only 33 per cent children were enrolled in the formal education system. Of the total children respondents, there were 12 per cent who never got enrolled in the formal schools, whereas 55 per cent children were the drop outs. It was also interesting to observe that the participation of girls in the formal education system was comparatively higher than the boys.
- Violence against children occurs in different settings were within family, at schools, at work and in the community.

- There were 23 per cent girls identified some adults within their community who were exhibitionist.
- Sixty three per cent of boys disclosed that their peer group members had faced sexual abuse. Most common form of abuse was masturbation, oral and anal sex.
- It was observed that children do various forms of deviant behaviours to cope and adjust with the street environment. Some of the practices adopted by these children were getting involved in gang culture, abusing and intoxicating substances, indulged in deviant sexual practices for survival, watching of pornographic films, gambling and living in a world of fantasies.
- Common perpetrators of abuse were the vendors (21%), leader among street children (24%) and other influential people (12%) in the community.
- Children reported that in most of the cases the perpetrators of sexual abuse were the known adults.
- Out of the total 100 girls, 74 per cent replied that they do not have any faith on the adult members of their surrounding community.
- Sexual abuse against street living boys was also familiar phenomenon. About 11 per cent of girls disclosed incidences of sexual abuse by known adults living in their locality. Another 58 per cent girls reported that they were aware of such abuse but still it did not happen to them.
- The incidence of physical abuse was higher (75%) among children working in some establishments than the self-employed children (62%). Of the children getting physically abused in their job at the establishment, more than 88 per cent cases were the victims of grievous hurt causing swelling leading to bleeding, burns and scalds.
- Because of immense exploitations by the employers, 58 per cent of the children preferred to be engaged in self-employed profession such as rag picking, vendors, rickshaw pulling and vegetable selling. According to these children, most profitable self-employed occupation is rag picking as it can fetch more money than others.
- The illegitimacy of the residence of families living on the street was the main stumbling block to access the required support from the law enforcement agencies. Even the police had a negative perception about the children living on the streets and

viewed them as drifter and criminals. Children reported to have face surprise raids at night, sudden eviction, harsh behaviour, physical assault and detention in the police station for no reason.

- There were 81 per cent of children who felt uncomfortable to live on the streets as their deprivation was exposed to outsiders.
- Children were forced to remain hungry throughout the day as the families were not allowed to cook food during day time. Thus, 59 per cent boys and 62 per cent girls opted for mid-day meal programme at the school. Children complained of getting humiliated by their teachers for belonging to the families living on the streets.
- More than 49 per cent children reported of family violence in almost every alternate day. Besides, there were more than 88 per cent cases children reported to have faced severe forms of physical punishment from father. About 69 per cent boys and78 per cent girls reported to have faced aggressive verbal assault from their parents. It was observed that in most of the cases, father adopted physical abuse as a means to release their own frustration on children. Similarly, verbal assault and aggression were most commonly adopted by mothers as well. For boys' causes of aggression were related to lack of sufficient monetary contribution to the family. Aggressive behaviour for girls were related with their inattentiveness in domestic work or sibling care. About 74 per cent boys perceived physical punishment from their family members as abuse but others perceived it as a means of parental control for their well-being. Girls perceived their family members as the only support system they have in the society. Thus, only 12 per cent of the girls perceived family members as abusers.
- It was observed that children and their families looked for the assistance of police administration to trace missing children and to lodge complains against sexual abuse. Children were widely use for anti-social activities and were victimized by the adult offenders as well as law enforcement bodies. It was also observed that children did not get fair chance from the justice authorities to safeguard their rights. The guidelines of the Juvenile Justice Administration were grossly violated by the law administration while dealing with children and juvenile offenders. Though the JJ Act, 2000 provided a greater significance on participation of children for the prevention,

adjudication and disposition of the matters for the best interest of the children, but children's opinion were not recognized by the law administration. Moreover, police officials were not equipped enough to deal with child related issues. More so, it was wearisome to observe that the Police Act drafted in the year 2006 did not make any effort to cover the role of police in the JJ Act, 2000; though it was amended long after the amendment of JJ Act.

- Children usually got involved in unskilled work and they were forced to change their jobs frequently. Being vulnerable and having no experience of the market tactics, children were not able to negotiate better wages while accepting jobs. Besides, they were forced to work for long hours and were exposed to hazardous conditions or chemical substances without any protective measures. As a result they suffer from various work related ailments and sometimes which are absolutely serious.
- In spite of the international and national promises, there were some children who were actively involved in economic activities. Of the total, 82 per cent boys and 100 per cent girls were found to be engaged in occupations or processes which are prohibited by the Indian Labour Laws/or under the Child Labour (Prohibition and Regulation) Act, 1986.
- Denied by the legal administration, children and their family members resort to various group-based protection mechanism. Affiliation to local political groups, settlement in clusters, and children's affiliation to powerful local groups were few examples of self-protection mechanisms. Besides, family members also tried to sleep in groups, tie their children with rope and engage their adolescents' girls in full time domestic help to protect their children from abduction and abuse. Girls were also oriented to take safety measures while interacting with strangers.
- While interacting with children regarding child friendly police system, they voiced their opinion about ensuring their right to lodge complaints in the police system without any adult. Children and their parents opined to make the use of audio recording system as an official protocol along with the written FIR (First Information Report) to facilitate children and illiterate adults to lodge complaint before the police. They emphasized that police should not be biased, listen to them, and give them

enough protection, so that they can disclose the truth and participate in the process. They also viewed that the legal proceedings should not be complicated and prolonged and they should have the access to free legal system to safeguard their rights.

To sum up, it was an effort of raising voice of the children of these street living families, who are still invisible in policy papers and hope to bring about a long-term change in the protection and overall development process through a synchronized effort.

Suggestions

Pavements are one of the main components of road transportation and infrastructure systems. By daily expansion of our ground transportation systems and higher cost of construction, maintenance and rehabilitation of pavements, highway agencies are facing challenges to keep serviceability of their pavements to an accepted level. Congested and over crowded pavements lead to safety problems of pedestrians and vehicle users. Thus, settlements on the pavements will not only cause problems in road transportation but will also deny people's right to safety as a whole. Unplanned urbanization has accompanied by dramatic increase in urban poverty. As discussed in the earlier sections that families migrate to the cities in search of alternative options. A large number of families settled on the pavements and other unauthorized areas because of lack of means to rent a place to stay in the city. Indeed, they are forced to live in with no shelter and suffer from absolute poverty. Thus, the unplanned urbanization and settlements not only cause problems to the pavement dwellers but also affects the rights of other city dwellers.

The study was an endeavour to understand different forms of violence against children of street living families face in different settings and also attempts to understand role of justice system for the protection of children of street living families. Within the gamut of whole justice system, the study sought to deal with police system which is one of the important agencies of juvenile justice administration. The study followed a holistic approach to understand the causal factors of child abuse of street living families and their coping strategies. Qualitative and quantitative techniques such as survey, focus group discussions, key person interview, physical observation and secondary data analysis were conducted to capture the opinion and experiences of street living children and their families. Based on these primary and secondary analyses of data, observations and the understanding of social work theories, the suggestions of the researchers have been summarized below.

- ★ All the street living families should be acknowledged as proper citizen of the country and they should not be denied of their basic citizen's rights only because of unauthorized land holding status.
- ★ It was observed that because of 'illegitimate' status of the street dwellers, their children are exposed to various risk and abuse. At the same time, they do not get fair chance from the justice authorities to protect their interest. This issue must be looked into passionately and they should be given due respect as a human being.
- ★ Over the past decade, the right to adequate housing has been consistently reaffirmed as distinct human rights by various bodies in the UN system. Appropriate plan should be developed in coordination with urban development bodies, Jawaharlal Nehru National Urban Renewal Mission and local NGOs for the proper rehabilitation of street living families with the basic amenities of life.
- ★ Holistic and synergic efforts among the governmental departments and civil society organizations should be given for proper rehabilitation of street living families and promote equitable condition.
- ★ District authorities of Kolkata should conduct a survey to enumerate total number of street living families and design an empirical map to identify source areas of this migrant population.
- ★ Voter ID and BPL cards were issued to the families against the residential address. Only because of the illegitimate residential status, these families were denied from their voting rights and also could not access facilities designed for the below poverty line families. Thus, a centralized ID system should be introduced in the country to protect legal identity and other rights of the citizen.
- ★ It was observed during the process of data collection that 77.5 per cent of the families were settled on the streets for more than 10 years on the same pavements. Government allowed them to settle on the pavement for decades. Thus, steps should be taken

to promote the legal identity of the pavement dwellers so that they could access their basic entitlements.

★ There is also need to look at the various dimensions of poverty that affecting the realization of basic human rights and rights of children at large. A multi-sectorial effort should be taken for the development of the street living families. An integrated rehabilitation package which will include regular housing, infrastructural opportunities, and income generation through micro credit facilities and safe saving and credit facilities will play a pivotal role in the protection of pavement dwellers and children in particular.

★ More than 1000 civil society organizations are working in Kolkata and mobilizing national as well as foreign investment for the development of underprivileged sections of the city. Each agency has different mandates and implements their project according to their own chosen directives. Each agency seeks to demonstrate their own achievements and do not believe in shared process venture. People affected by poverty have multifaceted needs. Without synergic efforts among the service providers, several activities are duplicated and their priority needs are neglected.

★ Moreover, there is no regulatory body to control over the funding and activities of these civil society organizations. Thus, state as well as the urban local bodies should form a multi-stakeholder committee to design macro plan, its strategies and financial requirements for the integrated development of the disadvantaged section of the respective area. Areas of intervention should be clearly distributed among the implementing bodies to supplement and complement efforts for a holistic and sustainable development of street families.

★ Coordinated effort should be taken among the authorities of rural and urban administration to design intervention to arrest further emigration of people from villages.

★ A steering committee should be formed within the urban local bodies for effective coordination, regulation and review of the progress of work within a stipulated time frame for the betterment of socio-economic status of these children and families.

★ People's representatives should also be oriented about the issue and active participation in the process should be ensured.

Education

- Due to nuclear family structures and lack of supportive system within the street living families, parents prefer to send their younger children to some institutions when they are not in work. Thus, accessibility to **ICDS** centers, crèches or pre-primary education centers should be promoted to create a safe place for children of working mothers as well as inculcate the habit of education among young children.
- Adolescent girls cannot attend school as they are to take care of their younger siblings at home. So, access to crèches/**ICDS** centres will also reduce dropout rate among them.
- Children and their parents cannot relate education with their daily life situation. They perceive that education is not meant for street children. One of the reasons of drop-out from formal school is that children do not get any supportive environment at home to complete their home tasks. Thus, complete renovation of the education curriculum is utmost important. Education curriculum should be modified to address the needs of children of different social strata.
- Broadly, the Constitution of India as well as **CRC** recognizes free and compulsory elementary education for all children up to the age of 14. Hence, it is bitter truth that a greater portion of the children of the country are not able to continue education further. The present curriculum does not incorporate the prerequisite skills of equipping children as responsible and productive citizen. Thus, the curriculum should incorporate the basic life skills required for the development of their abilities and talents to the fullest potential. The curriculum should take into account that it should equip a child to perceive his/her rights and responsibilities so that they can participate in any matters or procedure to protect their self-interest. The suggested incorporation in curriculum could be basic rights and responsibilities, basic legal literacy, reproductive and child health, basic health and hygiene education, different services of government including saving and credit facilities and different vocational skills.
- Issues related to child rights, protection and laws related to children should be discussed so that parents are aware of on those issues and can take legal measures to protect their own and children's interest.

- Basics of child rights and child protection issues should be incorporated in teachers training course so that teachers can facilitate children and their parents in their all round development process through education.
- As one of the care givers, teachers should be equipped to identify and handle child abuse cases. Training should be imparted to formal school teachers as well as non-formal teachers on child rights, abuse, protection issues, juvenile justice system so that they can also play an effective role in basic management and referral of child abuse cases.
- In their capacity as 'front-line workers', teachers often come into contact with children and families experiencing violence. Often, the only known signs of abuse and neglect are detectable by teachers. Fortunately, they can intervene effectively to diminish many of the potential adverse consequences of child maltreatment and refer the case to the concerned authorities.
- Teacher's attitude towards the people living on the streets is also a hindering factor in children's education. Thus, parents also do not get the confidence to interact with teachers regarding their child's problems. In most of the formal schools, parents-teachers meeting or mothers' meeting is one of the important components. The main objective of this system is to ensure parent's participation in the education process of their children.
- During the focus group discussion and data collection process it was found that rarely parents get time to attend the meetings. Many a time they are not informed about the date as it is not conducted on a fixed date. Moreover, they do not feel comfortable to attend these meetings as they know that their children do not perform better in school education. Thus, they feel inferior in front of other patents attend the meetings. Thus, teachers' attitude towards deprived children should be changed. Thus, this forum should not only be used for sharing student's performance in the education system.
- Teachers should be oriented about situations and other problems of street and deprived children so they can deal with the children and their parents more emphatically.

Juvenile Justice System

- "Illegitimate" status of street living families is the main constraint in accessing justice system. Thus, an identity number or card should be issued to the families who have already settled on the streets.

- As per the juvenile justice system of the country children can produce themselves in front of the Child Welfare Committee (CWC) for their own protection. But in India CWC is not physically accessible. Thus, children should also have the right to produce themselves before police station and lodge complaint to protect their interest.
- The awareness level among the common mass about juvenile justice system and CWC is also very low. Still, police are the first line of contact for the general population because of their administrative reach. Also, people have much more access and faith in police rather than other juvenile justice system. Thus, people expect support from police for any legal and protection issues. On the other hand there has been a widely held perception among police officials that child protection work is something that sits out beyond the fringes of "**Real Police Work**". So, police system should be redesigned to deal with juvenile justice issues.
- Police are more concerned about punitive aspect of crime rather than protective dimension. Juvenile Justice Act, 2000 has provided significance on treatment, care, protection and developmental needs of children by adopting a child friendly approach in the adjudication and disposition of the matters for the best interest of the children. Most of the police personnel have their own perception towards the child friendly approach which is largely predisposed by their own socio-cultural environment. Moreover, no standard operating procedure has been designed to deal with children. Thus, standard operation protocol should be designed to deal with child related cases.
- During the interaction with the police officials, it was observed that they were over burdened with different Acts and their Amendments. No official training was organized for these officials to update their knowledge about the recent amendments. Thus, most of the officials are not well aware of the special features of all enactments and their role in the implementation phase. Still the officials are not aware of the definition of child that India Government has amended. Most of the measures they take while interacting with children do not match with the standards set in JJ Act, 2000. Regular training course should be mandatory as per the service rule of all police personnel.

- The Police Act does not talk about forming Women and Child Protection Desk staffed by women personnel in each police station. No specific roles and responsibilities of the Women and Child Protection Desk have been designed. The following responsibilities of the desk should include:
  - Provide required assistance to children and other illiterate people to lodge complaint.
  - Maintain liaison with free legal aid services.
  - Provide referral services to the deprived families.
  - Maintain regular contact with the **Child Welfare Committee (CWC) and Juvenile Justice Board (JJB)** to take up the child related issues.
  - Maintain regular contact with civil society organizations running child protection services in their administrative zone and supervise their activities.
  - A number of agencies implement child protection projects and rescue children in distress. Though it is mandatory to produce children before Child Welfare Committee within 24 hours, but most of the NGOs do not adhere to this. Also they do not register those cases at the local police station. One of the roles of this desk should be to facilitate or force NGOs to stick to the legal guidelines.
  - Update child related information to the centralized data base.
  - Maintain date base of child related cases including rescue, referral and repatriation cases.
  - Maintain records of referral services including children's homes run by NGOs and change their legal status.
  - Facilitate NGOs to register all the child protection related cases, take legal action against the perpetrators.

- The JJ Act (Care and Protection), 2000 is a significant piece of legislation that sets the tone for the India's juvenile justice system approach. This Act is enormous improvement over the previous treatment of children and adolescents. It has also described the role and responsibilities of juvenile justice administration to deal with child related cases. It is surprising to observe that the Police Act 2006, which has amended after the ratification of the JJ Act (Care and Protection) 2000, did not give any emphasis on juvenile justice. The Act has also not incorporated the roles and responsibilities that have been mentioned in the JJ Act. Thus, no effort has still been made by the government to orient the police administration to implement juvenile justice system in the country. It reflects government's lack of commitment to combat with child protection issues. Gaps in implementation of juvenile justice administration will remain until government made any effort to combine these two Acts.

- Recognizing the Right to Information Act, the New Police Act, 2006 emphasizes that all the information required to be made public. As per the Supreme Court guidelines, details regarding persons arrested and held in lock-ups should be displayed. As per the suggestions of street living parents, list of all the missing and rescued children with their photographs should be displayed in police station so that people can trace their children.
- The JJ Act 2000 emphasizes to constitute two separate boards to deal with children:
    - CWC is to deal with children in need of care and protection.
    - JJB is to deal with children in conflict with law.
    - The offence against children bill emphasizes to constitute Children's Court (CC) under Commission for Protection of Child Rights to deal with offences against children.
    - Instead of separate boards for children, an independent justice board should be constituted to deal with all the cases related to children. The committee should have the legal knowledge, power and authority to give punishment to the perpetrators of child abuse.
    - A free legal cell should be constituted to protect the interest of children.
    - All the pedophilic cases may be registered in the police station.
    - Commission for child protection/child protection cell should be constituted under state police board in each state to monitor and supervise effective delivery of juvenile justice system of the state. Child protection cell should register, collate and monitor child related cases of the state.
    - The police force is also accountable for their deeds/ misdeeds. A grievance redressal mechanism should be

designed to look into all the grievances against police and justice system.

- The opinion and suggestions of children should be considered while designing child friendly operation protocol.
- Activities of the civil society organizations (CSO) should also be strictly monitored. A regulatory body may be constituted under the chairmanship of state and district social welfare officer to see the activities of CSOs working with children. All the CSOs should be forced to work under the purview of legal system of the country. So, the adherence of the CSOs should be monitored and regulated rigorously.
- Government should design micro-level plan on child protection and sensitize funding agencies to provide funds to complement the efforts of the government.
- State Child Protection Cell in collaboration with NGOs can design child protection strategy for the state and city and distribute the work among NGOs.
- The child line service was found to be very effective to reach the children in distress. The **CHILDLINE** service should be acknowledged as official body and should be incorporated in the law and order system.
- The calls to **CHILDLINE** should be acknowledged as official report.
- Like other countries a child protection worker receives and records the calls. The child protection worker will decide if an investigation is required and will refer the case to the concerned police station and other allied services as per the requirement.
- Government should restrain CSOs to implement child protection services without any coordination with law and order system. Many NGOs rescue children, provide shelter and also run illegitimate activities.
- Responsibility of managing Women and Child Help Desk in police station can also be provided to the selected CSOs.

BIBLIOGRAPHY

Action Aid (2008). *Homelessness in the City of Joy.*

Adams, R.; Dominelli, L. and Payne (2005). *The Legacy of Radical Social Work: Themes, Issues and Critical Debates*, Oxford University Press, London.

Agarwal, S. and Sagar, K. (2005). "Need for Dedicated Focus on Urban Health Within National Rural Health Mission", *Indian Journal of Public Health*, Vol. XXXXIX, July-September.

Amorso, Donald. M and Edward, E. Ware (1983). "Youth's Perception of Police as a Function of Attitudes Towards Parents, Teachers and Self", *Canadian Journal of Criminology*, Vol. 25, pp. 191-99.

BBC News (August 1st, 2006). http/news.bbc.co.uk/go/pr/fr/2/hi/south_asia/5235614.smt.

Beijing Rules, 1985.

Benedict Wim (1992). *Perception of the Police and Fear of Crime in a Rural Setting;* Utility of a Geographically Focused Survey for Police Services, *Planning and Assessment*, Eastern Illinois University Press.

Bhavnagri, Vaswani; Bhavnagri, N.P. and Vaswani, T.G. (1999). "Expanding Roles of Teachers for the Twentyfirst Century: An Indian Context", *Childhood Education*, Vol. 75, pp. 297-303.

Bureau of Democracy, Human Rights, and Labour, Canada (March, 2007). http:/www.state.gov/g/drl/ris/hrrpt/2006/78883.htm.

Child Labour (Prohibition and Regulation) Act, 1986, Government of India.

Children's Rights Movement, Retrieved on (2008). Wikipedia. http:/en.wikipedia.org/wiki/children's rights.

Civil Society Forum for South Asia (2003). *Promoting and Protecting the Rights of Street Children*, 12-14 March.

Civil Society Forum for South Asia (2001). *Promoting and Protecting the Rights of Street Children*, 12-14 December, Colombo, Sri Lanka.

Consortium for Street Children. http:/www.streetchildren.org.uk/resources.

Consortium of Street Children (2001). http:/www.streetchildren.org.uk/resources/details/? Country=64type=country.

Country Reports on Human Rights Practices by the Bureau of Democracy, Human Rights, and Labour; Norway, 1999.

D. Finkelhor (2004). "The International Epidemiology of Child Sexual Abuse", *Child Abuse and Neglect*, Vol. 18, No. 5, pp. 409-17.

Edward, Arnold and Corrigan, Paul (1978). *Radical Social Work*, Oxford University Press, London.

Environmental Health Programme and CINI ASHA, Situational Assessment of Slums of Kolkata, 2004.

Fink, Arther, E.; Everette, E. Wilson; Merrill, B. Cover (1955). *The Fields of Social Work*, Oxford University Press, London.

Flaim Amanda (2004). *Monograph on International Comparative School Education*, Stanford University Press.

Gauri Pradhan (2002). *Juvenile Justice in Nepal with reference to CWIN's Experience Working on Children in Conflict with Laws.* www.cwin.nepal.org

Glaser, P. and Frosh, A. (1988). "The Role of the Police as Amplifliers of Deviancy", in Cehens, S. (ed.), *Images of Deviance*, Penguin, USA.

Global Initiative to End All Corporal Punishment of Children, *Global Summary of the Legal Status of Corporal Punishment of Children* (2006). http/www.endcorporalpunishment.org

Giaretto, K. (1981). *British Social Work in the Nineteenth Century*, Routledge, USA.

Hollway, S. (2008). *The Formation of National States in Western Europe*, Princeton University Press, USA.

"Human Development Index (HDI) 2006", *Statistics in the Human Development Report*, UNDP.

Human Resource and Skills Development, Canada, *A Canada Fit For Children* (2004). http/www. Hrsdc.gc.ca/eng/cs/sp/sdc/socpol/publications.

"Human Rights Watch, Children's Rights Project, Police Abuse and Killings of Street Children in India", *World Report 2007*, India.

Human Rights Watch, *Guatemala Police Violence Against Street Children*, New York, 1997, p. 22.

ILO Convention 182 (1999).

ILO (2002). "A Future Without Child Labour", *Global Report*, Geneva,

ILO (2006). *The Global Trends in Child Labour.*

ILO (2006). *The End of Child Labour: Within Reach.* http:/www.oitcinterfor.org/public/English/region/ampro/cinterfor/news/rep_ib.pdf

ILO (2006). *The End of Child Labour: Within Reach*, Global Report.

Integrated Child Protection Scheme (ICPS) India, *Draft*, 2006.

Jawaharlal Nehru Rural and Urban Renewal Mission, 2008, Government of India.

Jones, K. (2001). The Case against the COS, Fabian Tract 158.

Juvenile Justice (Care and Protection of Children) Act, 2000, *The Gazetteer of India*, Published by Ministry of Law and Company Affairs (Legislative Department).

Kundu Nitai (2003). *The Cases of Kolkata*, Institute of Wetland Management & Ecological Design. http/www.ucl.ac.uk/dpu-projects/Global_ Report/pdfs/Kolkata_bw.pdf

Le Roux, J. and Smith, C.S. (1998). "Causes and Characteristics of the Street Children Phenomenon: A Global Perspectives", *Adolescence*, 33, pp. 683-88.

Lisa White (2007). *Children's Rights Australia*, Law Library of Congress. http/www.lov.gov/law/help/child-rights/australia.php

London Safeguarding Children's Board, "London Child Protection Procedures", *LSCB*, 3rd Edition, 2007. http:/www.londonscb.gov.uk/lscb_development_officers_network/lscb_development_officers_june_5thy_2007

Longres, John F. (1990). *Human Behaviour and the Social Environment*, Oxford University Press, London.

Marianne, Murdoch and Verwijs, Lim (1990). *Background on Juvenile Crime and the Legal Situation in the Philippines*, Free University Press, Amsterdam.

Minimum Rule for the Administration of Juvenile Justice (1985), Government of India.

Ministry of Women and Child Development, Government of India, "Save the Children", UK and UNICEF, (2007). *A Study on Child Abuse in India*.

Mrazek, S. (1983). *Culture and Society: 1780-1950*, Chatto.

Murali Kanta, *Food Insecurity in Urban India*, 22nd June, 2006. http/www.hinduonnet.com/fline/fl2001/stories/20030117007307500.htm

National Charter for Children, 2004, Government of India.

National Plan of Action for Children, 2005, Government of India.

Nicolas MC Bala Queens University, Joseph P. Hornick, Canadian Research Institute for Law and the Family Haward N. Snyder, National Centre for Juvenile Justice, *Juvenile Justice System — An International Comparison of Problems and Solutions*.

Optional Protocol to the Convention on the Rights of the Child on the Sale of Children, Child Prostitution and Child Pornography. www.unhcr.ch/hchn_un.htm

Petren, Alfhildetal, (2000). *Children's Rights Turning Principles into Practice*, Save the Children, Sweden and UNICEF, Stockholm, Sweden.

Police Act (2006), Government of India.

Rachel Masika and Arjan de Hannand Sally Baden (1997). *A Gender Analysis*, Swedish International Development Cooperation Agency (SIDA). http//www. Bridge.ids.ac.uk/reports/re54.pdf

Rafferty, Y. and Shinn, M. (1991). "The Impact of Homelessness on Children", *American Psychologist*, 46, pp. 1170-77.

S. Abdelgalil; R.G. Gurgel and S. Theobaldand L.E. Cuevas, "Household and Family Characteristics of Street Children in Aracaju, Brazil", *Arch DIs Child*, 2004; 89: 817-20. doi: 10.1136/adc.2003.032078

Save the Children, (1998-2001); Secure Care, Provincial Child Prostitute, Protection, Legislation, Commer. http/www.walnet.org/csis/news/securecare.html

Save the Children, Mirjam Van Reisen, Invisible Children, Children's Rights in EU and Member, States' Development Cooperation Policies.

SEAMEO Secretariat, (June, 2000). Legislative Framework and Law Enforcement, Chapter 8.3. http:/www.seameo.org/vl/combat/8chap3.htm

Sears, P. (2001). *The Quest for National Efficiency a Study in British Politics and Political Thought*, 1899-1914, Oxford: Blackwell.

Seed, P. (1989). *The Expansion of Social Work in Great Britain*, Routledge, USA.

Singh, K. (1982). *Social Work Theory and Practice*, Prakashan Kendra, Lucknow.

Standard Minimum Rules for the Administration of Juvenile Justice, 1985.

Street Children of India (1994), NCBI Publication.

Terry Nihart University of South Florida, Lersch Kim Michelle University of South Florida: Sellers, S. Christine, University of South Florida: Mieczkowski Tom, University of South Florida, "Kids, Cops, Parents and Teachers: Exploring Juvenile Attitudes Toward Authority Figures", *Western Criminology Review*, 6(1), 79-88 (2005).

Timmins Maria, Norfolk Constabulary (2007). *Child Protection Unit.* http//: www.norfolk.police.uk/articlelisting.cfm.

Umenda, Sayuri (August, 2007). Japan, Children's Rights, Law, Liberty of Congress-o4112. http://www.loc.gov/lsaw/help/child-rights/japan.php

UN Commission on Human Rights, *Street Children and Violence* (Updated 16, November, 2001).

UN Office for the Coordination of Humanitarian Affairs, IRIN IN-Depth (Monday 5, March 2007). *Youth in Crisis: Coming of Age in the 21st Century*, Humanitarian News and Analysis.

UNESCO (2003). *Bangkok Civil Society Forum, Promoting and Protecting the Rights of Street Children*. http:/cms.unescobkk.org/index.php?id=3336

UNFPA (2007). *State of World Population Report*, Chapter 1.

UNICEF (2005). *Changing a Harmful Social Convention, Female Genital Mutilation/Cutting*, Innocent Research Centre.

UNICEF (2005). *Female Genital Mutilation/Cutting, and a Statistical Exploration*.

UNICEF (2006). Innocent Research Centre, Florence, Italy, 25-28, GM/DVGC/2006/EP

United Nations (2005). *An End to Violence Against Children*.

United Nations Children's Fund (2005). *At a Glance, India: The Big Picture*.

United Nations General Assembly (2006); *Promotion and Protection of the Rights of the Children*, Sixty First Session.

United Nations, *Violence Against Children in Conflict with the Law*, Secretary-General's Study on Violence Against Children, GENEVA, 4-5, April, 2005.

University of Ljubljana, (2009). *Theories and Methods of Social Work*, Oxford University Press.

UNODCCP (1999). *Rapid Situation Assessment of Street Children in Cairo and Alexandria*.

U.S. Department of State (February 25, 2000). http/www.nationbynation.com/Norway/Human.html

West, T. (2007). *Women and the Welfare State*, Tavistock, U.K.

WHO (2006). *Violence Against Children*, Secretary General's Study on Violence Against Children adopted for Children and Young People.

Wratten, E. (1995). "Conceptualizing Urban Poverty, Urban Poverty: Characteristics, Causes and Consequences", *Environment and Urbanization*, Vol. 7, No. 1.

INDEX